Where the People Are: Language a
in the Poetry of W.S. Graham

MATTHEW FRANCIS is Lecturer in Creative Writing at the University of Wales, Aberystwyth. He is a poet and novelist whose most recent collection is *Dragons* (Faber, 2001). His work has won the TLS / Blackwell's Prize and the Southern Arts Literature Prize, and has been shortlisted for the Forward Prize (twice) and the Welsh Book of the Year Award. He is the editor of W.S. Graham's *New Collected Poems* (Faber, 2004).

Where the People Are

Language and Community in the Poetry of W.S. Graham

MATTHEW FRANCIS

University of Wales, Aberystwyth

SALT

CAMBRIDGE

PUBLISHED BY SALT PUBLISHING
PO Box 937, Great Wilbraham PDO, Cambridge CB1 5JX United Kingdom
PO Box 202, Applecross, Western Australia 6153

© Matthew Francis, 2004

The right of Matthew Francis to be identified as the
author of this work has been asserted by him in accordance
with Section 77 of the Copyright, Designs and Patents Act 1988.

First published 2004

Printed and bound in the United Kingdom by Lightning Source

Typeset in Swift 9.5 / 13

ISBN 1 84471 048 3 hardback
ISBN 1 876857 23 4 paperback

SP

1 3 5 7 9 8 6 4 2

Because always language
Is where the people are

Contents

Introduction

William Sydney Graham was born in 1918 in Greenock, Scotland. His father was a journeyman engineer, and the young Graham was apprenticed 'as a draughtsman to a Glasgow engineering firm'.[1] However, after attending evening classes at Glasgow University and spending a year studying literature and philosophy as a residential student at the Working Mens' College at Newbattle Abbey, he committed himself to a career as a poet.[2] After various jobs in Ireland and Scotland, he met the publisher David Archer, who had established an Arts Centre in Glasgow. Archer, the first of Graham's many patrons, allowed him to live in his flat in Sandyford Place, where several aspiring artists were already living rent-free. Archer's Parton Press published his first collection of poems, *Cage Without Grievance,* in 1942.[3] Over the next few years, Graham lived mostly in London and Cornwall with two long visits to the US. After 1955, he was permanently resident in Cornwall. He married Nessie Dunsmuir in 1954. They had no children, though Graham had a daughter, Rosalind, from a previous relationship, whom he saw occasionally. He died of cancer in 1986 at the age of 67.[4]

Although Graham took paid employment for brief periods as a young man, for most of his life he worked only at his poetry. He was dependent on the small fees and grants he received for his writing and on the generosity of friends. Nancy Wynne-Jones, for example, allowed him and his wife to live rent-free in a cottage she owned in Madron, Cornwall, and Robin Skelton for some time gave him a regular allowance in return for manuscripts.[5] After *Cage Without Grievance*, Graham quickly published two more books, *The Seven Journeys* and *2ND Poems*. His next collection, *The White Threshold*, was accepted by T.S. Eliot for Faber and Faber, who remained his publishers for the rest of his life. He was to publish only three more original volumes, *The Nightfishing, Malcolm Mooney's Land* and *Implements in Their Places*. In 1979, Faber brought out a *Collected Poems* which, significantly, omits some of the poems from the first four volumes, and in the same year, the Ecco Press published a *Selected Poems* in the US.[6]

At the beginning and end of his career, Graham was a poet of some reputation. In the 1940s, he lectured at New York University, received an Atlantic Award and took part in a reading tour in the US with Kathleen Raine and David Gascoyne.[7] His editor T.S. Eliot praised his work, with the flattering proviso that it 'was "intellectual" poetry and would go slow because people were lazy about thinking'.[8] The last two collections and the *Collected Poems* were widely noticed: *Malcolm Mooney's Land* and *Implements* were Poetry Book Society Choices and the prepublicity for the *Collected Poems* included an *Observer Magazine* interview with Penelope Mortimer.[9] In 1974, he was awarded a Civil List Pension, thanks to the efforts of Robin Skelton.[10] Nevertheless, Eliot appears to have been right – Graham's work has still not received the attention its power and originality deserves. Since his death, though, a revival of interest has been slowly gathering momentum, culminating in the annotated *New Collected Poems*, which I have recently edited for Faber. [11]

My own first experience of Graham was through the poem 'Johann Joachim Quantz's Five Lessons', which I came across in an anthology when I was an undergraduate, and found exceptionally vivid and powerful. Who was this poet, and why had I never heard of him before? Undergraduates often assume they have heard of everyone important, but my reaction turns out to be fairly typical, and 'Quantz' probably remains Graham's most popular poem. Like many anthology pieces, it is in some ways uncharacteristic of its author: a Browningesque dramatic monologue full of historical and regional colour, quite unlike the more obviously allegorical 'Malcolm Mooney's Land', it is about music rather than language, and deals with a type of relationship which Graham had little experience of in his own life (at least in a formal sense), that between a teacher and a student. Rereading the present study, I notice I have mentioned it only once, in passing. It is a fine poem, but it will always stand a little apart from the main body of work; one might even argue that, in its concern with the social dimension of art (or Art), it transcends its author's usual obsessions – though loneliness and silence are still there, hauntingly evoked. Years later, I found the *Collected Poems* in a bookshop and, opening it at random, read 'Imagine a Forest', which confirmed my impression that I had 'discovered' a major poet. By the time I enrolled for a PhD at Southampton University, there was only one possible subject for my thesis. My starting-point was an attempt to understand some of the statements about language in the late poems and, in particular, how they related to apparently similar statements I was encountering at the time in literary theory. The work I began then forms the basis of this book.

I was not, of course, Graham's discoverer at all. I have been much helped by the work of his earlier critics, above all by Tony Lopez's important and pioneering study *The Poetry of W.S. Graham*. Many other people have generously given help and support to the project in the ten years since it started: my research supervisor Peter Middleton; my advisor Stephen Bygrave; the School of Research and Graduate Studies, University of Southampton; the late Nessie Dunsmuir Graham; the late Robin and the late Sylvia Skelton; Ronnie Duncan; Malcolm Mackintosh; the late Alastair Graham; Chris Stephens; Anthony Astbury; Geoffrey Godbert; Alison Hill; the University of Glamorgan and the University of Wales, Aberystwyth; Chris Hamilton-Emery, John Kinsella and Salt; Chris Petter and staff of the Special Collections Department, University of Victoria, British Columbia; and staff of the John Rylands University Library of Manchester, the Harry Ransom Humanities Research Center at the University of Texas at Austin, the Poetry / Rare Books Collection at the University Libraries of the State University of Buffalo, the National Library of Scotland, and the National Library of Canada. Part of Chapter 6 has appeared in slightly different form in *W.S. Graham: Speaking Towards You*, edited by Ralph Pite and Hester Jones (Liverpool: University of Liverpool Press, 2004). My thanks to all of the above, and particular thanks to Michael and Margaret Snow, Graham's friends and executors, whose wisdom and experience has been a constant support. Finally I should like to thank my wife Creina for acting as research assistant and social secretary, and listening to innumerable draft chapters. This study is dedicated to her.

List of Abbreviations

The following abbreviations are used in the text.

AAN W.S. Graham, *Aimed at Nobody: Poems from Notebooks*, ed. by Margaret Blackwood and Robin Skelton (London: Faber and Faber, 1993).

'Clusters' Notebook 4, Robin Skelton Collection, c/o University of Victoria, BC,Canada.

CS Ronnie Duncan and Jonathan Davidson (eds.), *The Constructed Space: A Celebration of W.S. Graham* (Lincoln: Jackson's Arm, 1994).

ER *Edinburgh Review*, no. 75 (February 1987).

NCP W.S. Graham, *New Collected Poems*, ed. by Matthew Francis (London: Faber and Faber, 2004).

NFM *The Nightfisherman: Selected Letters of W.S. Graham* ed. by Michael and Margaret Snow (Manchester: Carcanet Press, 1999).

OED *The Oxford English Dictionary*.

PWSG Tony Lopez, *The Poetry of W.S. Graham* (Edinburgh: Edinburgh University Press, 1989).

SJ W.S. Graham, *The Seven Journeys* (Glasgow: William Maclellan, 1944).

TLS *The Times Literary Supplement*.

CHAPTER 1

Poet of Language

Failed Conduits

W.S. Graham is a poet of language, as a glance at the *New Collected Poems* reveals. This preoccupation is most apparent in the later poems, where the words 'language', 'words' and 'voices' recur many times, often in a negative context. In 'Malcolm Mooney's Land', language is described as an 'obstacle', while other poems – entitled 'What Is the Language Using Us For?' and 'Language Ah Now You Have Me' – lament the opportunities it presents for 'mistakes of communication' (*NCP*, p. 155, p. 200, p. 207). Some poems are extended metaphors whose tenor appears, more or less clearly, to be language. In 'Malcolm Mooney's Land' language is an Arctic waste, in 'Clusters Travelling Out' a prison, while in 'Ten Shots of Mister Simpson' it is both camera and gun, destroying what it describes. Many of the poems are haunted by monsters, 'The Beast in the Space' that destroys meaning, or the 'monster muse' that enters the act of writing the poem in 'Five Visitors to Madron' bringing the threat of death (*NCP*, p. 188). Language is never neutral; it has a will of its own which may be hostile to the speaker.

Language is undoubtedly a concern of the late poems; is it also important in the earlier ones? In the poems of *The Nightfishing*, the key words I have noted are already present. The poet is 'trusted on the language'; he tells us 'these words said welcome' and 'I heard voices within / The empty lines and tenses' (*NCP*, p. 122, p. 133). 'The Nightfishing' itself is a poem about fishing for herring, but it is also, more importantly, about fishing for words, about its own writing. In this metaphor, the sea stands for language, which is where poets do their fishing. This suggests it may also have the same significance in the slightly earlier poems of

The White Threshold, where the sea is the dominant image but its symbolism is more obscure, and indeed, phrases like 'the signed sea' and 'the long shore printed / With arrow steps' suggest that this analogy is being made (*NCP*, p. 82, p. 81). So does 'the white threshold', the phrase that occurs in 'Three Poems of Drowning' as well as giving the title to a poem and to the collection as a whole (*NCP*, p. 85, pp. 92–98). The threshold in question is the foamy surface of the sea, through which sailors pass when they drown, but white is also the colour of the pages of a book, a fact that later provided the Arctic metaphor of 'Malcolm Mooney's Land', and the phrase 'the white language' in 'What Is the Language Using Us For?' (*NCP*, p. 199). If we go back to the poems of Graham's first published collection, we find, in such poems as 'Of the Resonant Rumour of Sun, Impulse of Summer', the vocabulary of 'sign', 'index' and 'writing', applied this time to landscape (*NCP*, p. 18).

In seeing language as a problem, and as one of overriding importance, Graham is participating in the linguistic turn which is such a feature of twentieth-century thought. From Saussure's founding of a synchronic linguistics to Chomsky's project of identifying the cognitive basis of grammar, from Nietzsche's insistence that truth is 'a movable host of metaphors, metonymies and anthropomorphisms' to Derrida's attempts to use writing as a lever to crack open the categories of Western metaphysics, from Sapir and Whorf's speculation that cognition may depend on the potential for it offered by the structure of a native language to Lacan's claim that 'the unconscious is structured in the most radical way like a language', this has been the issue to which modern and postmodern thinkers have obsessively returned.[1] I have not been able to discover a philosophical pedigree for Graham's own pursuit of this theme, though I began this study hoping to do so. Tony Lopez states that he studied philosophy as well as literature at Newbattle Abbey.[2] The titles of famous philosophical texts are mentioned in a number of his notebooks from different periods of his life, and some of his friends have told me that he used to speak at times of Heidegger and the pre-Socratic philosophers. On the other hand, the poems do not feel – to me, at any rate – like the products of a trained philosophical mind. Poets and artists are sometimes in mentioned in them – Section 50 of 'Implements in Their Places' lists David Jones, Kandinsky, Shelley, Crane, Melville and Eliot, for example – but there are no references to philosophers (*NCP*, p. 251). Graham's notes on philosophy are largely lists of texts and authors for future reading, and they seem to me like the fantasies of a man daydreaming about a systematic education he is never likely to get round to. There is a touchingly schoolboyish tone to such notes as:

'read Hume who at the age of 26 shocked all Christendom with his highly heretical TREATISE ON HUMAN NATURE – one of the classics and marvels of modern philosophy.'[3]

To be fair to Graham, the quotation marks in this passage are his, implying that he is quoting someone else. Nevertheless, seen in the context of his extensive notes on the correct use of the comma, his quotations from definitions of technical poetic terms from *Nelson's Encyclopaedia* and his explanation to himself of sonata form, they suggest an enthusiastic novice rather than a scholar.

I hope to show in the course of this study that Graham's ideas on the nature of language are both complex and – so far as I have been able to tell – remarkably original. They were not, of course, formed in a vacuum. Rather, they were put together from three main ingredients: the literary and critical commonplaces current when he was a young man, the psychodynamics of his personality and his own perception of the position of the writer. From an early age, Graham chose to be a poet. His understanding of this vocation was conditioned by the work and views of older writers, such as T.S. Eliot and Dylan Thomas. These were congenial to him because they offered an escape from, and at the same time, a return to, his family and social origins. (The explanation of this paradox should become clear in time.) His perception of the position of the writer is thus inevitably connected both with that of his predecessors and with his own psychological needs and desires. But it also gives an insight into the nature of text – or rather, since text is part of history like other cultural products, into the nature of text in the late twentieth century.

In this chapter, I shall be concentrating on the view of language implied in the late poems, because it is their explicit concern with this theme that first prompted me to undertake this study. (The late poems are also considered in Chapter 5.) However, the attitudes directly revealed here are present throughout his work, though often in a more cryptic form, as Chapters 3 and 4, which deal with the early and middle-period poems, will show. In the following discussion, I shall be exploring the implications of the metaphors Graham has used to illustrate his subject, some of which I have already listed. I shall suggest that he is deploying these as a critique of a commonsense view of language which is itself metaphorical, a view which Michael J. Reddy has called 'the conduit metaphor'.[4]

Reddy's argument has been well summed up by George Lakoff and Mark Johnson:

> Reddy observes that our language about language is structured roughly by the following complex metaphor:
>
> IDEAS (or MEANINGS) ARE OBJECTS.
>
> LINGUISTIC EXPRESSIONS ARE CONTAINERS.
>
> COMMUNICATION IS SENDING.
>
> The speaker puts ideas (objects) into words (containers) and sends them (along a conduit) to a hearer who takes the ideas/objects out of the word/containers.[5]

Reddy convincingly demonstrates the metaphor's pervasiveness by listing a large number of English expressions which imply that communication functions like a conduit.[6] But, as he points out, the idea is a strange one. Clearly words are not receptacles with an outside and an inside, even though we habitually speak of them as if they were. Nor are thoughts themselves passed across space, 'since these are locked within the skull and life process of each of us'.[7] His alternative account is that language allows one person to construct for another a set of instructions which can be used by the latter to generate thoughts. These thoughts will not be the same as those of the originator of the message, but they will be equally compatible with the instructions. The differences are due to the mental and circumstantial differences between sender and recipient and to the indeterminacy of language (a topic on which I shall have more to say later in this chapter).[8]

Reddy is far from being the only theorist to offer a critique of commonsense models of communication like the conduit metaphor. In structuralist and poststructuralist theory, particularly in the somewhat simplified accounts of these designed primarily for English-speaking university students, it is normally argued that common sense assumes a transparent language. This image is not quite the same as the conduit metaphor; it downplays the fact that common sense (if we take Reddy's examples from everyday speech as conclusive evidence) sees language as a thing, albeit one with the remarkable property of being able to transfer ideas or sense-impressions from one person to another. Of course, a pane of glass is a thing, too, but one whose thingness can be ignored, and it is this refusal to acknowledge thingness or materiality which is the great error of common sense according to writers like Catherine Belsey and Colin MacCabe.[9] On the other hand, Antony Easthope, in making the same point, more accurately depicts the popular view of language as a material entity successfully deployed for the transference of information when he ironically compares Roman Jakobson's account of communication with the carrying of coal by trucks.[10] It seems to me, however, that poststructuralist theory, though it rightly disputes the telepathic or magical features of such models, is actually a product of the same preconceptions. Language is, of course, as 'material' as every other aspect of this material universe, but this truism is easily confused with claims for its 'materiality' in another, more contentious sense of the word. I shall argue shortly that Graham's portrayal of language as a thing ultimately derives from the textual bias of twentieth-century Western culture, and this is a bias in which most literary theory participates.

Reddy's critique of the conduit metaphor, in contrast to poststructuralist theories, is a humanist one. For him, the fact that language does not physically convey ideas between people only serves to emphasize the human role in meaning creation. The conduit metaphor obscures this role, making meaning seem a property of language itself:

> In the simplest of terms, the conduit metaphor lets human ideas slip out of human brains, so that, once you have recording technologies, you do not need humans any more.[11]

He emphasizes the importance of education, insisting that communication depends, not on efficient technology and the volume of messages transmitted, but on the abilities of the human beings involved. We must put less trust in media and more in minds.

Nevertheless, in making this case he inadvertently undermines it. Our obsession with technology, he argues, is a result of the conduit metaphor: the language we use about language irrevocably influences the way we think about it. This view, which Reddy inherits from Whorf, makes language a powerful agent rather than a passive conduit. However it is inconsistent with his humanism since it takes away much of the responsibility for thought from human beings and gives it to an autonomous language instead. While it is not possible for people to put ideas into language, it would seem that language can put ideas into them. Reddy allows only the possibility of 'brief, isolated and fragmentary' evasions of the conditioning imposed on the mind by language.[12]

There is, however, an alternative approach which avoids the necessity of positing a dehumanized language. This is that of Lakoff, Johnson and Lakoff's more recent collaborator, Mark Turner, who see metaphor as a cognitive phenomenon rather than a merely linguistic one.[13] For them, the conduit metaphor is one of many metaphorical concepts by which members of a culture structure their lives. Such concepts are systematic and coherent; a basic metaphor like 'time is money' generates an indefinite number of phrases which are coherent with it but whose exact wording is not important.[14] Metaphors are not arbitrary, but are grounded in culture and experience.[15] The 'time is money' complex, for example, has its roots in the practice of Western industrial society, 'where work is typically associated with the time it takes and time is precisely quantified'.[16] No metaphor can be fully adequate to its object, or it would cease to be a metaphor at all; it follows, therefore, that metaphors highlight certain features of the concepts they describe while hiding others.[17] For example, the metaphorical view of labour as a resource, also a consequence of industrial capitalism, hides the difference between meaningful and meaningless labour.[18] This theory offers a more convincing answer than Reddy's to the question of how it is possible to offer a critique of language using language. Because metaphors are not complete, they do not wholly control our thought; because they are cognitive, there remains a base of human experience with which they can be compared and, on occasion, found inadequate, as when Lakoff and Johnson point to aspects of time and labour that are hidden by the 'time is money' and 'labour is a resource' metaphors.[19]

Lakoff, Johnson and Turner provide a theoretical position from which it is possible to criticize not only the conduit metaphor but also other metaphors which, though they seem to be opposed to it, share its portrayal of language as a thing or a place. Metaphors like this come into being because they highlight some aspect of an experience. In so doing, they hide others. When we encounter the metaphorical descriptions of language in Graham's poems, we must ask ourselves why he has chosen to emphasize some aspects of linguistic experience at the expense of others.

Such descriptions are to be found not only in Graham's work, but also, as I shall show in later chapters, in a wide range of writing in the broad modernist tradition which influenced him as a young man. Graham does not simply take over these metaphors from his predecessors; rather, he struggles to remake them in an attempt to satisfy his own complex sense of what language is. Lakoff and Turner argue that the metaphors of poets are often more powerful and intricate versions of those that are generally current in our culture.[20] Just as the common metaphor of death as departure gives rise both to clichés such as 'He passed away' and to poems such as Emily Dickinson's 'Because I could not stop for Death', so the images in Graham's poems are based on the metaphors from everyday speech listed by Reddy.[21] Graham is no more satisfied with these than Reddy is, but because he is a poet rather than a theorist his response is not to analyse their inadequacies but to try to rewrite them in a way that does satisfy him.

Some of the poems literally depict language as a form of conduit, the electric cable down which telephone signals are sent. In 'What Is the Language':

> I lean my back to the telegraph pole
>
> And the messages hum through my spine.
> The beaded wires with their birds
> Above me are contacting London.

> (*NCP*, p. 202)

In 'Dear Who I Mean', 'the five high singing wires', (which also suggest a musical stave) trap the kite of the poet's message (*NCP*, p. 160). In 'Implements', there is again an analogy between music and wires – the strings of the bazouki in a Cretan taverna are 'buzzing plucked wires' (*NCP*, p. 256). Graham is using the wire as a symbol of language but bringing it into juxtaposition with other images which complicate its function. (We shall see the significance of the birds shortly.) The telegraph wire, the most perfect model of a linguistic conduit that our technological society can provide, keeps turning into something else. Graham is hinting that language does not function like a conduit, but, like the Freudian unconscious, he negates imagistically, by adding negative symbols to his positive ones.[22] If the vibrations are music, this transformation of the message appears benign. But this is only one image of the failure of the conduit.

In what Graham refers to as the 'constructed space' of the poem, 'I' and 'you' – that is, the writer and reader – 'face / Each other now across this abstract scene / Stretching between us'. Any communication that takes place between them must be passed *across* the intervening space. The preposition is an important one. As Lakoff and Johnson convincingly demonstrate, prepositions often give vital clues to the topography of a metaphorical concept.[23] The word 'across' occurs in Reddy's example sentences:

'It's very hard to get that idea across in a hostile atmosphere.'

[. . .]

'If you salesmen can't put this understanding across to the client more forcefully, our new product will fail.'[24]

In the conduit metaphor, ideas or understanding are passed across a space. In Graham's poem, the interlocutors attempt to see each other across such a space, so what is, or should be, passed is visual recognition. Later in the same poem, Graham states that it is language that must be moved across:

I say this silence or, better, construct this space
So that somehow something may move across
The caught habits of language to you and me.

(*NCP*, p. 162)

The words in 'Approaches to How They Behave' are also sent across a space: 'to go across / In roughly your direction.' (*NCP*, p. 178.) There are similar movements 'across' in many of the poems. In 'Sgurr Na Gillean Macleod', the poet characterizes himself as 'a man who rows / This light skiff of words across Silence's far cry' (*NCP*, p. 224); in 'Enter a Cloud' it is the cloud itself which moves across a separating space to the poet's friends in Cornwall and London 'bearing changing / Messages' (*NCP*, p. 217). In 'What Is the Language', the King of Whales goes 'mushing across the blind / Ice-cap between us in his furs' (*NCP*, p. 202). If, as Tony Lopez claims, the voyage is Graham's most important image, then the attempt to portray this movement from writer to reader is a possible explanation.[25]

This movement is always problematized in one way or another. One impediment to it is the vastness of the distance involved. Graham constantly complains of the distance contained within the poem; Malcolm Mooney's Land is governed 'by the laws of distance', the reader is a 'Dear Pen / Pal in the distance' (the line break emphasizes the spacing between them), and the words contain 'a great greedy space / Ready to engulf the traveller' (*NCP*, p. 154, p. 159, p. 227).

The spacing that vitiates communication is symbolically identified with wildernesses of various kinds: the sea, the Arctic, the wood of poems such as 'The Secret Name' and 'Implements' and its exotic equivalent, the jungle of 'Language Ah Now You Have Me'. These are elaborations of the metaphor implicit in the preposition 'across'. They are not only vast spaces but also unexplored ones, spaces in which the writer and his message can get lost. Each offers its own concrete characteristics to enrich the metaphor. The sea has a massive and lethal energy of its own; the Arctic has the frozen immobility of words on a page; the wood is dark, so that those who meet there cannot see each other's faces; the jungle is teeming with colourful and possibly dangerous life. But they are all spaces, and as such represent a threat to any communication which might cross them.

It seems, though, that distance itself is not a sufficient symbol of this threat to communication. The intervening space may be inhabited. As I have mentioned, the jungle of 'Language Ah Now You Have Me' has an indigenous life of its own, 'pigmies', 'a pleasure / Monkey', 'great and small breathers', 'a creature with its eggs' (*NCP*, pp. 208). In another poem, a 'great creature' lives in the space, biting, padding, sniffing and lapping up the poem's meaning (*NCP*, p.p. 157–8). In 'Dear Who I Mean', the message is a crashed kite which is intercepted by a 'god' who bears a close resemblance to a dog, carrying the message in 'spittled jaws' and being vainly whistled by the poet (*NCP*, pp. 161). The orthographic inversion which turns a dog into a god is, as I shall show in Chapter 6, a typical device; here it represents an inversion of the master-servant relationship between language-user and language. But whether the inhabitant of the textual space is subhuman or superhuman hardly matters. The important thing is that it is alive – it represents a third agency in the intended dialogue of addresser and addressee. Space, that is, has become animated, space with an agenda, but whether it is friendly, hostile or indifferent remains obscure. For this reason, Graham prefers vague words for it, 'creature', 'breathers', and, above all, 'beast', a word which ambiguously suggests both juvenile mischief and mythical predation (*NCP*, p. 208, p. 157).

A third device used to problematize the crossing of the textual space is the placing of objects in the way. There may be a 'barrier', or an 'obstacle' that prevents communication from passing (*NCP*, p. 159, p. 155). The Arctic of 'Malcolm Mooney's Land' and other poems intimidates by its opacity as well as its distances; its mountain ranges, glaciers and crevasses block movement and vision. The same is true of the trees in the forest poems. Another way of depicting the textual space as obstructed is to use the image of a prison or cage, which gives its title to Graham's first published book *Cage Without Grievance*. The quintessential poem of confinement, however, is 'Clusters Travelling Out', in which the captive speaker has to signal by tapping on the pipes or waving his arms in semaphore from the prison roof (*NCP*, pp. 191–5).

Distance, intercepting animals and barriers are all ways of troubling the 'across' part of the conduit metaphor. They are not necessarily consistent. If the poem is a space, how can it also be an 'obstacle' – empty and full at the same time? If it is a lifeless waste, why is it so full of inhabitants? (Malcolm Mooney's Land has so many voices, ghosts, hunters and explorers as to be positively overpopulated.) The contradictions are due to Graham's reliance on a metaphor which he finds inadequate but which he is unwilling to abandon. He continually gestures towards what is going wrong by using the metaphor negatively – the message is not passed, the conduit is not working – but in doing so he continues to use it.

The conduit metaphor depicts the message as a receptacle into which thoughts are placed by the writer / speaker to be taken out again by the reader / listener. When Graham talks about a word that 'said / Something it was never very likely / I could fit in to a poem in my life', he is seeing the poem as a receptacle for meaning, just as in the example listed by Reddy: 'That thought is in practically every phrase!' (*NCP*, p. 180).[26] The receptacle may be language as a whole as in 'certain experiences seem to not / Want to go in to language' (*NCP*, p. 199). On a more detailed level, it may be the specific words that 'try to come / The tin man with me' (*NCP*, pp. 252). The allusion here is to the tin man in *The Wizard of Oz*, who had no heart, and the meaning is the same as Reddy's example 'Your words seem rather hollow'.[27] Alternatively, the words may be full, but their contents remain inaccessible. This is the origin of the image of hiding, as in 'Each object hides in a metaphor' (*NCP*, p. 201). Language is seen as having an outside and an inside, but at the same time its interior is made useless, either because meanings cannot get in or because they cannot get out. Again, this image satisfies Graham's sense of the inadequacy of the conduit metaphor without actually abandoning the terms of that metaphor.

Just as the space the message was to pass across could be seen as inhabited or personified, could become an agency itself, so the receptacle can have ideas of independence:

> At times a rare metaphor's
> Fortuitous agents sing
> Equally in their own right.   (*NCP*, p. 246)

The singing here reminds us of the telegraph wires which may be singing the messages that are sent along them or humming a little tune of their own. It may even remind us of those other songsters, the birds the poet noticed sitting on the wire. Words and poems are depicted in Graham's poetry as birds, animals, or people. In 'The Fifteen Devices', and several other poems, words are equated with the rooks flying over the poet's roof, 'blown, black wobblers [. . .] from a better high flocking / Organization than mine' (*NCP*, p. 183–4). In 'Implements', the poem is a horned creature in a zoo as well as a 'great Art-Eater / Licking [its] tongue into the hill' where, no doubt, it dines on ant-like words (*NCP*, p. 248–9). In 'Approaches to How They Behave' and 'Implements', words, like impudent children, make faces at the poet (*NCP*, p. 178, p. 248). The same vague and ambiguous vocabulary which refers to animated space also applies to the animated utterance. Words are 'beasts', 'the very devil' or simply, as in 'Approaches to How They Behave', 'They' (*NCP*, p. 252, p. 246, p. 178–82).

In the conduit metaphor, as we have seen, there is a space that has to be crossed and an inner space within language. While the image of a conduit, pipeline or wire is the most obvious way of visualizing the relationship between these two spaces, there are times when the difference between the two is elided and language is seen as distance and interiority simultaneously. The phrase 'The Constructed Space' implies both the interiority of a 'constructed' receptacle and a separating distance, and indeed, the poem tells us that it stretches between writer and reader, and that 'lonely meanings' are read 'in' it (*NCP*, pp. 161–2). Similarly, prison and cage imagery simultaneously negates both elements of the metaphor, the crossing of distance and of the boundary between inside and outside.

The imagery we have looked at accepts the idea of a spatialized, reified language which is the basis of the conduit metaphor. That metaphor is a way of reconciling our sense of communication as the crossing of space with our sense that words are things or that language is a thing. If communication is the passing of things across space, then any information must be inside the things. This is a very optimistic view of language, one that allows room for the possibility of human interaction within its supposed substantiality. The conduit is passive and harmless, a medium through which messages are passed. Its role in communication is simply not to get in the way. It is this optimistic attitude that Graham's poems do not accept.

The attempt to reconcile a reified language with human participation is always likely to present practical problems. It is easy to demonstrate that words do not contain meanings, but that on the contrary meanings depend on context. Lakoff and Johnson give as an example the sentence 'Please sit in the apple-juice seat', which can only be explained by the context in which it was uttered, that of a hostess offering her guest the place with the glass of apple-juice at the breakfast table.[28] Another well-known example of a sentence whose meaning depends on context is Stanley Fish's 'Is there a text in this class?'[29] Again, there is J.L. Austin's query as to whether or not France is hexagonal, to which the answer can only be that it depends what you mean by hexagonal.[30] Clearly in these cases the meanings are not conveyed by the words alone.

The conduit metaphor, then, is inadequate to these situations, and no doubt to many instances of language use that are more significant. This is the point made by Graham's imagery; he is drawing attention to 'communication's // Mistakes in the magic medium' (*NCP*, p. 200). The aspect of the formula whose existence he never questions, however, is the 'medium'. His metaphors portray language as stretching between us, both space and object. If meaning is not getting through, it must be because of some property of the medium, its 'magic'. Instead of being a traversible space, language is a wilderness; instead of an accessible container, it is a prison; instead of a passive receptacle, it is an active agent, a meaning-devouring monster. But why should he choose to see it as a space or a thing or an agent at all? The answer, I suggest, is that it is text that encourages us to see language in this way; both the conduit metaphor and Graham's attempts to negate it are products of textuality.

Sydney Ought to Be Given Away

Metaphors, I have argued, are grounded in culture and experience – and, obviously, the culture to which one belongs shapes to a great extent the experience one has. We live in a literate culture, and much of our experience of language is textual. This inevitably influences the way we look at language in general. Indeed, members of nonliterate cultures cannot *look* at language at all; it is not, as Walter J. Ong has pointed out, an enduring physical presence to them.[31] Words come to be seen as things when they are written down or printed.[32] In societies where this technology does not exist, they are events, or rather actions, since they never exist separate from the person who utters them.[33] (The issue of 'secondary orality', the cultural developments made possible by new long-distance and / or permanent forms of oral communication such as radio, telephones and television, is by no means irrelevant to Graham, who broadcast on the radio and whose poem 'Wynter and the Grammarsow' mimics a tape-recording. However, it is not a major theme, and since its cultural implications are only gradually becoming apparent, I shall not be able to consider it here.)[34]

Ong shows that the implications of this textual bias are manifold, and that some of them are buried so deep in our culture that they are hard for us to detect. The oral universe is human-centered, since all knowledge is located in individuals. It is therefore inseparable from human needs, activities and priorities. 'Objective' knowledge is a meaningless concept in orally-based societies. But literacy has given us a sense that knowledge is in some way autonomous, that it can be detached from the human lifeworld. Writing may continue to exist long after the occasion that produced it is finished. It thus acquires an oracular status, seeming to utter itself and to generate meanings which transcend particular circumstances.[35] This sense of autonomy has been reinforced by the development of print, which presents text as an artefact.[36] Books may be seen as 'utterances', but their 'speakers' remain out of reach, and their 'listeners' are always eavesdroppers, since books are not directed at specific individuals.[37] Writing and print bring with them the sense that language exists in a separate domain from the human beings who use it. The idea of language as a closed, self-governing system is very powerful, reinforced, as Ong shows, by texts such as grammar books and dictionaries.[38]

The conduit metaphor, which depends on a reified language containing meaning, can only apply in a literate society, in which words – or the paper they are written on – can be given away, scrutinized, picked up, put down or left lying around. Furthermore, books, which are boxlike in shape and can be opened and closed, provide a concrete symbol of the interiority which is so important a part of the metaphor. As we have seen, this textually-derived sense of language as a physical entity with an outside and an inside persists even in accounts, such as Graham's, that ostensibly reject the conduit metaphor.

His view of language partakes, then, of this general textual bias. When he writes of 'language', he often seems to mean 'text' or even specifically poetry. To picture language as white, as he does in 'What Is the Language' is to picture it as a page. Confusingly, though, he does not ignore speech or dismiss it as inferior; instead, he regularly compares writing and speech in his work, to the detriment of the former. Writing must always fail in its attempt to emulate speech because:

[. . .] we want to be telling

Each other alive about each other
Alive.

(*NCP*, p. 200)

Sound is portrayed as natural and fulfilling while sight is artificial and alienating, yet in becoming a writer Graham has condemned himself to an endless attempt to bridge the unbridgeable gap between the two and suffer the resultant loneliness and silence:

I speak as well as I can
Trying to teach my ears
To learn to use their eyes
Even only maybe
In the end to observe
The behaviour of silence.

(*NCP*, p. 171)

'Silence', that constantly reiterated word, is identified with the alienation he associates with writing. It is 'the northern dazzle' that watches Malcolm Mooney, the 'terrible shapes' of the invisible audience listening curiously to the flautist Karl, the food and residence of the beast in the space (*NCP*, p. 153, p. 229, p. 157). Writing is a kind of speech ('I speak as well as I can') which never quite manages to fulfil the role of speech, so that the silence it tries to break is ultimately unmarked by it (*NCP*, p. 182).

Graham's sense of what language is derives primarily from his experience of text, but when he tries to explain this experience, he does so by contrasting it with speech. He appears not to regard speech as language at all; to write, on the other hand, is to give oneself up to a world of pure language. He would no doubt have been surprised by Jacques Derrida's refusal to accept conventional distinctions between speech and writing:

It is as if the Western concept of language [. . .] were revealed today as the guise or disguise of a primary writing: more fundamental than that which, before this conversion, passed for the simple 'supplement to the spoken word' (Rousseau). Either writing was never a simple 'supplement', or it is urgently necessary to construct a new logic of the 'supplement'.[39]

This approach seems directly opposed to that of Ong, who indeed attacks it for its 'historically unreflective, uncritical literacy'.[40] Nevertheless, the effects of Ong's investigation into the difference and Derrida's deconstruction of it are rather similar. What Derrida shows is that literacy has generated a mythology of speech; precisely because speech is displaced by writing to an inaccessible distance, it becomes a symbol of a perfect conjunction of meaning and being which is in fact nowhere to be found. This is Derrida's concept of presence.[41] *Physical presence*, in its common-sense meaning, is, of course a condition of speech (except where telecommunications or tape-recording are involved), and I shall not forget the adjective when I wish to refer to this fact. The Derridean or transcendent presence is what physical presence symbolizes in the logocentric myth. Graham never arrives at Derrida's deconstruction of the speech / writing opposition, even though in his preoccupation with the effects of writing he seems to inhabit a Derridean world. Time and again he returns to a logocentric position, in which speech is affirmed as not only primary, but almost sacred.

The conduit metaphor, I have claimed, is optimistic; it attempts to put the thing-like language at the service of human beings. People are still a part of the process it depicts, one to put the meaning in and one (the reader is usually imagined as singular) to take it out again. Furthermore, the 'across' part of the metaphor, the distance the message has to traverse, appears to be modelled on speech. In conversation, people have a physical sense of the distance between them. As this increases, they have to speak louder in order to be heard. As it grows still further, communication becomes impossible. Writing solves this problem – instead of trying to shout across the intervening space, I can put my message in a letter and send it. My words can be read by people on the other side of the world. It would be possible, then, to see writing as an enhanced form of speech, one with a long-distance capability.[42]

It is perhaps easiest to believe this of letters, which are typically written from one known individual to another and traverse a definable separating distance. Graham had a considerable investment in this form of communication. He was, unlike most people of a later generation, a prolific letter-writer, and enjoyed the sense of long-range intimacy which writing them gave him. In many of his letters, he evokes and requests signs of physical presence and love from his correspondents (just the sort of thing that cannot be sent through a conduit of this type), while at the same time reminding them of the distance across which these tokens must be miraculously sent: 'Here I am. Alone in this place and I write to you across the night shires of England. [. . .] Hold me in your four arms, you two.'[43] Many of his poems take the form of, or borrow some of the conventions of, letters, from '1st Letter' and '2nd Letter' (*NCP*, p. 20, p. 27) through the 'Seven Letters' of *The Nightfishing* (*NCP*, pp. 121–40) to 'Yours Truly' (*NCP*, p. 159), 'Dear Who I Mean' (*NCP*,

p. 160) and 'A Note to the Difficult One' (*NCP*, p. 206). Graham also takes full advantage of the literary convention whereby published poems may be addressed to individuals. The *New Collected Poems* contains addresses to his brother (*NCP*, p. 98), father (*NCP*, p. 99, p. 222), mother (*NCP*, p. 100) and wife (*NCP*, pp. 78, p. 166, p. 263), to Peter Lanyon (*NCP*, p. 163), Don Brown (*NCP*, p. 174), Roger Hilton (*NCP*, p. 177), Bryan Wynter (*NCP*, p. 184, p. 258), Norman Macleod (*NCP*, p. 223, p. 225) and Robin Skelton (*NCP*, p. 234).

If a text can be as personal as a letter, its ability to cross the shires or even the ocean is a simple asset. But at the same time as making distance traversible, text makes it meaningless. A printed text does not cross one particular distance separating two interlocutors; it exists simultaneously in many places, and the decisive factor separating readers from writer is not physical distance but their ignorance of each other's circumstances. As Ong and Derrida both point out, the writer may even be dead.[44] The physical distance which can impede speech is overcome by writing, but at the same time it is transformed into an eerie metaphorical distance (the mutual invisibility and inaudibility of the correspondents) which never changes. We have already seen that Graham uses images of vast distances to symbolize the threat to communication. A speech that carries its own distance around with it becomes a kind of despairing shout. The author has 'reached the edge of earshot', the brink of an abyss where his attempts to communicate receive only echoes in reply (*NCP*, p. 154, p. 227). At the end of one of his meditations on the nature of writing, he becomes so oppressed by its silence that he feels the urge to shout:

> [. . .] Hello
> Hello I shout but that silence
> Floats steady, will not be marked
> By an off-hand shout.

> (*NCP*, pp. 182)

Graham accepts that words cannot pass thoughts or emotions, though he certainly wishes they could. Indeed, for him, as we have seen, nothing less will do than the passing of physical presence itself, a four-armed hug, 'a moth-kiss [. . .] in the hollow under your left ear', 'a light kiss on the outside of the right buttock'.[45] The lack of physical presence threatens even the personal communication promised by the letter form:

> Because we are not physically seeing each other one believes by memory

and hope that one still has some connection with another. That is true, that's how it works. WOW! What a mouthful. Are you there? Are you there?[46]

Writing and reading, as Ong notes, are solitary activities.[47] To choose the life of a writer is inevitably to choose to be alone for much of the time. Even when Graham writes to his friends, he is conscious of his solitude. In poems, he frequently complains of this loneliness. The page is a place with 'no love', and the poet asks only 'to be by another aloneness loved' (*NCP*, p. 205, p. 177). It is as if he has given up all the consolations of human society in return for a bodiless communication with someone of whose presence he can never be certain. In the case of a published poem, even a named addressee must share the text with an unknown audience of 'gentle and un / Gentle readers' (*NCP*, p. 227). The irony of this situation is painstakingly explained in 'Private Poem to Norman Macleod':

> The idea of me making
> Those words fly together
> In seemingly a private
> Letter is just me choosing
> An attitude to make a poem.

> (*NCP*, p. 227)

The poems struggle to be direct, personal communications but they must always accede to the absence that characterizes text. Most of the 'letter' poems do not have a named recipient, and many of those that do have one who is in no position to reply, since he or she is dead. The poems to his mother, father and Lanyon, and the second of each of those to Hilton and Wynter, are in fact elegies. The condition of textuality makes every poem an elegy, Graham claims, because the reader is never present. As he writes to his dead friend Wynter:

> Speaking to you and not
> Knowing if you are there
> Is not too difficult.
> My words are used to that.

> (*NCP*, p. 258)

If texts do not contain ideas, it is even more apparent that they do not contain people. But because Graham models communication on the face-to-face encounters characteristic of speech and, at the same time, insists on imagining text as space, the poem metaphorically becomes the scene of an uncanny meeting in which neither of the participants is physically present to the other. (The Freudian theme of the uncanny is discussed in Chapter 4.) One way of symbolizing this mutual absence is to have the meeting take place in darkness:

> And who are you and by
> What right do I waylay
> You where you go there
> Happy enough striking
> Your hobnail in the dark?

(NCP, p. 167.)

It is largely for this reason that Graham is a poet of the dark, a specialist in nocturnes. He cannot hope to know the circumstances in which the poems might be read, or the identity of the generalized reader, the 'Dear Pen / Pal in the distance' or 'Dear Who I Mean' who can only be visualized as a monstrous figure with the 'vast unseen eyes' already referred to and a 'deadly face' (*NCP*, pp. 159, p. 160, p. 181, p. 213). As for his own circumstances, he tries his best to pass these on. He writes at an 'Untidy Dreadful Table', usually 'in the small hours' (*NCP*, p. 205, p. 188). He uses a typewriter, which provides him with images like the 'taps' of the Muse, 'the strike of the [. . .] key' and the typing exercise which generates the phrase 'quick brown [. . .] god' (*NCP*, p. 188, p. 256, p. 161).[48] He knows, however, that by the time the reader reads the poem, he may be somewhere else entirely. In 'Clusters Travelling Out', he asks 'Has it been a good Wednesday? Or is yours Tuesday?' (*NCP*, p. 194).

From the reader's point of view, it is the author who is absent. Graham, one feels, rejects the conduit metaphor primarily because he has found it impossible to send himself through the conduit – as his girlfriend Julian Orde said of him, 'Sydney ought to be given away with every copy of his book.'[49] To write is to imagine one's own absence, a process akin to imagining one's death; his poems remind us that 'I am not here,' (*NCP*, p. 158, p. 257).[50] Graham is now really dead, but his poems still exist, repeating their statements about thought, memory and desire long after their author has ceased to be capable of these functions. In a sense, this cessation begins as soon as the words are written. The poems have not changed since their author's death; they are as indifferent to him as they always were. Unlike Roland Barthes, for whom 'the death of the author' is the dissolution of an oppressive myth and the empowerment of the reader, Graham might be said to take the phrase personally, and to consider himself bereaved of himself:[51]

So I spoke and died.
So within the dead
Of night and the dead
Of all my life those
Words died and awoke.

(*NCP*, p. 120)

'Those / Words', which end Graham's longest poem, 'The Nightfishing',
have a final ring about them. It would seem that once he had acknowl-
edged so explicitly this painful truth about writing, there could not be
much more to say. The choice is either to accept it or to give up. After
the poem's publication in book form there was a long gap, in which his
publishers apparently assumed he was literally dead. Yet when he
returned to print, it was with poems that reiterated the same lament,
that nagged away at the death of the author as though they hoped to
resurrect him by sheer persistence:

[..]what is the good
Of me isolating my few words
In a certain order to send them
Out in a suicide torpedo to hit?
I ride it. I will never know.

(*NCP*, p. 248)

The meeting between writer and reader not only takes place in the
dark, but also in a timeless zone because of the permanence of written
language. Continuing to model his understanding of text on speech,
Graham explains this permanence as a consequence of the freezing of
real-time conversation in order to turn it into the space of text, another
reason for the Arctic imagery of some of the poems. In 'Malcolm
Mooney's Land', the passage of time has become a 'diary of a place', and
each section of the poem represents a day (*NCP*, p. 156).

The world of things is a problem, too. The linguistic sign works by
pointing to the absent, 'half of it always "not there" and the other half
always "not that"' in Gayatri Chakravorty Spivak's neat phrase.[52] In
speech situations, this absence can be supplemented by literal pointing,
a method known to philosophers of language as 'ostensive definition'.
(This is not, of course, a foolproof solution to problems of reference, as
Wittgenstein noted.)[53] Spoken language typically takes place in a known
and shared context and is provided with a number of connecting words
called 'deictics' used by speakers to relate it to this context. These
include the personal and demonstrative pronouns and adjectives, and

act like hooks attaching language to the perceived and demonstrable world. In a conversation, we either know what our interlocutor means by 'this' or we can soon find out by asking a question. In text, however, 'this', like 'I' and 'you', becomes problematic; the deictics float on the page unconnected to any shared context.[54] Their use in a poem, therefore, involves a kind of trust. Poet and reader have to believe they are 'seeing' – that is, imagining – the same objects.

In one of Graham's late poems, he asks the reader to 'imagine a forest / A real forest', and proceeds to describe one:

> [. . .] Go on between
> The elephant bark of those beeches
> Into that lightening, almost glade.

(NCP, p. 204)

The 'context' here has been created by the poet's effort of will. As if by magic he has created a world, instructing the reader by the use of imperatives ('imagine', 'go on') to participate in it. If the reader co-operates, he or she may seem to recognize the objects with which Graham has furnished this imaginary world, 'those beeches' and 'that [. . .] glade'. But this quasi-recognition demands an effort of will on the part of the reader also. It is no coincidence that the situation to be imagined is that of a traveller lost in a forest. The glade may be 'almost' because it is overgrown or because it is, after all, only the product of verbal illusionism. The deictics are a confidence trick – a trick, that is, to gain the reader's confidence – and in the next two lines this is apparently achieved:

> And he has taken
> My word and gone.

'Real' is a word Graham uses when he wants to draw attention to the failure of the poem to contain things or people (which, as we have seen, it cannot do because it is not a container). Reality is something we must all provide for ourselves; the poet must simply trust us to relate the words 'real' and 'forest' to our own experience of words and trees. Equally, when he says of a character in a poem, 'he is a real man', he cannot indicate the man concerned and so compel us to believe him (*NCP*, p. 219). In his poems there are statements about Bryan Wynter and others about Malcolm Mooney. It happens that Bryan Wynter was 'a real man', an artist and friend of Graham, while Malcolm Mooney is a fictional character, whose name Graham took from a chain of pubs run by Guinness.[55] The author cannot ultimately be responsible for the reader's knowledge of such distinctions.

Language's failure to provide vicarious experience is demonstrated in 'Imagine a Forest' by the example of death. The poet describes the body of a dead stranger to remind us of the death we will all have to face on our own, but no amount of telling us about this adds up to an experience of it. As Graham remarks to his dead friend Wynter in another poem:

> [. . .] I couldn't really
> Have died for you if so
> I were inclined.

> (*NCP*, p. 258)

The impossibility of transmitting an experience linguistically from one mind to another is a concept referred to as the indeterminacy of language.[56] Many people find the idea difficult to accept, but Reddy's essay shows that it is possible to apply it without making communication unviable.[57] Language is not a container for thoughts but a device by means of which people construct their own thoughts, referring the words as best they can to the world as they experience it.[58] Communication is not a simple process of sending and receiving messages; instead, sender and receiver work at achieving an approximate degree of understanding, one that will be suitable for the purposes they each have in mind. This understanding is never 'right' nor is it ever the same from one receiver to another. It is also subject to revision when circumstances require it. There is no objective standard by which the success of such a communication can be measured – it is part of the complex system of all our social relations. It is only the attempt to cut language off from these relations by insisting on its autonomy that makes indeterminacy a cause for despair.

'Imagine a Forest' brilliantly expounds this indeterminacy, a theme which Graham summarizes elsewhere in the phrase 'the words are mine [. . .] the thoughts are all / Yours' (*NCP*, pp. 181). And yet, as we have seen, he cannot be content with it. He is constantly having to remind himself that language does not contain the 'real'; instead, in another of his key words, it is 'abstract'. In 'Five Visitors to Madron' he depicts himself in the act of writing 'with my chair drawn / Up to the frightening abstract / Table of silence (*NCP*, p. 188). In 'The Constructed Space', writing is an 'abstract act' which the poet himself *becomes* (*NCP*, p. 162). He was fascinated by the phrase 'It Must Be Abstract', the title of the first section of Wallace Stevens's long poem 'Notes Toward a Supreme Fiction'.[59]

The indeterminacy of language and the poet's failure to send himself through the conduit together make his original intention in writing the poem irrelevant. He does not know how the reader will interpret his words. Graham depicts this uncertainty, in the poem 'The Dark Intention', as a dark wood:

> My first intention was at least not this
> That darkly gathers over the ground.
> The dark discloses us in different ways.
>
> Here in this wood can I be this disguise
> Wielding a muffled light without a sound?
> My first intention was at least not this.

(NCP, p. 270)

The critique of intentionality here reminds us that Graham was a younger contemporary of the New Critics, and indeed met some of them on his trips to the United States. 'The Alligator Girls' is dedicated to John Crowe Ransom (*NCP*, p. 277).[60] But he did not need to learn this theme from literary theory – it follows from all I have been saying about his experience and understanding of the isolation of text. It is not surprising that 'The Dark Dialogues' opens with the words:

> I always meant to only
> Language swings away
> Further before me.

(NCP, p. 167)

The poet's intention cannot guide the poem, but must always vainly pursue a perversely independent language.

The only reality he can describe with the confidence of being understood is the physical reality of page and words. The last lines of 'Malcolm Mooney's Land' refer us to:

> Words drifting on words.
> The real unabstract snow.

(NCP, p. 157)

The phrase is puzzling at first – the 'snow' is no more real than any other feature of the poem's landscape. But it is not snow that is unabstract but the snowlike drifting of words. The poem, like nearly all of Graham's poems, is self-referential; among the many things it points to is itself. We might wish to call it a metapoem.

A metapoem is a poem that takes itself as its own object of reference. It is the poetic equivalent of a metafictional novel, such as Italo

Calvino's *If on a Winter's Night a Traveller*, which describes the efforts of a reader to read 'Italo Calvino's new novel *If on a Winter's Night a Traveller*.'[61] Perhaps because fiction in the twentieth century has been the dominant literary genre and hence its role in the social construction of reality has been more significant than that of poetry, critics have paid more attention to metafiction than to metapoetry.[62] In studies by Robert Alter, Patricia Waugh and Linda Hutcheon, the consensus is that metafictional novels, by drawing attention to their textuality, dispel the illusion of reality which is the aim of more traditional fiction. They reveal, that is, the materiality of language. The process is ingenuous, an abandonment of artifice.[63]

Seen in relation to Graham's desire to capture in words the physical presence that is a condition of speech, to send and receive hugs and kisses down the conduit of text, an alternative explanation of his metapoems suggests itself. Far from being a demystification of the materiality of language, they are an attempt to master its indeterminacy, the last stand of intentionality. You must know what I mean, he says: I mean *these words, here*. In 'The Nightfishing', he interrupts his narrative to tell us 'These words take place' (*NCP*, p. 110). In 'Enter a Cloud', 'the real ones' he thanks for their contribution to the text include the 'good words' that have helped him write it (*NCP*, p. 219). And in 'The Dark Dialogues', he shows an exasperated awareness of his failure to escape more than momentarily from self-reference:

> This is no other place
> Than where I am, between
> This word and the next.
> Maybe I should expect
> To find myself only
> Saying that again
> Here now at the end.

> (*NCP*, p. 174)

It is as if metapoetry is a vortex that inevitably sucks him in sooner or later. The consolation of words that suddenly seem to have lost their duplicity, their refusal to be tied to the poet's intention, is achieved at a price. The repetition entailed by his self-referential compulsion seems to have frustrated even him. 'Is where you listen from becoming / Numb by the strike of the same key?' he asks in 'Implements', and it is sometimes tempting to answer 'yes' (*NCP*, p. 256).

Graham is a remarkable poet but this obsession makes him a limited one. In 'Five Verses Beginning With the Word Language', for example, his attempt to deal with the Vietnam War by writing a poem about the death of a North Vietnamese soldier proves unable to balance its linguistic and political concerns, so that eventually 'the jungle metaphor' becomes irritating in its artificiality (*NCP*, pp. 331–3). In its final version, 'Language Ah Now You Have Me', (*NCP*, pp. 207–9) the setting is no longer Vietnam but 'damp paper / In the rain forest beside the Madron River' (that is, in the author's Cornish home). Contrasting this with the original plan, as quoted by Robin Skelton and Margaret Blackwood in their notes to *Aimed at Nobody*, one can only feel disappointed:

> ... the very beginning of this poem sprung from me trying to write about a soldier dying on the Paddy fields of Vietnam of a belly-wound and the flies at his face and wanting his mother and not knowing what he was fighting for.
>
> (*AAN*, p. 66, quoted in *NCP*, pp. 368–9.)

Coming as the culmination of such a project, 'Language Ah Now You Have Me' is a cry of defeat.

Graham's poems are about language, but they take text as the epitome of language. To summarize, his claim about text is that it substitutes for the real-time, personal, meaningful encounter between living human beings, an impersonal, timeless space. In such a space, communication can never really take place because the text is indeterminate: the interlocutors see neither each other nor the same objects. This condition is contrasted with speech where language does not have to do all the work on its own; meaning can be ascertained by reference to a shared context. Even more important, in such face-to-face encounters physical signs can be used, especially those which convey love, such as a hug or a kiss. The only physical world writer and reader have in common is that of the page itself, and Graham's texts endlessly refer to this in an attempt to defeat the indeterminacy of language. But in so doing, he is aware of the realities, political and otherwise, he leaves untackled. As he is forced back yet again to statements about 'these words', he cannot help feeling that language is calling the tune. It has him in its power.

The Playground of the Text

Throughout this discussion, I have insisted that certain views of language are only metaphors. The conduit metaphor is an easy target; as we have seen, it has been subjected to a searching critique not only by

Reddy but also by Graham's poems. But I have gone further, arguing that all views of language as object or space, closed or autonomous, are metaphors which, like those considered by Lakoff, Johnson and Turner, highlight some aspects of linguistic experience while hiding others. They are grounded in the experience of reading and writing. Is not Graham right, therefore, to contrast the features of text I discussed in the last section with the condition of speech? What aspects of the textual experience are his metaphors hiding?

He is in a sense quite accurate in seeing text as impersonal and frozen – but it is impersonal and frozen not by its essential nature but by the conventions of our culture. 'The author cannot be reached in any book,' Ong tells us, but the idea that a book is a protected space is not universally acknowledged.[64] Salman Rushdie was held to account for *The Satanic Verses* by an Islamic community which refused to accept, and perhaps could not understand, the Western convention whereby books are considered to some extent independent of their authors. For them, a book was to be understood primarily as the act of an individual as, according to Ong, oral cultures regard utterances primarily as acts.[65] Again, we assume that texts are static, but poems like 'Clusters Travelling Out' and 'The Thermal Stair' in fact went through a great many drafts. It is only by convention that we see these as imperfect and abortive prototypes of a final text. Why should not the entire portfolio be read as a text which constructs itself before our eyes? The answer, of course, is to do with the conventions that govern the publishing industry in our society. The book is a complete product which exists independently of both its author and the processes of writing and manufacturing by which it was produced. Even the margin round a poem, the snowy space which Graham takes to be one of his few reliable objects of reference, is contingent, an artificial rather than a natural and inevitable symbol of the text's separation from the world. The text as place or thing, rather than act or process, is one of the metaphors we live by.

What Graham sought in writing was control. If text is, as our culture tells us it is, a bounded, protected place, then the writer can play freely there without interference from anybody else. He can turn it into 'a place I can think in / And think anything in' (*NCP*, p. 168). But the price he pays for this control is loneliness: the playground of the text appears to be an extension of his own mind. And so in his writing he dreams of speech, and of the intimacy that can take place between people who are physically present to each other. This, of course, is easy enough to obtain in everyday life. That intimacy, though, is not always blissfully unencumbered; it carries with it responsibilities and dangers. To love is to give up part of one's will to the loved one. Graham, hiding in what he regards as the safety of the text, tries to achieve intimacy through it, to make contact with others, while at the same time retaining control. The only way he can do this is through self-reference, because this is the only literary trope in which the writer's intention wholly governs the meaning. This limits his field of play even more severely – 'these words' may be material, but they are a poor substitute for hugs and kisses.

Reddy's solution to the problem of the indeterminacy of language is reciprocity. As the original sender and receiver continue to exchange messages, they become aware of the difference in each other's circumstances and their mental images approximate more and more closely. Interestingly, his model of this exchange is a textual one, in which the correspondents leave written messages at an agreed point.[66] Our conventional model of text, on the other hand, does not permit reciprocity:

> I am always very aware that my poem is not a telephone call. The poet only speaks one way. He hears nothing back. His words as he utters them are not conditioned by a real ear replying from the other side.[67]

It is the objectifying margins of the poem and covers of the book that allow poets to believe that a text is a totally isolated utterance whose author 'hears nothing back'. The same man who complained that no one replied to his texts also said of his reviews: 'My verse seems to rile reviewers into almost personal spite or result in a whole-hearted acclaiming'.[68] The text is part of a constant exchange of messages in which the author is only one participant. The social nature of all language, including text, together with its indeterminacy means that meaning is always subject to negotiation.[69] Control by one individual, even an author, is as impossible in a poem as it is in a face-to-face, 'real life' encounter with other people. Following the publication of the *New Collected Poems*, the meaning of Graham's work, far from being limited by his original intention, continues to be renegotiated in the public arena years after his death. The present study is an attempt at making a useful contribution to this negotiation.

In the chapters that follow, I shall persist in ascribing thoughts and feelings to Graham, in defiance of the post-New-Critical tradition which reminds us (as does Reddy) that we cannot see the inside of his head. This limitation, after all, affects not just our relationship to the author of a text but every relationship we have. If a poem is a social act, as I believe it is, we are entitled to treat it as one, and the fact is that we are all happy to continue our social interactions with an assortment of opaque individuals on the basis of nothing more than our speculative insights into their motives; if these insights seem debatable, our response is to debate them rather than to condemn such speculation as epistemologically inadmissible. I am not insisting on my determinate knowledge of Graham's intentions, but I *am* insisting on my right to propose a provisional account of them just as one would for any human act. The poems are not a conduit conveying thoughts from his brain to ours, but they may be the smoking gun or, to use a less incriminating image, the smouldering ashtray, from which, like detectives, we can retrospectively construct a story. My approach is similar to Reddy's description of the process by which his hypothetical correspondents arrive at a picture of each other's circumstances.[70]

Graham was seeking control but he was also seeking love. Throughout his work, as I shall show in the next chapter, he states his desire to surrender to the will of others – but he does so from a safe distance. Just as he uses writing to praise speech, so he spent a life of comparative isolation celebrating community. He travelled as far from his original home as it was possible for him to get without leaving the country, and then wrote poems full of yearning for home. He attempts to reconcile these discrepancies by displacing his feelings about home and other people on to language. In an ingenious trope which is, in my view, central to his oeuvre, he turns language itself into a community.

CHAPTER 2

Poet of Community

An Indeterminate Love

Graham is a poet of language but he is also a poet of community. This word will require further definition; for now, though, it is enough to point out that his poems constantly affirm the value of relationships with other people. As in the case of language, this is easily demonstrated by even a cursory reading of the *New Collected Poems*. I have already noted that many of the poems are addressed to individuals, living or dead: to his wife, his brother, parents and friends. In effect, they are love poems, offerings from one individual to another, like 'I Leave This At Your Ear', which was presumably left by Nessie Dunsmuir's bedside while she slept (*NCP*, p. 166). (Graham was in the habit of sending poems as presents to his friends, and the poem-addresses in the *New Collected* represent only a small part of the writing he produced in this vein.) Some of the poems stress the poet's affection by means of endearments; Nessie Dunsmuir is 'my dear', while Norman Macleod is 'my dear Norman' and 'my boy' and the dead Roger Hilton is also 'dear' (*NCP*, p. 166, p. 225; p. 227, p. 237). Gestures of love are also important, in the poems as in the letters: he takes 'a moth kiss' from his sleeping wife and asks the dead Lanyon for his hand (*NCP*, p. 165). But, as I have remarked, the perpetual frustration of language is that such physical contact cannot be made through it; explaining abstraction to Hilton, he contrasts it with the intimacy that signifies love: 'We either touch or do not touch' (*NCP*, p. 177). The most direct of his protestations of love are reserved for situations where contact is ruled out. The loved person may be dead, like his father ('I think I must have loved him' – *NCP*, p. 223) or Hilton ('I loved him' – *NCP*, p. 235). Alternatively, the poem may be an expression of love for a reader who is not and can never be known. The anonymous addressee of 'Are You Still There?' is loved indirectly – the poem opens with the statement 'I love I love you', suggesting the possibility that the phrase itself (and hence words in general) has absorbed some or all of the poet's love. It is useless for the reader to expect a hug, but the verbal substitute provided may even transcend such gestures – 'I love you more than that' (*NCP*, p. 207).

Language, as we shall see in the course of this chapter, transcends physical intimacy in some respects and falls short of it in others. What is immediately clear, however, is that for Graham both language and art stand or fall by their ability or inability to express love. The indeterminacy which problematizes meaning has the same effect on love, and indeed it is for this reason that he finds it such a threat. Pleasure alone is not enough for him:

> What shape of words shall put its arms
> Round us for more than pleasure?

> (*NCP*, p. 201)

Instead the artist has a duty to provide a permanent monument to love:

> [. . .] His job is Love
> Imagined into words or paint to make
> An object that will stand and will not move.

> (*NCP*, p. 164)

This involves diverting love from its natural flow between known individuals. 'The Beast in the Space' is, as we have seen, a figure of the inhumanity and distance of text, but Graham nevertheless asks the reader to 'give him your love' (*NCP*, p. 158). What he cannot know is whether his own textualized love, like textual meaning, ever arrives at its final unseen destination. The page is a place 'with no love' (*NCP*, p. 205), and he complains:

> Dammit these words are making faces
> At me again. I hope the faces
> They make at you have more love.

> (*NCP*, p. 248)

It is love, then, rather than pleasure or such other ideals as beauty, truth and religious faith, that he takes as the ultimate criterion of textual value.

Of course, love of one kind or another is a traditional theme of poetry. Sexual love is the kind most frequently associated with it, but Graham is not, on the whole, a great poet of passion. In the two late poems to Nessie Dunsmuir, for example, there is no attempt to describe his feelings for her, apart from the conventional endearments I have mentioned (*NCP*, p. 166, pp. 263–5). Throughout his poetry, however, one can find sexual imagery. In the early poems it is one among many possible targets for the poet's restless creative energy. Vague female figures abound, a 'bride', the 'gentle queen of the afternoon', 'a peartree girl', together with Nessie Dunsmuir herself, 'my warfare wife', though they were not in fact married at this time (*NCP*, p. 17, p. 18, p. 23, p. 51). Sex and landscape are intertwined, and both are seen as potential poetic material:

> Who, with a map of picnics primed for April
> Could probe humanity and hoist a sign of veins?

> (*NCP*, p. 18)

The question here is whether the poem, an explosive map incorporating the conventional materials of pastoral, is an abstract substitute for sex that can penetrate the human species in general. Is the 'sign of veins', that is, the linguistic representation of flesh-and-bood humanity, a superior version of that other hoisted sign of veins, the erect penis? The sexual act in this case stands for all human contact, and the masculine energy of the poet's writing is the best evidence he can offer that communication may be possible.

Later in his career, however, there is more ambivalence in his treatment of sex. In 'Letter VI', the encounter between two lovers provides a model of perfect communion:

> I moved and caught the sweet
> Courtesy of your mouth.
> My breath to your breath.

> (*NCP*, p. 135)

In such an encounter the boundary between individuals is abolished. Or rather, since this is an impossibility, a particular gesture of contact or penetration, by transgressing that boundary, symbolically abolishes it. Such gestures, which include the touch, the kiss, sexual intercourse and, in religious ritual, the eating of symbolic food, can only be temporary, but they stand for a total and permanent union. This kind of border-crossing is dangerous, and the ritual nature of communion is necessary to protect individuals from the violation of their integrity that it may entail. So the encounter between lovers depicted here begins by describing the kiss as an act of 'courtesy', reminding us of the limits which circumscribe the woman's offering of herself. Within those limits, the temporary ecstasy of mutuality can be enjoyed. The kiss is a substitute for speech in which the separation of the roles of speaker and listener has ceased to exist.[1] Instead of a transaction between mouth and ear, there is a meeting of mouth and mouth, a shared breathing more intimate even than speech. But the kiss is not only a wordless form of speech; it is also a metonymy for sex, in which the joining of mouths hides the difference that is fundamental to the act, that of penis and vagina. Focusing on the kiss allows the illusion that sex can be a total union of identities rather than an act in which male and female retain their separate identities and different sexual functions. The lovers are 'halfway / Your body and my body', the boundary between them elided. Already, though, this communion is in the past, as the use of tenses shows. In the last three lines, the shift to the present and the concluding question suggests that it has been succeeded by responsibility, doubt and guilt:

> The great verbs of the sea
> Come down on us in a roar.
> What shall I answer for?

We shall see again and again in Graham's work that communion, though fervently believed in, is always situated in the past, and that language is blamed for its loss – the sexual encounter 'without a word' is succeeded by 'the great verbs'.

The poems of the last period often show a rather jaded attitude to sex. Marital intercourse is as regular and boring as factory work, a case of 'punching the sexual / Clock' (*NCP*, p. 241). Love is turned sour by 'dirty milkbottles', and there are hints of joyless adultery in Sections 8, 9 and 47 of 'Implements' '(*NCP*, p. 244, p. 241–2, p. 251). There is more emphasis on the discomforts and disharmonies of sex, a numb right arm in 'Implements' and, in 'The Lying Dear', the poem which most strikingly exemplifies this dissatisfaction, a lover who calls out the wrong name (*NCP*, p. 256, pp. 158–9). Sex is already imperfect, involving deceit (the woman's 'acting flutters') and power (the man's 'pinning arm') rather than the communion celebrated in 'Letter VI'. Nevertheless, the imperfection here, like the fall from grace in the earlier poem, is blamed on language, with the difference that this encounter, instead of taking place 'without a word', is already verbal as well as physical. The dead right arm of 'Implements' recalls the left leg of the narrator of 'What Is the Language?', which 'has no feeling' because of the frozen impersonality of text, and 'The Lying Dear' is a symbol of the reader, whose idea of the poet stands in for the real man: 'some image not me' (*NCP*, p. 200, p. 158). The ecstasy of the lovers in the latter is displaced and disorientating, a vertiginous though not unpleasurable sleigh-ride into 'a new language'. The sexual encounter, based as it is on difference, is an allegory of language, and it is for this reason that sex itself can symbolize a fall from the possibility of communion.

The love of family is a more important theme in the poems than sexual love. Nevertheless, it is largely implicit in the early poetry, manifested above all in the depiction of a tranquil pastoral landscape within which he situates home. A poem like 'Say That In Lovers With Stones For Family', cryptic as it is, contains obvious elements of domesticity – a husband, a wife, children and, apparently, the imagery of a seaside holiday:

[. . .] she speaks beside a boatless sea
To minnow children milling cliff to sand.

(*NCP*, p. 23)

'Here Next The Chair I Was When Winter Went' describes the poet leaving his home in the spring and looking for a new one. Moving across the landscape like the smoke of the late winter bonfires, he shelters in his own grief:

Like making a hut of fingers cupped for tears
Love burned my bush that was my burning mother.

(*NCP*, p. 21)

The burning bush identifies him with the exiled Israelites, and in its association with a prophetic vocation is a rhetorical device by which he justifies his leaving.[2] (It is linked with the mother by way of the old wives' tale that babies are found under gooseberry bushes.) Love is behind him in his home and in front of him, the object of his search, for, despite the typically mystifying syntax of the first sentence, it seems to be the poet rather than winter who goes 'looking for distant bothies of love'. His means of doing so is poetry, which explains the proximity of his writing chair, and his one hope (deemed unlikely at the end of this poem with its fear of a lonely evening in the open and of the icy death that is textuality) is that writing will create for him an alternative to the home he has given up – song, as another poem puts it, will become his home (*CP*, p. 26).

It is in *The White Threshold*, whose very name denotes a boundary between home and elsewhere, that family love becomes central. Many of the poems in that book, as I shall show in Chapter 4, depict drowning as a paradoxical return to home and family. Others treat more directly his relationships with his mother, father, brother, childhood and native place. As in 'Here Next the Chair', he seems to be trying to justify his leaving: 'All journey, since the first / Step from my father and mother' (*NCP*, p. 59). It is his mother above all who is the focus for his love and guilt; the 'Three Letters' are dedicated to her memory, and he pays tribute to her in 'The Search by a Town':

> This step sails who an ocean crossed
> And mountain climbed, who apprenticed
> For this while quietly to bearing me
> Put forth a rose and my name to die.
>
> (*NCP*, p. 64)

The poem is a step on the journey which has taken Graham away from his mother, but it also affirms his relationship with her. She now bears him as a ship bears its passengers, an image which both celebrates her heroic passivity and insists that the poet has not deserted her.

In the later poems the fantasies of return which are already present in *The White Threshold* are more obvious. 'The Dark Dialogues' makes an implicit analogy between the working of text and that of dreams; the words themselves enable him to revisit the scenes of his past exactly as a dream might do (*NCP*, pp. 167–74). In several other late poems he depicts himself literally dreaming of return and reconciliation. In 'Greenock At Night I Find You' he returns to the local pub, the Cartsburn Vaults, where he meets his father, brother and several relatives (*NCP*, p. 219–20). In 'Loch Thom', he revisits a favourite beauty spot of his childhood; there are no other people present this time, but he carries with him a token of maternal care: 'I am here with my mammy's / Bramble jam scones in my pocket' (*NCP*, p. 220). In 'To Alexander Graham', he dreams of meeting his dead father: 'who seemed pleased to see me' (*NCP*, p. 222). As in the poems of *The White Threshold*, love and harmony are in the past, inaccessible except in dreams and in poetry.

From this brief survey, then, we begin to see what community means to Graham. It is something he believes he has lost. Sexual love is one possible ideal of closeness to another human being, and in 'Letter VI' he depicts such love in familiar romantic style as part of an unrecoverable past. But sexual love was also part of his present; he knew not only its ecstasies but also its imperfections. His poems suggest to me that it was above all the community of his childhood which he mourned – Greenock, his home, his family and, most of all, his mother. He mourned them with special intensity because he felt that they were lost not in the usual way through growing up and the passing of time but by an act of conscious rejection on his part. His complaints about the impersonality of text, the impossibility of using it for hugging and kissing, whatever their theoretical basis, conceal a more pragmatic sense in which text was an obstacle to his relations with others. He had distanced himself from his family in becoming a writer. The guilt consequent on this decision is one of the major themes of his poetry.

Organic Edens

The longing in Graham's poems is directed both at a group of people and a way of life. The Clydeside of the 1920s and 1930s when he was growing up must have been very different from the English literary and artistic world in which he spent his adult life. I shall refer to it as a 'working-class' community, but this is a term of convenience rather than a rigid category. As the son of a shipyard engineer, Graham came from a white-collar background, and there were no doubt considerable social differences between his family and those of manual workers. Their situation, closely linked as it was to a dominant heavy industry, is not easy to define from the point of view of a later, largely post-industrial Britain. However I am not concerned with the situation as such but with the way Graham remembered it and described it in his poems. He referred to himself as 'lower working-class', and the poems, as I shall show, create a mythical community in which distinctions such as that between the families of engineers and of labourers are elided.[3]

   Graham's poetic descriptions of this lost working-class community have parallels in Richard Hoggart's more academic account of his own working-class childhood in the 1930s, though Hoggart's was spent in Leeds. The life Hoggart depicts is centred on the home and the family; food and warmth are important, and family relationships are close, with little privacy. 'The father is a part of the inner life of the home' while 'the mother is the working-centre, always with too much to do'.[4] Graham's writing agrees with these accounts; we have already seen the important part played in it by the mother and father, and the home itself is powerfully evoked. One Hope Street was a Scottish tenement or 'land', as described in 'The Dark Dialogues' (*NCP*, pp. 168–70). The most telling images of the tenement itself are the fire (Hoggart remarks that the working-class home is usually overheated) and the set-in bed, a bed built into the thickness of the wall in the main living room.[5] This kind of accommodation plays a part in 'The Nightfishing', in which the speaker is actually born in one, and in 'Baldy Bane', where a husband and wife are about to make love in it – unless the wife chooses to clean the grate instead (*NCP*, p. 107, p. 145). Such an arrangement would obviously contribute greatly to the intimacy and lack of privacy described by Hoggart.[6]

Nevertheless, Hoggart's image of home as 'a burrow deeply away from the outside world' does not entirely fit Graham's Greenock tenement, which, central and intimate as it is, is also penetrated by the outside.[7] The mother in 'The Children of Greenock' stands at the window 'in a listening shape' and is aware of all the sights and sounds of the town, the 'shouting games and faces' of the children, the smoke and industry of the shipyards, the sparrows on the sill, the chiming of the town hall clocks (*NCP*, pp. 67–9). Some of Graham's most powerful memories seem to be of this interpenetration of home and outside. In particular, the adult world of work is a constant presence in his accounts of his childhood, not only in the daytime but also at night. Images of nocturnal industry abound in his poetry, suggesting that even when lying in bed he could not fail to be aware of the economic and social structure of which he was a part. The first two sections of 'The Nightfishing' are set at home, with work present as a summons – the speaker is 'called' by the quay night bell to go fishing (*NCP*, pp. 105–7). But it is above all the sounds and fires of the shipyards which are recalled:

> Younger in the towered
> Tenement of night he heard
> The shipyards with nightshifts
> Of lathes turning their shafts.

> (*NCP*, p. 123)

Greenock presents itself to his memory as the 'loud [. . .] long rope-working [. . .] rivetting town' where he is still 'lying / Half asleep hearing the rivetting yards / And smelling the bone works' and seeing 'the welding lights in the shipyards flower blue' (*NCP*, p. 219).

For Hoggart as for Graham, however, the working-class child can always participate in the outside world simply by stepping out into the street:

> Home may be private, but the front door opens out of the living-room on to the street, and when you go down the one step or use it as a seat on a warm evening you become part of the life of the neighbourhood.[8]

In other words, the boundary between home and elsewhere works only one way, affording protection against intrusion, but allowing egress at will. This world of the street offered to an eleven-year-old boy a seductive combination of a sense of freedom with one of belonging:

> Here he passes a shop where they never grumble at being asked to sell pennyworths of sweets, here a pal's father smoking in the doorway in his shirtsleeves, after the last shift before the weekend; here a broken-down wooden fence out of which large spiders can be teased; here the off-licence with its bell clanging as someone comes out with a small jug of vinegar.[9]

The street links the interiors of the various houses, the doorways always seeming to be open. Like the fence, the barriers which might prevent the boy gaining access to some part of his world all seem to be down. The adult is reassuringly familiar, 'a pal's father', the sweetshop is not barred to him by his limited finances, and even the off-licence, which presumably remains out of bounds, is selling something non-alcoholic as he passes, as if to protect him from the knowledge that prohibitions exist in his world. One can compare this picture with the dream described in 'Greenock At Night I Find You', where the poet drifts from his set-in bed down to the Cartsburn Vaults, the local pub:

> [. . .]I walked from Hope Street
> Down Lyndoch Street between the night's words
> To Cartsburn Street and got to the Cartsburn Vaults
> With half an hour to go. See, I am back.

> (*NCP*, p. 220)

The litany of streets evokes a townscape that must have been almost as familiar as his own home, and which is indeed seen as an extension of the home. The people the poet meets in the pub are almost all members of his family. Two of them are his father and his brother; 'Sam' is also encountered in the street in 'What Is the Language', where he is described as 'a far relation on my mother's /¦ West-Irish side', while Brigit appears in 'Clusters Travelling Out', 'Implements' and 'The Greenock Dialogues' as not only his childhood sweetheart but also his 'half-cousin' (*NCP*, p. 201, p. 194, p. 252, p. 319).

The street in Hoggart's Leeds had a culture of its own. It had its own games, 'with the lamp-post taking the place of the tree on the village green'. These were accompanied by 'rhyming chants': '"eeny – meeny – miny – mo": "one – two – three-a'lairy:" "tinker – tailor – soldier – sailor": "I like coffee, I like tea. I like sitting on a black man's knee"'.[10] Such children's games are recalled in Graham's poems. In 'Listen. Put on Morning', the children play 'tig' and skip with 'playropes' (*NCP*, p. 60). In 'The Dark Dialogues', the speaker shouts 'you're not het' (it) to an invisible playmate and plays hide-and-seek, a game which, here as in 'Greenock At Night', symbolizes what he regards as his culpable rejection of community, his evasion of its gaze (*NCP*, p. 169, p. 219). In many of the poems, as I shall argue in Chapter 5, the sight and sound of children playing is an unbearably nostalgic summons to return to the community of his childhood. And it is above all the rhyme game 'Water Water Wallflower', quoted in 'Letter II', which encapsulates this children's street culture for him (*NCP*, p. 124).

Another outdoor activity of children described by Hoggart is the outing, that significantly named custom that takes them one step further away from the home than the street:

> Of 'outings', those recreations which involve spending a few coppers or leaving the home ground, the sequence is determined almost entirely by the seasons. There are outings with jam-jars to a dirty stream a mile or so away, for sticklebacks and red-throats; blackberrying, also with jam-jars, even farther afield, past the church with the whalebone arches; raids on the nearest rhubarb and turnip fields, or a little birds' nesting.[11]

Just as the home gives naturally on to the street, so the town is open to the surrounding countryside. Expeditions 'farther afield' link the community to nature and their seasonal character gives them a reassuringly cyclical structure; we understand that they were part of the rhythm of life in the days when life had a rhythm. Similarly, Graham's poetry refers frequently to the landscape of his native region, to outings and walks. As I have already noted, an outing is described in 'Loch Thom', where the child's brief departure from home has the parental approbation of his 'mammy's / Bramble jam scones' (*NCP*, p. 220). Graham's father is seen in the dream of 'Greenock At Night' carrying 'the stick he cut in Sheelhill Glen' (*NCP*, p. 220). We have already seen a reference to picnics in an early Graham poem, and there is a walking theme in 'Since All My Steps Taken' with its hobnail and rucksack (*NCP*,

p. 18, p. 59). To walk in the country is not to leave home; it carries the blessing of both his picnic-making mother and his stick-cutting father. The return in 'The Dark Dialogues' is not just to the tenement at One Hope Street, but also to the local countryside with its 'old rainy oak / And Cartsburn and the Otter's Burn', a setting he seems to associate with his father, just as he associates the tenement with his mother (*NCP*, pp. 170). It seems there was no moment of his childhood when he was not enfolded in the community. So unified and protective was his home that he could not leave it even by taking a rucksack and setting off into the country. (Hoggart notes that hiking was a popular working-class activity in the 1930s, the decade when Graham was in his teens.)[12]

Hoggart and Graham both offer seductive images of a working-class way of life in which individuals are bound together by kinship and common interest, where the home is a protected space but the outside is not forbidding, alienated or fissured. The alien or frightening elements of the community, its potential for conflict, are not entirely ignored, but they are seen as insignificant in comparison with the unity which enfolds it. Hoggart's raids on the orchard may well have brought about confrontations with its owners, and 'double-breasted Sam' had certainly been 'thrown out of the Cartsburn Vaults' but these crises are absorbed into the cosy structure of the familiar. A conflict that takes place in a thoroughly understood context, that is identified with the seasonal cycle and the traditional behaviour of children or family black sheep, is understood paradoxically as a reinforcement of communal harmony instead of a danger to it. They are the kind of occurrences one chuckles over nostalgically, as evidence of the triviality of old problems. Like Barthes's 'Operation Margarine', they innoculate the myth against possible objections.[13] Furthermore, dangers are tamed by hindsight since their threat is circumscribed by the knowledge of their actual and limited consequences, which one could not have known at the time.[14] Remembered dangers are very different from dangers experienced in the present, and their significance may even be reversed.

This account of a unified community is echoed from the point of view of social science by an influential study published in the same year as *The Uses of Literacy*, Michael Young and Peter Willmott's *Family and Kinship in East London*. In the community of Bethnal Green studied by Young and Willmott, 'length of residence' and 'localized kinship' combined to 'create a network of local attachment'. They depict 'a familiar society, filled with people who are not strangers'.[15] The very attractiveness of this depiction has made contemporary researchers suspicious of it. According to Graham Crow and Graham Allan, for example, Young and Willmott's study is one of several which have helped to propagate a 'mythical representation' of the warmth and closeness of working-class community:

> Stereotypes of the Bethnal Green mum at the centre of an extended kin network [. . .] fit the historical realities of life in traditional working-class communities at best only approximately. At worst, their exaggerated features are wilful in their neglect of dimensions of local social relationships which do not conform to the idealized versions of community norms which [the authors] promulgate.[16]

Descriptions of community, as we shall see, have a tendency to be infiltrated by myths of community, and they do so because community itself depends on such myths for its continued survival.

Much of the work of Raymond Williams was an attempt to separate these historical and mythical dimensions of the term; if the attempt was not altogether successful, it nevertheless provides a valuable basis for subsequent analysis. In his entry on 'community' in *Keywords*, Williams makes a distinction between senses of the word which 'indicate actual social groups' and senses which indicate 'a particular quality of relationship'. A community is people living together, and it is also how they live together. The term's complexity, he continues, can be attributed to 'the difficult interaction' between these two broad areas of meaning. In both, however, it is 'warmly persuasive' and 'seems never to be used unfavourably'.[17] To think about community, then, is to think at the same time about the actual and the ideal. The communities in which people live, with their tensions and conflicts, their frustrations and instabilities, are in constant juxtaposition with the virtual communities of the communal imagination, which lack all such flaws.

Williams had been influenced by his teacher F.R. Leavis's version of such an ideal. Leavis's book *Culture and Environment* (co-written with Denys Thompson) argued that an agrarian society based on the 'organic community' of the village had recently ended, and that its values must somehow be reclaimed from the industrial wasteland that had succeeded it. (This metaphor, and the opposition of the organic and the mechanical on which it is based, is not confined to the theory of community. It is also a term in the criticism of art and literature, and I shall discuss this in Chapter 3.[18] In Graham's thought and that of his contemporaries, this aesthetic use cannot be entirely separated from the social sense I am considering here; nevertheless, I shall postpone my consideration of their interdependence until my later discussion.) In

Leavis's case, the myth of the organic community is used in the service of a broadly conservative, anti-industrial philosophy:

> The great agent of change, and, from our point of view, destruction, has of course been the machine – applied power. The machine has brought us many advantages, but it has destroyed the old ways of life, the old forms, and by reason of the continual rapid change it involves, prevented the growth of the new.[19]

This argument had a great influence on Williams, whose rejection of it was 'a personal crisis lasting several years'.[20] His response extends over several of his writings, suggesting that he was still too attached to it to dispose of it finally. Its attraction to him was that he, too, was driven by a nostalgia for community. Ultimately, however, he could not accept it because its anti-industrialism did not fit the values of the community he grew up in.[21] *The Country and the City*, his study of the interactions between pastoral convention and English rural history, surveys a number of accounts, from different periods, of a supposedly recent break in communal tradition. The attempt to pin down the organic community historically involves an continual regression into the past on a sort of 'escalator' which probably never stops 'until we get to the garden of Eden'.[22] Community, to put it in poststructuralist terms, is 'always already' fallen.

The Eden in Leavis's account was the age of agrarianism before the Fall represented by the Industrial Revolution. Like so many of the terms analysed by Williams in *Keywords*, 'organic', in both its social and aesthetic senses, is closely tied up with the intellectual reaction to modernity whose history he traced in *Culture and Society*. In the romantic period, Williams tells us, 'organic' came to be analogous to 'natural'. The term implies that community is purely the domain of organic life and thus represents an attempt to guard this domain from the encroachment of the machine.[23] Williams, like Graham and Hoggart, was a product of a working-class industrial community, and thus well-equipped to expose the mythic nature of Leavis's anti-industrialism.

Nevertheless, the organic community is not primarily a myth about the countryside but one about boundaries. The metaphor implied by the adjective 'organic' can be summed up thus: a community is (or was, or should be) a living being. Its members correspond to the organs of the body, which perish when removed from the organism, and are thus wholly dependent on it. The distinction made by Coleridge, as Williams reminds us in his article on the term in *Keywords*, was between the organic, in which 'the whole is everything and the parts are nothing' and the inorganic (later to be replaced by the mechanical) in which 'the whole is nothing more than a collection of the individual parts'.[24] A living being has only one important boundary, that which separates the body from the rest of the world. It is true that internal boundaries separate the organs, but the liver and kidneys and brain are not generally thought of as individuals with needs and priorities of their own, but as parts of a whole. As we have seen, this is the implication not only of Leavis's argument but also of the descriptions of community in the writings of Hoggart and Graham: like a body, the community has a single boundary separating it from the outside world, and any internal boundaries between individuals, between home and outside, between kin and others, or between town and surrounding country, are regarded as insignificant. Young and Willmott's study, by emphasizing the threads of kinship uniting the inhabitants of Bethnal Green rather than the differences between them, lent itself to such a mythology. Even Williams, despite his demythologizing mission, insisted on the organic properties of his own home community.[25] The working class, in his writings, seems an undivided organism. Its achievements, he tells us in *Culture and Society*, are collective ones and its particular mode of community is solidarity.[26] The organic community he situates in his personal past 'with its emphases of neighbourhood, mutual obligation and common betterment' provides the basis for his vision of an ideal society of the future.[27]

The anthropologist Anthony P. Cohen has argued that communities define themselves by the construction of symbolic boundaries. The word itself, he maintains, implies both similarity between the community's members and difference from the members of other groups; his book *The Symbolic Construction of Community* is a study of the way in which members reinforce these internal similarities, despite the differences which separate one from another, by insisting on an external boundary between them and the non-members with whom they come into contact. Such boundaries are symbolic, and the value of symbols to a community is not a matter of common meanings but of a capacity for supporting differences of meaning: it is the symbols themselves rather than their precise meanings that are shared between members. This process of symbolic boundary-building allows communities to retain internal differences while still understanding themselves as an organic whole:

It continuously transforms the reality of difference into the appearance

of similarity with such efficacy that people can still invest the 'commu-
nity' with ideological integrity.[28]

In Cohen's analysis, then, communities elide their internal bound-
aries by constructing and maintaining an external boundary. But the
models of community we have looked at, in Graham's poems and in the
writings of Hoggart, Leavis and Williams, are rather different, and the
external boundary in these cases is not easy to detect. It is, in fact, the
boundary that divides present from past. The 'symbolic construction of
community' we are considering is not like that by which Shetlanders
define themselves in opposition to outsiders or gypsies in opposition to
'gorgios' – it is not defined by its members, from the inside, but by its
non-members, from without. Community, for these writers, is consti-
tuted by an act of self-exclusion which also excludes their readers, for it
is time that separates us from the organic community.[29] The imagined
integrity of this lost community can be even greater than that of those
defined from within, for we are not inside it to experience its internal
differences. While all communities are constructs, this is clearly a
construct of a different order; it is appropriate to define it as a myth,
since it represents an unattainable perfection.

This mythopoeia, though, is not in itself a new or unusual phenome-
non. As Jean-Luc Nancy has argued :

> Until this day history has been thought on the basis of a lost community
> – one to be regained or reconstituted [. . .] always it is a matter of a lost
> age in which community was woven of tight, harmonious and infrangible
> bonds and in which above all it played back to itself, through its institu-
> tions, its rituals and its symbols, the representation, indeed the living
> offering of its own immanent unity, intimacy and autonomy.[30]

The consciousness of a lost community, Nancy claims, 'seems to have
accompanied the Western world from its beginnings'.[31] Furthermore,
like the symbolic construction of a community of the present, it is itself
communal in origin: 'Myth arises only from a community and for it'.[32]
We may surmise that this is complementary to the process described by
Cohen – one of the symbols which unites the community is that of its
own perfection, now lost as a fact but still available as an ideal. Those
internal differences that the community cannot elide it explains away
as a consequence of its fallen state.

The model of community we find in Graham's poems is a myth, and
it is not entirely of his own creation, but closely analogous to the myths
of an organic community we find in Leavis, in Hoggart, and even as a
residual presence in the critic of organicism, Williams. These accounts

retrospectively create a community in which there are no fissures. The street, full of relatives and with all its doors open, *is* the home; the country, goal of parentally or traditionally sanctioned excursions, is the home, too. This organic unity is contrasted with the distances and barriers of modernity, but the contrast, in one form or another, is an old one, part of the mythology of community. In Graham's work, however, this myth had a personal relevance: the fall from community was blamed not only on modernity but also on himself.

Paradise Regained

The ideal communities of the past are forever inaccessible. Because they are a kind of Eden, we are separated from them by the Fall. 'Fall', in fact, is a favourite verb of Graham's, one whose symbolic resonance is not always apparent. 'Enter a Cloud', for example, depicts the poet 'lying / In a bower of bramble / Into which I have fallen', which sounds matter-of-fact enough (*NCP*, p. 216). This accident seems to be the same one he describes in 'Dear Who I Mean' as 'the lonely stumble / In the spiked bramble', where the adjective hints that the fall referred to may have a deeper meaning (*NCP*, p. 160). The same phrase, 'lonely stumble', occurs in the early poem 'Soon To Be Distances' (*NCP*, p. 34). Certainly the image of a trip or stumble suggests that the poet may be to blame for it, since the same words are often used of wrongdoings. The Christian terminology associated with loss of grace has a euphemistic character which can prove invaluable to those hesitating between guilt and self-exculpation: the words enable Graham to accept the blame and deny it simultaneously.[33]

The sin responsible for this stumble is writing, which has separated him from his family both symbolically, by imposing its distances and barriers between them, and pragmatically, because he has had to abandon the values of his family in order to practise it. To be in language is to fall down to the level of the page:

> We fall down darkness in a line of words.
>
> (*NCP*, p. 27)

> [. . .]He fell
> He falls. (Tenses are everywhere.)
>
> (*NCP*, p. 199)

What has been lost by the fall is suggested in the unfinished poem 'A

Dream of Crete', some versions of which include an account of a drowning which is also described as a fall:

> And wakened into dream to find
> Myself falling with ancient speed
> Slowly through the dark dividing
> At my headlong approach. [. . .]
>
> Mother I have tripped and fallen
> [. . .]Why did you let
> Me out of you both to land here
> Not knowing?

(NCP, pp. 343–4)

The mysterious word 'both', as I shall show in my detailed discussion of the poem in Chapter 6, refers to both of Graham's parents and the fall here fuses two departures from a state of grace, being born and leaving home. 'A Dream of Crete' is about the unfinished and perhaps impossible attempt to recover the community he has lost through this fall.

Hoggart's account of the 'scholarship boy' whose achievements will eventually separate him from his family and friends gives us some idea of the human reality which may have underlain Graham's imagery:

> He has to be more and more alone, if he is going to 'get on'. He will have, probably unconsciously, to oppose the ethos of the hearth, the intense gregariousness of the working-class family group.[. . .] The boy has to cut himself off mentally so as to do his homework. [. . .] [34]

Hoggart is obviously writing from personal experience here, though the experience must have been a typical one for gifted children from such backgrounds at the time. Graham's early departure from his intended career to study first art appreciation and then literature and philosophy must have been even more disruptive to his family – indeed, Lopez tells us it caused 'dismay'.[35] Graham's subsequent career at Newbattle Abbey and in the artistic bohemias of Glasgow, London and, eventually, Cornwall (with only a brief interlude of regular employment) was much less secure and predictable than the move into professional life described by Hoggart.[36] In some ways this must have had its compensations; bohemian life is itself communal. Nevertheless, to embrace such a life must have put far greater barriers between him and his native community than any caused by a middle-class career, since it can hardly have been comprehensible. We also know that Graham for all his friendships with such artists as Roger Hilton and Bryan Wynter did experience the difficulty of belonging to 'another group' which Hoggart describes as characteristic of the scholarship boy. Lopez writes of 'Graham's uneasiness at what he took to be his rather humble social position' and maintains that 'he was comfortable only in the company of close friends'.[37] Graham himself wrote in a letter to one such friend, Ronnie Duncan: 'I am not really a good man socially for more than about two or three days'.[38] His sporadic heavy drinking seems to have been related to this social insecurity.[39]

It is understandable, then, that Graham should look back to his original community as to a lost Eden, blinding himself to the barriers and conflicts that it must have contained, and that he should blame himself for leaving it and rejecting its values. It was the desire to write that caused this Fall, and writing looks a poor and flimsy thing when contrasted, as Graham regularly does contrast it, with human love. To one who has actually lived through the journey from a world in which 'working-people still draw [. . .] on oral and local tradition' to a literary life, the connections between speech and love on the one hand and loneliness and writing on the other must seem so natural as to be almost tangible.[40] Certainly both Hoggart and Graham emphasize the evocative power of the spoken word. Phrases like ''unger's the best sauce' and 'she gave me a meaning look' for the one and 'fairly his mile' and 'anyhow here's Mary will tell you right' for the other have an emotional appeal that seems disproportionate to their meaning.[41] This loyalty to an oral tradition underlies Graham's occasional use of Scottish words and phrases such as 'airts' (compass bearings or locality), 'caa' (to drive), 'the Dancing Men' (the Northern Lights), 'messages' (shopping: a pun in 'What Is the Language' – *NCP*, p. 199) and 'land' (tenement building).

The Fall, being mythical, is not merely an event in time, an allegorical rendering of a particular biographical incident – it is re-enacted in every poem, since to write words is to cause them to fall from the air to the page, from the live world of speech to the dead world of writing. The argument of my first chapter must be borne in mind here. Text for Graham is closed and impersonal, forever cut off from the human intimacy he associates with orality. In condemning himself to an attenuated existence as a pronoun on a piece of paper, the poet has lost the physical companionship of others which is, apparently, the thing that matters most to him. Like the Ancient Mariner, he is condemned to go on relating to anyone who will listen the story of his failure and alienation.

This is a depressing picture of Graham's life's work. If this were all, his poems would be condemned to a negative tone and a simple, static structure, and he would have no convincing excuse for continuing to write them. In fact, however, his entire oeuvre is an attempt to overcome this state of affairs. His poems are written on the premiss that the organic community still exists in a fallen form in which, while it may not be fully recoverable, it may still be available as a source of magical power.

Such an idea is compatible with the myth of community, which is often a dream of the future as well as of the past. Nancy's passage about the lost community quoted above describes it as 'one to be regained or reconstituted'. 'Reconstituted' may seem an odd choice of word here, but it is an exact one. In the next sentence, he describes the community as 'lost, or broken', and this choice of adjectives is not due to uncertainty on his part but to an ambiguity in the myth itself.[42] What exactly happened to the community, and where is it now? Instead of seeing it as lost, we may see it as broken, the relations between its members shattered and the members themselves dispersed. Scattered in this way, community would in a sense still be here – that is, all its components would be here, and it might be possible, by some magical or political means, to 'reconstitute' them.

Graham's poems exist in a constant state of tension between his views about the limitations of text and a persistent conviction that his decision to become a writer can be justified in communal terms, as an act of love. This tension gives the poems their tonal variety and complexity of structure. More than that, it gives them a dynamic: they are continually striving towards, though they can never finally arrive at, the creation of a satisfying substitute for the organic community in language. If that goal could finally be attained, the Fall into writing would turn out to have been a fortunate one and Graham's sin a *felix culpa*. Paradise would be regained.

The title of the present study is taken from a passage in 'The Dark Dialogues' in which the narrator finds himself standing in a dark outdoor landscape which he situates 'between / This word and the next'. He addresses the reader:

And you, whoever you are,
That I am other to,
Stand still by the glint
Of the dyke's sparstone,
Because always language
Is where the people are.

(*NCP*, p. 168)

'The Dark Dialogues', like so many other poems, asserts Graham's long-ing for the intimacy of personal contact. To the extent that language has a place in such contact, it is in the form of speech – the mother murmuring to her children, the child calling to his playmate (*NCP*, p. 169). In live speech it is literally true that 'language is where the people are'. In the case of writing, though, the statement is more prob-lematic. It must be distinguished from my own claim, made in Chapter 1, that writing is a social phenomenon whose meaning must be under-stood, and if necessary renegotiated, according to the differing social contexts in which it finds itself. Graham has not abandoned his insis-tence on the autonomy of written language. For him it remains cut off from social relations, but it allows a magical access to the social itself: it is 'where the people are' – and the definite article is not to be over-looked. The lost or broken community is manifest in language, for those who know how to look for it.

This assertion is an apparent contradiction of the beliefs which I attributed to Graham in Chapter 1. To make sense of it we have to accept that his writing is not the exposition of a settled philosophy, but a battleground; like a Freudian dream or neurotic symptom, it attempts to reconcile conflicting forces. I have called one of these forces control, the desire for a life totally subordinate to one's will, and the other love, the desire to share that life with other people. From the viewpoint of the crowded sort of childhood described by Hoggart and evoked in some of Graham's poems, control must have looked particularly desirable, and writing seemed to offer it. Text was a fenced-off playground which the writer hoped to be able to 'think anything in', unaffected by the will of others (*NCP*, p. 168). But to fence himself off in this way was to deny himself the companionship he needed. This autonomous space, which we might call the mythic text, was the domain of total control and total absence of love. Opposed to it, and the object of his nostalgic dreams, was the mythic community, the domain of total love and total absence of control. We can detect this yearning in his use of the word 'other' in the poems of the middle period; it stands in his work for community in general, the principal of selflessness, and in particular for his mother, the other in whom the self was once totally absorbed. The 'Saint Other' of 'The Search by a Town' and 'The Lost Other' is thus a Mother, the apotheosis of the Other (*NCP*, p. 65, p. 77). (To contemporary readers, this word carries almost irresistible echoes of Lacan and literary theory in general, but Graham probably took it from his youthful study of Greek philosophy. In his *Timaeus*, Plato describes how God created the soul from a mixture of the Same and the Other.)[43]

Graham yearned simultaneously for both these impossible extremes, for the peace to be found in his own will and that to be found in the will of others. His instinct was always to seek solitude and control, but at the same time he needed to appease the communal will, to insist that his intentions were ultimately harmonious with it. What he was principally trying to appease, no doubt, was his own internalization of communal values, the family in his mind. He attempted to do this through the rhetoric of his poems.

The simplest rhetorical device by which he could justify his position would be the conduit metaphor. If writing could be seen simply as a vehicle for the transmission of interpersonal love, then Graham's practice of it would be a basically sociable activity. We already know that he could not view it in this way, and indeed I have suggested that he sought it out precisely for the insulation it afforded from such contact. Nevertheless, he had to try, and his repeated enactments of the failure of the conduit are protestations of the genuineness of his desire to communicate. One of his personal mottoes was 'try to be better' or 'TTBB', and many of his poems insist on the efforts he is making in the direction of others.[44] 'I try to pay for my keep. / I speak as well as I can', he cries in 'The Dark Dialogues', in terms that surely recall and respond to an early parental accusation of irresponsibility (*NCP*, pp. 170–1). 'Try' is another of his favourite verbs, and even when the context is displaced (he had a habit of recommending his own precept to other people), the repetition is a reminder of his obsessive self-exculpation:

[. . .] I try to find

Whatever is wanted by going
Out of my habits [. . .]
To ask [. . .] how I can do better.

(*NCP*, p. 202)

I am only trying to get home.

(*NCP*, p. 311)

[. . .]My father,
I try to be the best

(*NCP*, pp. 222–3)

Try. Try. (No offence meant.)

(*NCP*, p. 250)

I am trying to be better

(NCP, p. 260)

These efforts to communicate, praiseworthy in themselves, may fail through his own inadequacies and thus remain 'unheard by a fault' (*NCP*, p. 172). But on the whole it is language which is to blame for them; it is seen as erecting barriers between people, both the epistemological barriers of textual indeterminacy and the social barriers of an isolating career. While this may excuse him to some extent, the excuse becomes thin when stretched over a whole lifetime. If language cannot accomplish what he claims to want it to, surely he must abandon it. The only defence to this argument is to find at least the possibility that language is more than communication, that it is in some sense a form of community in itself.

Lakoff and Turner remark that 'given any well-structured concept, an inventive person can probably find a way to understand another concept using it', even such a frivolous conceit as 'Death is a banana'.[45] Graham's justifications of his metaphor are many, but it is a correspondence that, at first sight, appears one of the most far-fetched that constitutes probably his most fundamental reason for believing in a genuine structural resemblance between the two entities. Community, stripped of its cosiness, is nothing more than collective power – other people may offer love but they demand in return the right to influence or even thwart the individual will. Language, like community, is collective, 'a social fact', as Saussure notes, and it too is resistant to the individual will.[46] For Saussure, this resistance is manifested in the inability of the individual to modify the structure of language itself. The 'community's natural inertia' is responsible for restricting 'freedom of choice', and while language does indeed change over time, this is not due to any conscious effort, even by the community as an organized whole, but to the 'social forces' which continue to act upon it.[47] But Graham, as we have seen in Chapter 1, regards language as an agency which does more than resist changes to its own structure. It intervenes in the act of communication, preventing him from accomplishing the personal contact he desires, changing not only his 'message' but the very identity of the communicators. Its collective nature brings about the indeterminacy with which he struggles; meaning is not located in any individual mind, but in the resources of the language as a whole and the understanding of unknown readers. Language's collective will dominates his individual will, and in this crucial respect it resembles community.

It is worth pausing to reflect on the strangeness of this idea. Graham's sense of responsibility requires that, if he is to devote his life to language, he must use it to communicate – that is, to extend the community's reach. As a good son of that community, he internalizes its collective will and desires nothing more, by his own account, than to fulfill it, not just for its satisfaction but for his own as well. But his attempts to do this are frustrated by a second embodiment of the collective will, language, which forbids him to communicate in the direct, personal way that his family and friends might reasonably expect of him. His situation is similar to that of a boy who runs away from home to join the army – he has rebelled against one form of authority by embracing one even more potent. If he is right that language is such a tyrant, he has the perfect response to accusations of delinquency; instead of trying to escape discipline, he has chosen a sterner form of it. However this excuse appears disingenuous if we suspect that he originally opted for language precisely for the protection he thought it could offer from the claims of the communal will. His hidden feelings are given away by the fact that the property of language which epitomizes community for him is its authoritarianism. If he loved community as much as he maintains, he would not need to protest so much. However we must also remember that the excuses he is making are for his own benefit as much as for anyone else's. Like other people, he has social needs and a genuine desire for love some of the time; if his insistence that he is 'a good boy' whose desires are totally aligned with those of others is unfounded, so too is his guilty fear that he is a bad boy whose only motives are selfish ones. (Graham was fond of the phrase 'Good boy' which he originally addressed to his cat and then transferred to people, even his wife.[48] That this habit was a displacement of his own desire for parental approbation is suggested by many of the poems, for example 'To Alexander Graham' where he asks 'Dad [. . .] / Are you proud of me?' and concludes by expressing his own love in a tentative phrase that suggests its ambivalence: 'I think I must have loved him' – *NCP*, p. 223.)

Language clearly has a logical connection with the community which collectively evolved it and continues to use it. Strictly speaking, this means that the statement 'language is a community' is a metonymy rather than a metaphor, but, for Graham, the connection has been severed by the Fall into writing, and in practice he sees the relationship as metaphorical, two separate domains linked by a structural isomorphism.[49] Language is treated autonomously as a metaphorical social world in itself rather than as part of the literal social world.

Nevertheless, the similarities are not a mere coincidence of properties but a consequence; language might be said to have a family resemblance to community, or to bear within it the mystical signature of its communal origin. 'The shape of all of us is in this language,' Graham wrote in his most important piece of theoretical writing, the essay 'Notes on a Poetry of Release', first published in 1946. Language has the shape of community because community has transferred its own shape to it; alternatively it is seen as carrying stigmata, 'scored and impressed by the commotion of all of us since its birth'.[50]

The thorough explication of the metaphorical equation of language and community will be the work of the remaining four chapters of this study. For now, I shall content myself with a brief outline of the correspondences. Most important is the point I have already made, that language is a collective entity that rebukes the individual will. Secondly, it is bigger than the individual, a world of 'vast' dialogues, a 'terrible surrounder of everything' (*NCP*, p 167, p. 248). Thirdly, it has inherited the communal 'commotion', a state of continual change which accounts for the elusiveness of meaning. This flux is the condition of language in general but not that of words 'on the dead-still page' and Graham's lifelong struggle to reconcile these two opposing states is one of the themes we shall trace in ensuing chapters (*NCP*, p. 181). 'The language is a changing creature continually being killed-off, added-to and changed like a river over its changing speakers', but the poem must be 'a still thing, a mountain' (*NFM*, p. 380, p. 382). This transformation of soft material into hard object is a threat to his metaphor and its implications which requires all his rhetorical skill to account for. Fourthly, just as the working-class community centres on and is embodied in the mother, so language itself, with its voluptuous fluidity, can be seen as maternal, the mother-tongue. Its changeability is described as 'dying and bearing', and in one of his late pieces of automatic writing, to be discussed in Chapter 6, he addresses it as 'fluxy mother'.[51] These feminine characteristics also make it possible for him to treat it as a lover (the Muse), with ambiguous implications. Sex is both the epitome of communion between living beings and the act which takes the children of a family away from it. The poet therefore flaunts his sexuality (as the speaker of 'The Broad Close' boasts of slipping 'the Muse a length for she / Appreciates the starkest man / Her length and breadth to be') because it demonstrates his ability to humanize language, while at the same time revealing an Oedipal anxiety that in so doing he may be dealing a 'deathblow' to the parental authority of community (*NCP*, p. 141). And

the last correspondence between language and community is also a
specifically masculine concern: just as language demands an appropri-
ate male sexual response to its femininity, so its materiality also insists
that a man fulfil the traditional role of manual worker. Hence the work
imagery of 'Notes', relating the labour of writing a poem to more physi-
cal forms of labour. The making of a poem is like that of a table, and
many of the terms in which writing is described are drawn from the
crafts and engineering. A poem is 'a construction of words', 'an appara-
tus' and 'charged to the power of release' like an electrically operated
machine, while the poet is 'the labourer carrying the bricks of his time
and on the scaffolding of an unknown construction'. (*NFM*, p. 379,
p. 382, p. 381.) It as if the child in the Greenock tenement had after all
grown up to go and join the workers he heard outside his window.

These correspondences between language and community are only
the most significant of the many links between the two which I shall
trace in the remainder of this study. Such tropes cannot, of course,
recreate the mythic community of Graham's childhood memories.
Indeed, it is essential to the myth that it remain forever out of reach, for
its fragile substance would crumble if it were ever exposed to the air of
the real world. It is part of his mission as a writer to fail, because in so
doing he confirms the perfection of the Eden he has given up. But the
failure must be glorious, or his career would be a disaster and his deci-
sion to leave home unjustifiable. The Fall must not be simply an error or
a crime; it must also be a sacrifice, undertaken in the interests of the
community itself, perhaps even demanded of him, and in this respect
the masculine rhetoric of adventure comes to his aid. As our earlier
consideration of 'Here Next the Chair' suggests, a man must leave home
to find a new one, and he may also be expected to travel for the sake of
trade, war or discovery. The poet is 'that explorer who shoots the sun,
carries samples of air back to civilization, and looks his forward', 'a new
searcher with his direction changing at every step', and he tries 'to
remember those adventures along the lines of words'. (*NFM*, p. 380,
p. 382.) In this way the boundaries of the community are extended, but
the traveller may also be lost or killed and the extended community
changes its nature because of the distance that is incorporated within
its borders. It becomes distributed, exceeding the old community in
range and in the authority which was one of its main characteristics,
but lacking its human comforts. It is both transcendent and inadequate,
a fallen Paradise, a shattered body whose very corporeal insufficiency
proves that the powers it still possesses must be magical.

   Graham's poems have a remarkable thematic unity. As the rest of this study will show, the contrast between a mythic text and a mythic community is present in the earliest published work and dominates his entire career. It would be fair to call the poems obsessive, but it would not be fair to call his work as a whole monotonous. There is a variation of style, from the density of the early poems to the *faux naïf* starkness of the late ones; there is a variation of imagery, dominated by pastoral and machinery in the early poems, the sea in the middle ones, the Arctic, the forest and nostalgic dreams in the late work; finally, the emphasis can shift from one term to the other between poems. The early poems insist on the boundaries of the text, its cagelike qualities. At this stage of his career, Graham was still overcome with enthusiasm for this new space and the richness of the world that might be contained in it. The community of language is seen largely in sexual terms, and his embracing of it has the energy of youthful rebellion. In the middle period of his work, the years of *The White Threshold* and *The Nightfishing*, he begins to show a sense of unease about how much he may be giving up to enjoy this textual playground. The poems thus move on to the defensive. They continue to celebrate the pleasure of the text, but now it is more important to them to justify this pleasure in communal terms. It is at this stage that he begins to develop the metaphor of a community of language in detail and to concentrate all the forces of his rhetoric on to the task of proving its validity. In the late poems this unease becomes overwhelming, so that his argument for a transcendental synthesis becomes harder and harder to sustain. Instead he longs more and more for a simple reversion to the community he has lost, which is now only available to him as an illusion, in his dreams. The poems try to treat language as a conduit by engaging in a dialogue with the reader and thus demonstrate both his eagerness to be social and the superiority of the forces which thwart it. But there is an alternative corpus of late work represented by some of his unpublished writings of the late 1960s. The automatic writings in particular are his most direct attempts to communicate with language itself, the 'fluxy mother' for whose sake he has exiled himself to the textual wasteland. But in their exuberant wordplay they also look back to the celebration of textual autonomy in the early poems, and thus conceal a solipsistic desire for control beneath his protestations of communal love. In the remaining chapters of this study I shall examine these four stages of his career.

CHAPTER 3

Electrifying the Cage
The Early Poems

Journeys Into Text

Graham's early poems have been the subject of much hostile comment. Dennis O'Driscoll, for example, states that *Cage Without Grievance* 'displayed some of the worst obfuscatory characteristics of its time' and sees the poet's career as a 'struggle towards lucidity'.[1] This was not Graham's own view. He defended his early poems all his life, for example in a letter to Michael Schmidt:

> I would be pleased if you should discern not just the poet struggling from early wordiness up to maturity. There is a quality in the early poems a bit special which I won't be able to put out again. [2]

Lopez is one critic who refuses to dismiss them; his treatment of them is to a great extent polemical, designed in part to weaken their damaging association with the still unfashionable work of Dylan Thomas and in part to emphasize their links to international modernism in the arts generally.[3] He makes a convincing case. Thomas is by no means the only influence on this work, and, besides, is not himself the isolated eccentric he is sometimes made to seem in hindsight, but representative of a British avant-garde of the time that was far less cut off from international influences than was to be the case subsequently.[4] There is no doubt that Graham saw himself as experimenting with words in much the same way that modernist painters, many of them his friends and acquaintances, experimented with paint. But to say all this does not take us very far in our understanding of the early poetry. Now that these experiments have been put more accurately into context, we still have to determine what they were intended to achieve, and whether or not they were successful.

In making an analogy between these poems and the work of cubist, fauvist and abstract painters, Lopez is criticizing one art form in terms of another, a strategy also employed by the poet William Montgomerie in his introduction to Graham's first book, *The Seven Journeys*. Montgomerie claims that Graham makes 'his poems out of words, as a cathedral is built out of squared stone'. To demand a meaning from them is 'not so much a practical question, as a metaphysical question, as we might say, What is the meaning of St. Marks in Venice?'. Quoting some lines, he argues 'We are sharing the movements of a word-ballet [. . .] all in waltz rhythm'. Later, he compares the movement of the reader's eye over Graham's rhymes and other sonic effects to that of a skater, and adds, 'The same thing has been demonstrated in painting.'[5] All these comments employ metaphors – comparisons between items from different categories.[6] If, as the art critic Clement Greenberg maintained, the guiding principle of the avant-garde has been to make each art into its own subject matter, then a comparison between writing that explores the nature of writing and, say, painting that explores that of painting is obviously valid but in an obviously limited sense.[7] To proceed any further it is necessary to discuss the writing in its own terms, that is in literary ones, and here both Montgomerie and Lopez provide an incomplete analysis. Both note that the poems, by defying the norms governing the sense of sentences, frustrate the reader's attempts to establish a reference for them. Like Chomsky's 'colourless green ideas sleep furiously', they are apparently well-formed in grammatical terms but deficient in meaning.[8] 'Meaning is not primary but secondary' and a poem 'does not "mean" in the sense of prose meaning'.[9] But describing the poems in terms of a deficiency leaves the critic with little to discuss. Once the comparison with other art forms has been made, all that is left is to indicate the 'secondary meaning' (which must inevitably be a shadowy area not susceptible to precise definition), as Montgomerie writes of the Scottish connotations of 'The First Journey', and to draw attention to the sound patterns made by the words, a game which, as I.A. Richards long ago pointed out, is suspiciously easy to play.[10]

I believe the most fruitful approach to this body of work is through its meaning. Perhaps the question vetoed by Montgomerie, 'What does it mean?' is too difficult to start with, but we can at least ask what Graham is doing to the signifying function of language to cause this difficulty – we can ask 'How does it mean?'. To do this is to treat words as words rather than as a substitute for paint or music. Consider, for example, the opening of 'The First Journey':

> Launched three windy neptunes high from a gargoyle scree
> My birth in a spittle of glass like the death of a lark
> In a settling largo falls from the crucified height
> Or in motion fearfully loves the rainbow waterspout
> And climbs the myth, the tented miracle.

(NCP, p. 4)

On consideration there seems to be an excess of meaning here rather than a deficiency. The words point us to several different areas of experience. Some are taken from physical landscape ('windy', 'scree', 'rainbow', 'waterspout'), others from human art and artifice ('gargoyle', 'glass', 'largo', 'tented'), while others still have mythic connotations ('neptunes', 'crucified', 'myth', 'miracle'). These varied terms are arranged together in an obscure relationship by the syntax of a single sentence. One's first instinct on reading it may be to panic and assume that the words have been thrown on to the page at random, but in fact the sentence is well-formed in the sense that Chomsky's 'Colourless green ideas [. . .]' is well-formed.[11] 'Launched three windy neptunes' at first has the look of a main clause lacking a subject, like one of those diary entries with the first-person pronoun left out ('Went to the shops' etc.), but further consideration shows that the first line is a subordinate clause. The subject of the main clause is 'my birth', and there are three active verbs: 'My birth [. . .] falls [. . .] or [. . .] loves [. . .] and [. . .] climbs [. . .]' The hesitation here is caused by 'three neptunes', which looks like the object of 'launched' but actually indicates the height to which 'my birth' has been launched, a height of three neptunes, however high that may be. The fact that the syntax yields to analysis, that there is a right way and a wrong way of reading it, is already an encouraging sign. It suggests that the poem has a structure of some kind.

If this complex sentence does not yet give us much clue as to the relationship the poet is attempting to establish between its elements, we can nevertheless isolate smaller syntactical units which may be easier to deal with. The passage is strongly adjectival. Most of the nouns in it are matched with a corresponding adjective ('windy neptunes', 'gargoyle scree', 'settling largo' etc.). This is characteristic of the early poems as a whole, and in particular of those in *The Seven Journeys*. The early pages of the *New Collected Poems* are strewn with adjective-noun pairs such as 'sculptured cuckoo', 'hiccuping hero', 'constructed festival', 'choral vagaries', 'country crimes', 'holy somersaults', 'harmonic orchard', 'slang gland', 'milking bleeder', to select three pairs from each of the first three original volumes. (*NCP*, pp. 3–4, p. 17, pp. 47–8). An over-reliance on adjectives is often considered to be a poetic fault, and this may indeed be one reason why the early poems have been generally dismissed. But if we put aside this prejudice, we may go some way towards understanding the view of poetry which informs the work. The use of adjectives here is neither slipshod writing nor dispensable orna-mentation; for the early Graham, the adjective-noun pair might be called the fundamental unit of poetry itself.

The first point to notice is that the pairings are mostly incongruous. Given the task of finding an adjective for the noun 'scree', 'gargoyle' would be among the very last one thought of – indeed, I doubt if the noun 'gargoyle' has ever been used adjectivally before. Since we are bracketing for the time being the question 'What does it mean?', we must not speculate on what a 'gargoyle scree' actually is. More impor-tant is the ingenuity of the phrase, which exemplifies the clashing of words belonging to different conceptual categories that I remarked on in the passage as a whole. A gargoyle and a scree are both stony, but whereas the first is sculpted by human artifice into a single meaningful object, the second is natural, formless and multiple. The phrase resem-bles an oxymoron, but that word really refers to a figure that cancels itself out, leaving, as it were, no remainder; oxymorons like Shakespeare's 'heavy lightness' or Horace's 'jarring harmony' are clashes between abstractions, where the resolution of the paradox, its applicability to the experienced world, has to be supplied not by the phrase itself but by some other part of the text.[12] In 'gargoyle scree', the clash is between two concrete images that do not seem to belong together. A more appropriate term is 'catachresis', the 'deliberate wrest-ing of a term from its proper signification for effect'.[13]

A catachresis need not be an adjective-noun pair, but an example of one that is came up in a recent conversation when I was considering this subject: a child tired of sightseeing with her parents complained that she did not want to visit any more 'broken churches'. In citing this I am defying *The New Princeton Encyclopedia*'s stricture that the trope should be 'deliberate' and used 'for effect' – the girl simply did not know that the vocabulary used for buildings in a state of disrepair is different from that used for toys or household objects. In making her mistake, however, she has reminded us that the terminological difference hides a real similarity, and a poet might well use the same expression with the deliberate intention of defamiliarizing the concept of ruin in a building.

The catachresis in the preceding example is arguably an inadvertent correction of one of the perversities of English usage, the removal of a conventional but unnecessary barrier between one set of words (those used for buildings) and another (those used for many other functional artefacts). Virgil's use of the Latin verb reserved for the building of houses to describe the construction of the Trojan Horse achieves much the same result. 'Gargoyle scree', on the other hand, seems itself perverse. 'Gargoyle' as an adjective, unlike 'broken' or *'aedificant'*, is not a standard term from one context transplanted into a new one. Nevertheless, all these examples work in a broadly similar way, linking the vocabulary of different conceptual categories on the basis of a resemblance between them (disrepair, construction or stoniness), and extreme effects like Graham's are indeed covered under the same heading in *The New Princeton Encyclopedia*'s article: one such is Milton's 'Blind mouths! that scarce themselves know how to hold a sheep-hook.' [14] In effect, they are a form of metaphor, but whereas metaphor, according to Lakoff, Johnson and Turner, is essentially cognitive, this trope is defined at the lexical level, just as a simile is a form of metaphor which is recognized by the use of the verbal formulae 'as', 'like' and so on. The defining feature of catachresis is the appropriation of terminology from the source domain of the metaphor to the target domain.[15] 'Death is a banana' is not a catachresis because there is no borrowing of vocabulary, but to talk about 'peeling' death would be.

I can now expand on my earlier claim that the adjective-noun pair is the basic structural unit of the early poems: pairings like 'gargoyle scree' encapsulate the process of qualification by catachresis which goes on throughout these texts. Other structures that perform such qualification in 'The First Journey' include the use of double adjectives ('young shouldering east'), the noun-'of'-noun combination, where the noun in the possessive really works as an adjective qualifying its companion ('my cinder of striding', 'my winter's edge'), and adverbial and adjectival clauses such as 'Launched three windy neptunes high' and 'screeched from a mountain pap'. The impression of syntactical complexity derives from the fact that almost every word or phrase that can be qualified is qualified. The simple 'my birth falls' is followed by an adverbial phrase describing how it falls: 'in a spittle of glass', and the whole phrase then receives the further qualification 'like the death of a lark'. Since each of these qualifications is strongly imagistic and has the incongruity of catachresis, the end result is a kaleidoscope of clashing images without any apparent logic.

Michael Riffaterre has used the concept of catachresis as a component of his theory of poetry in general. According to him the mimetic function of a poem, its claim to describe the world in all its complexity, is only a pretence. This realist aspect of the poem, which he calls its 'meaning', is complex and multiple; it is distinguished from the 'significance', which is simple and unitary, so much so that it can often be defined in a single word. The process of reading a poem is the imaginative leap from one level to the other, from meaning to significance. In reading 'Malcolm Mooney's Land', for example, there comes a moment when one realizes that this Arctic landscape with all its concrete details of glaciers, bears and sleeping-bags (the meaning) is a way of describing language (the significance). For Riffaterre, this shift of levels, simultaneously undermining the meaning and leading the reader towards the significance, is brought about by deviations from standard linguistic usage that he calls 'ungrammaticalities'. He describes these as resembling 'a series of inappropriate twisted wordings' whose effect is on the poem is that of 'a generalized, all-encompassing, all-contaminating catachresis'.[16]

The problem with his approach has been pointed out by Jonathan Culler. Its restrictive model of poetry in which the reader has no choice but to move from one level to the other, falsifies the multifarious experience of reading. This is all the more ironic in that Riffaterre supports the theory with some brilliant interpretations of nineteenth- and twentieth-century French poems. If reading were the unvarying process he claims, these would be superfluous, since every intelligent reader would already have reached the same conclusions.[17] And indeed the theory is incompatible with the indeterminacy for which I have argued in Chapter 1. Nevertheless, it is relevant here because it is so strongly grounded in the practice of symbolist and post-symbolist poetry. The fact that Riffaterre uses catachresis as a synecdoche of poetic tropes in general tells us much about the poets he analyses, Rimbaud, Mallarmé and the Surrealists among them. While all varieties of metaphor contain elements of both similarity and dissimilarity, in catachresis of the extreme literary kind it is the dissimilarity which is more striking. The difference between gargoyles and screes is more evident than their shared property of stoniness. Instead of giving voice to a structural resemblance between two domains that is deeply and generally felt, the poet is more likely to be seen as bringing about their conjunction for the first time; catachresis exemplifies the post-romantic cult of originality. It is the product of a special mind, that of the artist, or a special state of mind, the liberated unconscious. It breaks down the barriers by which conventional thought separates items into different domains but because it does so at the level of words, by yoking together apparently incompatible terminology, it sets up another barrier, the one that separates the magical world of the poem from humdrum, compartmentalized reality. (This issue of the autonomy of the poem is complex and will be discussed in the third section of this chapter.)

It seems, then, that qualification by catachresis is one of the poetic strategies of the modernist era. Graham would certainly have noted its use in the more extravagantly surreal passages of Dylan Thomas, such as 'Altarwise by Owl-Light',where we find adjective-noun pairs like 'rocking alphabet', 'naked sponge', 'bald pavilions' and 'ringing handprint' and the noun-'of'-noun combinations 'teats of music', 'house of bread' and 'sound of shape'.[18] Thomas is, I believe, the most immediate and forceful presence behind the early poems, but Lopez is right to point to other influences on both the early Graham and Thomas himself. Hart Crane's 'Voyages' revels in its glamorous adjectives ('silver snowy sentences', 'sceptred terror', 'spindrift gaze') and a passage quoted by Lopez does indeed resemble Graham's early writing in its compound qualification using both adjective-noun pairs and noun-'of'-noun phrases:

> And onward, as bells off San Salvador
> Salute the crocus lustres of the stars,
> In these poinsettia meadows of her tides, –
> Adagios of islands [. . .][19]

The poetry of Gerard Manley Hopkins, another influence cited by Lopez, also surprises with its abundance of unusual adjectives, as in the lines:

> Wiry and white-fiery and whirlwind-swivellèd snow
> Spins to the widow-making unchilding unfathering deeps.[20]

From all these sources Graham would have received the idea of the adjective as an instrument of poetic power. In Hopkins, its power is that of revelation – in its energy and sensuousness, the adjective acts on the noun to reveal 'the grandeur of God' in the created world of nature.[21] For Crane and Thomas, the power begins to transform the world. Thomas creates a magical world of fused adjective-nouns whose relationship to the objective world is not at all clear, and in so doing celebrates not merely God's creation but also his own creativity, the poetic imagination. In the case of Crane, with his obvious debt to Rimbaud, the adjectives qualify an allegorical sea which represents the imagination's ability to bear one away from the dry land of everyday reality altogether. Adjectival catachresis exemplifies the transforming imagination of the post-symbolist poet, bringing about 'the silken skilled transmemberment of song'.[22]

A similar approach can be found in the work of those other heirs of the symbolist movement, the Surrealist poets, whose influence was at its height in Britain at about the time of the early poems.[23] According to Anna Balakian:

> The Surrealist image has to be a far-fetched – or rather deep-fetched – chance encounter of two realities whose effect is likened to the light produced by the contact of two electrical conductors.[24]

The Surrealist practice of automatic writing to liberate the imagination from its logical constraints undoubtedly influenced Graham, as I shall show in Chapter 6. Another of their poetic strategies was a game called 'Exquisite Corpse' in which they jointly constructed sentences by supplying the required parts of speech (adjective, noun, verb and so on) without being able to see the rest of the sentence. Such a method makes any mimesis sporadic and merely fortuitous – the sentences so constructed cannot coherently describe pre-existing facts. Every phrase produced must, in effect, be a catachresis, since the words it contains will almost certainly come from different categories and combine to form a unique and incongruous image. The very title of the game, which was generated in one of its early sessions, is an adjective-noun pair of this kind.[25] The poems in *The Seven Journeys*, with their formulaic syntactical structures, extravagant diction and obscure sense, read almost as if Graham composed them using a similar system.

Nevertheless the passage we have been considering is not a simple aggregation of adjective-noun pairs; while the qualification by catachresis is its most striking feature, there is a narrative element operating, too. The poem calls itself a journey, but it begins with a birth. We may conclude from this that one of Lakoff and Turner's basic metaphors is operating here, that of life as a journey.[26] The narrative is a sort of autobiography, but the Surrealist mode of writing precludes any mimetic account of a Greenock childhood. The poem is allegorical of itself – the birth it begins with is that of its own narrative voice. (Compare 'The Narrator' – *NCP*, pp. 3–4.) It is significant that this birth is described as a fall; even at this early stage of his career, Graham was preoccupied with the theme of writing as self-inflicted loss. It is not, however, an unqualified loss, since, as we have seen, nothing in the poem is unqualified. The jumble of conflicting categories we noted at the outset is brought about by an aesthetic that sees poetry as the place where all categories meet. Thus it is not only a fall but also a launching. The mysterious word 'neptunes' fuses the name of a planet with that of the god of the sea: one is the apotheosis of height, the other of depth. (Its main function, I suggest, is as a hyperbolic indication of height, meaning three times as high as the planet Neptune, but it is overdetermined by the word 'launched', suggesting the departure of a ship.)[27] And in fact the five lines we have been considering are structured round the antithesis of rising and falling movements: a launch, a birth, a fall, a waterspout and a climbing. Birth is the fall to which all myths of the Fall can be traced, the expulsion from the paradise of the mother's body. Here, however, it is combined with images of a contrasting bodily expulsion, the ejaculation of semen, which is 'launched' to a hyperbolic height and then falls like spittle. The 'rainbow waterspout' is a second ejaculatory image. The identification of masculine sexual symbolism with poetic inspiration suggests Coleridge's 'sacred river' with the graphological name which was 'forced' from the rocks in a 'swift, half-intermitted burst'.[28] Another influence was the erotic diction of Thomas's particular brand of the egotistical sublime; the poem clearly echoes the tone of such lines as:

> Beginning with doom in the ghost, and the springing marvels
> Image of images, my metal phantom
> Forcing forth through the harebell,
> My man of leaves and the bronze root, mortal, unmortal,
> I, in my fusion of rose and male motion,
> Create this twin miracle.[29]

The poet is self-born from his own ejaculation. The birth takes place, as Montgomerie noted, in a Highland landscape, with scree, wind, the song of a lark, mountains, rowans, brambles and so on. But the language of artifice and myth which qualifies this implies that the birth is a cultural rather than a natural event. The scree from which the poet / sperm / foetus is launched is made of gargoyles – that is, it is not only artificial but also monstrous. (I would interpret the scree as the poetic or cultural tradition, 'a heap of broken images' in Eliot's phrase, or Pound's 'two gross of broken statues'.)[30] The falling of the sperm on the ground is associated with the death of the natural world (the lark) and with the martyrdom of the artist ('crucified height', 'largo'). Instead of having the fluidity of real sperm, a quality Graham associates with the extratextual lifeworld, the ejaculate has the hardness and brittleness of glass. And indeed, at the end of the poem, the poet created from it is broken by the timeless perfection of art:

SHEER I break AGAINST those EVERMORE GLITTERING SEASONS.

Between the ejaculation / birth which begins this journey and the breaking which ends it, the poet, whatever else he may be doing, is certainly walking. We see him 'strideful', lifting his 'tenderly mimicing [sic] feet' and on a path. His shoulder prances 'in air'; he has 'a map of journeys' and a 'pilgrim compass'. Lopez, as I mentioned in Chapter 1, sees voyaging as Graham's most important theme, and demonstrates his debt to such literary treatments as 'The Wreck of the Deutschland', 'The Rime of the Ancient Mariner' and *Moby-Dick*. This is apparent in the seafaring passages of *The Seven Journeys* (*NCP*, pp. 6–7, p. 10).[31] But walking is just as important, for various reasons: it is, as I noted in Chapter 2, associated with his upbringing in an environment within easy reach of the countryside in a period when hiking was a hobby rapidly growing in popularity; in contrast to this, it represents his own departure from home towards a new and very different life, in which sense it is a walking *away* from something; and it exemplifies the crossing of the space between addresser and addressee that is fundamental to the conduit metaphor, being in this sense a walking *towards* someone. It thus applies equally to each of the three stages of the dialectic enacted by the poems – the freely traversible space of original community, the leaving of that community and the approach towards a textual alternative to it. At the beginning of his career, the emphasis falls on walking away: the poems are largely celebrations of travel as a manly accomplishment which of necessity takes one away from home but which is – or at least should be – sanctioned by the community. In fact, as I shall show in my discussion of *The White Threshold* and *The Nightfishing* in Chapter 4, even the imagery of seafaring can be justified in terms of communal values, particularly by someone who grew up in a community largely dependent on it for income, as Graham did. In 'The First Journey', however, the relationship between language and community is schematized as a bracing hike along roads and through the countryside.

In Riffaterrean terms, then, the poem is a mimesis of a journey on foot through a Scottish landscape. This mimetic 'meaning' is disrupted by catachresis. The landscape is a monstrous one with its gargoyles, medusa, idols and giant; it is full of strange and artificial features, a scree made of gargoyles, spittle made of glass. The traditional association between life and journeys suggest that the significance here is autobiographical: instead of a real journey we are shown the journey of life. Certainly the poem celebrates the poet's youthful energy, his 'young shouldering east'. (The same metaphor appears in a poem by Nessie Dunsmuir in which she writes of the 'early east' of children.)[32] It is appropriate that one of the landmarks he passes is Sgurr Nan Gillean, a mountain on Skye whose name means 'the peak of the young men'. However this autobiographical theme is not enough by itself to explain the poem's many catachreses. These show off the poet's ingenuity, his ability to yoke together the most incongruous images imaginable, and in so doing they advance a view of poetry as a powerfully original transgression of categories, a 'transmemberment' of reality. Its artificial world is one of masculine endeavour and prowess; instead of being born of woman, the poet brings himself into being by sheer virility. But while we are invited to admire this quality, we must also feel sorry for him, since the fragile glassy world through which he must travel is both uncomfortable and dangerous. Instead of the comforts of a real mother, he must make do with a 'mountain pap', and there are monsters along the way; at the end, he is broken by art. These are the sacrifices that provide the poem's religious diction, from the 'crucified height' of the opening, through 'faith' and 'amen' to the 'pilgrim compass' at the end. The implication is that the artist's journey is a sacred duty, one that he cannot neglect, however much he might wish to.

Already in this poem written in his early 20s we encounter all Graham's main concerns. The complex rhetoric is obviously being enjoyed for its own sake, as an exercise in exuberant catachresis, a game of 'Exquisite Corpse', but at the same time it is being used for the purpose of self-justification. If the later rhetoric appears more direct, it is not because his view of poetry had changed, but because the task of self-justification had become more urgent.

Making a Table Out of Water

It is in the early poems that we see the beginning of Graham's lifelong attempt to reconcile his view of text as closed and static with his insistence that in writing he was in some way participating in the flux of the lifeworld. His need for control was manifested in images of cages and objects, while his need for love gave rise to the fluid imagery of water and electricity. As long as he continued to view poetry as the inspired fusion of apparently incompatible entities this complex of images provided him with an almost inexhaustible supply of poems.

Graham's first published book (though not the first to be written) has a cryptic title: *Cage Without Grievance*. The enigmatic impression produced by this phrase is due to a catachresis. One expects 'cage without parrots' or 'cage without bars'. A cage cannot contain a grievance, be constructed from one or nurse one, so the title seems to be the pointless negation of an absurdity.[33] However, this impression will be seen to be illusory when the phrase is replaced in its original context, as I shall do shortly. It is, in effect, a condensed version of some such statement as 'I inhabit this cage without grievance', but the reader of the book is unlikely to realize this, as the original context occurs in Graham's previous book, which had not yet been published when *Cage Without Grievance* appeared. It seems probable therefore that Graham relished the catachresis and intended an effect of mystification. Similar tropes are characteristic of Surrealism, as Balakian has noted (and exemplified) in the phrase: 'The image lends to the abstract the mask of the concrete'.[34] The mismatch between a material object and an abstraction is intended because, as we shall see, Graham finds himself trapped in such a mismatch, unable to reconcile his view of text with his view of the self.

The phrase 'Cage Without Grievance' is a quotation from 'The Seventh Journey'. I shall come to the passage which includes the phrase in a moment, but I shall start my analysis a little earlier:

> Beyond my dawnrung footgems tilts a stellar phrase
> Preaching a discovered hallow to my world's toe-stars
> Till my truth's accident builds a sealed tropic of love
> Girt with a cage of latitudes no gauge destroys
> And exiled in a molecule no liberty selects.

(NCP, p. 12)

It is possible to distinguish a number of threads of imagery here. Some of the words are associated with discourse: 'phrase', 'preaching', 'truth', 'hallow' if we take this to be a pun on 'hallo'. Others are celestial: the 'dawn' of 'dawnrung', 'stellar', the 'stars' of 'toe-stars'. A further strand is to do with exploration, reminding us that this, too, is a journey: the 'foot' of 'footgems', 'discovered', 'world', the 'toe' of 'toe-stars', 'tropic', 'latitudes'. The first line allows us to visualize this explorer's gemlike footsteps ringing as he sets off in the dawn with the stars still visible in the sky. A fourth strand involves construction and containment. Something 'builds' something else that is 'sealed', which is in turn 'girt with a cage' that cannot be destroyed and 'exiled', which in this case appears to mean 'imprisoned', since the exile is to the smallest imaginable space. The 'cage of latitudes' sounds like the world, which is crossed by imaginary lines of latitude, but this huge cage seems itself to be contained in a 'molecule'.

A possible interpretation of this passage, then, is that the poet pictures himself as an explorer who sets off on an expedition guiding himself by the stellar phrases which reach him from outside (these could be the words of other poets, but I suspect it is the externality of language in general that is meant), providing him with sacred verbal insights ('a discovered hallow') until by a process of serendipity ('truth's accident') he constructs a poem. This poem is autonomous ('sealed') and although it is inspired by love it remains confined within its complex boundaries, which are both global and atomic, that is, microcosmic. The passage simultaneously celebrates and laments this confinement: 'tropic', 'love' and 'latitudes' suggest that the poem is a warm, passionate and expansive place (and we should note that 'latitudes' is another pun – it can mean 'freedoms' so that 'cage of latitudes' is an oxymoron), while 'cage', 'exile', 'molecule' and the phrase 'no liberty selects' emphasize its restriction. The cage cannot be gauged: it is liberating and confining, vast and small. At the same time it is the product of measurement (gauging). The 'latitudes' are simultaneously contained in it (where the word is a metonymy for great distances) and the marker of its boundaries (where they define the restrictive grid of lines on a map).

This image of the map requires a comment in passing: it is of great importance in Graham's early poetry, and has the metapoetic implication of a cage confining the poet to a paper world. As Valentine Cunningham points out, its use by Graham's immediate predecessors, the writers of the 1930s, already reflects an interest in the theme of textuality itself as well as the apparently more characteristic one of travel and global politics.[35] In 'Explanation of a Map', however, the emphasis, typically, is on the map's inadequacy as a description of reality (*NCP*, pp. 33–4).[36] 'The Serving Inhabiters' questions the idea that the map can be communal and organic: 'Can blood admit a people's map / Together district to a common shape?' (*NCP*, p. 36). The microcosmic image which ends 'His Companions Buried Him' identifies the map with each explorer's personal reality (*NCP*, p. 38). Finally, in 'The Narrator', the poem is evoked at the moment of generation, when it is still an 'unmapped spell' being passed from the poet's brain through his body (*NCP*, p. 3).

The passage I have discussed is the first appearance of the cage in 'The

Seventh Journey', but I have still not quoted the passage in which the phrase 'cage without grievance' occurs:

> Somewhere in distilled harmonies a tumult spins
> One for each human constellation in a skull,
> And blows a world of faculties in a watched bubble
> And ribs my magpie comet in a cage without grievance.

(NCP, p. 12)

Since Graham adopted the phrase as the title of his next book, it was obviously important to him. If we assume that the cage is once again the poem itself, we can read the passage as a statement of faith. The poet accepts the confinement of the poem. A rough paraphrase of this passage would be: the poem, though it appears to be harmonious, is in fact a tumult of different readings, one for each reader (since every reader has a different universe in his or her brain), and these various worlds appear reflected in its bubble – as for me, the poet, my soaring writing (black and white like a magpie) is given human form ('ribs') by these readers, and although this is also a form of imprisonment, I do not resent it. In other words, the passage insists on the indeterminacy of poetry. Such insistence, of course, is a paradox, but, as I have argued in Chapter 1, it is a paradox typical of Graham's metapoetry. The poet, by describing the only reality shared by writer and reader – that is, the text itself – seeks to impose his will on it, while at the same time celebrating the 'latitudes' it allows.

The imagery of cages and imprisonment occurs in many of the early poems. 'The Narrator' refers to 'anarchy within a cage', while in '2nd Letter' there is 'a lamp that cages / My head in heliotrope' (*NCP*, p. 3, p. 28). In 'There Was When Morning Fell', the speaker appears to be in prison ('Day through my prison walked'), and in 'I, No More Real Than Evil In My Roof', 'children cartwheel from prison in procession' (*NCP*, p. 22, p. 29). Nessie Dunsmuir, on being transformed into the subject of a poem, is 'locked round with making', and the application of this imagery to writing is clear enough in 'Soon To Be Distances', where the poet's experience is about to be transformed into silent and distant text, 'Soon to be distances locked sound' and 'What I learn turns barrier to voice' (*NCP*, p. 51, p. 34). Language, as I argued in Chapter 1, is seen as blocking interpersonal relations, and this imagery of barriers or walls coexists with that of distance, or the exile evoked in such a poem as 'By Law of Exile' (*NCP*, p. 49). But the cage or prison fits particularly well the conduit metaphor's attributes of interiority and substantiality.

The cage is a rigid outside immobilizing a vital inside. It is therefore an image of artifice when this is seen as a means of oppressing and confining nature, the occupant of the cage, which may represented by a wild beast or a bird. One of the most famous uses of the image is that of Rilke in his poem 'The Panther', which he wrote in Paris under the influence of the 'severe and salutary discipline' which Rodin had imposed on his working methods.[37] Rilke's response to this discipline was to go to the *Jardin des Plantes* and use the panther as a model for a poem in the same way that Rodin used models for his sculpture:

> His vision, from the constantly passing bars
> has grown so weary that it cannot hold
> anything else. It seems to him there are
> a thousand bars; and behind the bars, no world.[38]

Clearly at some level this study of confinement is a response to the discipline imposed on the poet by the sculptor. To write to order is to be a caged panther. But the response is paradoxical: told to go out into the world and practise mimetic art, Rilke has obeyed the instructions only to discover in that world a symbol of the autonomous poem. For the symbolist poet as for the panther the world remains out of reach.

Another use of the image of a caged beast is that of André Breton in his 'Manifesto of Surrealism':

> [. . .] Experience itself has found itself increasingly circumscribed. It paces back and forth in a cage from which it is more and more difficult to make it emerge.[39]

Whether or not Breton's cage owes something to Rilke's, we see in this passage how the cage enters Surrealist theory, from where it was able to influence British avant-garde writing of the 1940s.[40] Neither Breton nor Rilke in these examples explicitly equates the cage with language itself, but, another Surrealist, Robert Desnos, in his *L'Aumonyme*, uses the term 'FORMES-PRISONS' to describe syllables and words. The French word *mots*, which he uses, refers to words as part of the system of language (*langue*), as distinct from *paroles*, which refers to the words actually uttered by the individual. Such *paroles* must always be chosen from the *mots* available. It is the arbitrary and inescapable contraints of language which imprison the poet.[41]

In the 1930s, the period when Graham received his literary education, the cage was a familiar symbol both of the physical privations and sufferings which were being endured by many on the continent of Europe, and of the sense of epistemological confinement felt by intellectuals. For Spender, Eliot and others, 'the destructive modernist belief-chaos composed a cage.'[42] However, in this instance as in the imagery of drowning and ice which I shall explore in later chapters, Graham refocused a symbol which could represent a wide range of themes on to his own main concerns.

The theme of the poem as simultaneously a cage for the poet and a release for the reader occurs in the essay 'Notes on a Poetry of Release', which I discussed in Chapter 2. (This essay was published in 1946, when Graham was working on the poems of *The White Threshold*, but elucidates much of the imagery of the early poems). The metaphor is clearly present in the title of the essay. For Graham the belief in language as a prison, a permanent and inescapable outside, problematizes any concept of expression. How can there be any release at all if *paroles* have to be selected from *mots*, the very bars of the cage?

> The most difficult thing for me to remember is that a poem is made out of words and not of the expanding heart, the overflowing soul, or the sensitive observer. A poem is made of words. It is words in a certain order, good or bad by the significance of its addition to life and not to be judged by any other value put upon it by imagining how or why or by what kind of man it was made. It is easy to strive to make a poem out of the wrong material like a table out of water.
>
> (NFM, pp. 379–80)

Graham is struggling here to reconcile the materialist account of language as a thing with a view of consciousness as flux which we shall discuss shortly, while at the same time preserving the opposition between the 'inside' and 'outside' of language on which the conduit metaphor depends. For Derrida, 'the outside ⋈ the inside'; without the same theoretical ingenuity, Graham is forced to use a series of metaphors to try to reconcile the personal meaningfulness of writing with the externality of language.[43] The 'poetry of release' is nothing so straightforward as a discharge of the poet's interiority into the world. This is prohibited by his commitment to an opposition between a static, material writing and a self pictured as interior and fluid. The poem, since it is 'made of words', cannot represent such a self, an admission Graham, makes with the utmost reluctance: it is 'the most difficult thing [. . .] to remember'.[44] The poem is a made object, a 'construction'. (The word is used several times in the course of the essay.) It is represented by images of solidity: a table, a mountain, a building in the phrase 'the labourer carrying the bricks of his time and on the scaffolding of an unknown construction' (NFM, p. 380, p. 382, p. 381). The poem is thus seen to be well and truly outside, constructed as it is of the same materials as walls and prisons. (A more positive image is the 'squared stones' of Montgomerie's introduction to *The Seven Journeys*.) But if the poem is on the outside, so is the reader. Graham therefore displaces the metaphor of release from the poet to the reader:

> The poem itself is dumb, but has the power of release. Its purpose is that it can be used by the reader to find out something about himself.

> (*NFM*, p. 381).

This emphasis on the creative role of the reader, with its implication of textual indeterminacy, is similar to Reddy's account of communication, but it lacks the crucial elements of reciprocity and context which would allow the poem to be used along with other evidence 'to find out something' about its author. Graham is working with the ingredients of the conduit metaphor, an inside and outside and the 'release' of meaning, whether from addresser to text or from text to addressee, but he has rearranged them:

> A poem is a mountain made out of the containing, almost physical language, and with the power to release a man into his own completely responsible world larger than that outward solid geography.

> (*NFM*, p. 382)

Since the reader is already on the outside, he or she can only be released inward. But the walls of the poem cannot be breached in either direction, so that the release must be into something else entirely. An inward release implies a paradoxical reversal of spatial properties – the inner world is 'larger than that outward solid geography'. A release into something other than the poem (into the reader's 'own completely responsible world') leaves the poem's 'power' to effect it unexplained. One thinks of Eliot's image of the poet as catalyst, but Graham's preferred image to explain a power that is both material and apparently magical is that of electricity:[45]

> A poem is charged to that power of release that even to one man it goes on speaking again and again beyond behind [*sic*] its speaking words.

> (*NFM*, p. 382)

Something roughly corresponding to the poet's emotional output is released from the poem; the water which the poet could not make tables out of is here transformed into another fluid, an electrical current.

One of the claims of 'Notes' is strikingly contradicted by a poem written some twenty years later. Graham, as we have seen, insists that to make a poem out of 'the overflowing heart' is like making a table out of water. But in 'Enter a Cloud', this is exactly what he does:

Enter a cloud. Between
The head of Zennor and
Gurnard's Head the long
Marine horizon makes
A blue wall or is it
A distant table-top
Of the far-off simple sea.

(*NCP*, pp. 216–17)

Later, as if catching himself in the contradiction, he accuses himself as follows:

It is funny I got the sea's
Horizontal slightly surrealist.

(*NCP*, p. 218)

This allusion to Surrealism points us once again to a movement that had an important influence on Graham. If to mistake water for a table is to be 'slightly surrealist', then Surrealism is located at the intersection of solid and liquid (or, to decode the metaphor, of objects and emotions) where Graham in 'Notes' showed himself so ill at ease. Paul C. Ray has argued that 'the Surrealist program to discredit conventional reality included an attack on the object, the basic, irreducible component of that reality'.[46] In speaking of an 'attack', Ray is no doubt going too far. It is an obsession with the way objects can catch up and hold human emotions, whether of loathing or of love. There is a strong element of fetishism in the Surrealist treatment of objects.[47]

So far we have looked at the tension between the solidity associated with the poem as object on the one hand and on the other a number of concepts associated with liquid imagery. The poet's emotions are an internal liquid whose relationship to the hard material outside is problematic. However, liquid imagery is also to be found on the outside. In the first paragraph, for example, Graham writes of 'the environment flowing in on me from all sides'. Shortly afterwards, he describes history in terms which clearly allude to Heraclitus's famous aphorism about stepping into a river: it 'does not repeat itself' and 'continually arrives [. . .] differently'.[48] This terminology is then reapplied in the next paragraph to language, which is 'continually being [. . .] changed like a river over its changing speakers'. The outside, whether it is called 'the environment' or history or language (and it might also be called the community, since Graham refers to it as 'a crowd' and 'the people who wait outside [the poet's] gates') attracts to itself the vocabulary and imagery of flux (*NFM*, p. 380). The solidity of the 'Art Object' acts as a shell or wall between two shapeless oceans, one inside the poet and one outside.

This tension between flux and stasis was characteristic of the modernist period as a whole. Randall Stevenson has written of 'modernism's contrasts or reconciliations between fragment and flow, between atom and wave, between the divisions of the clock and the continuity of consciousness', while Sanford Schwartz shows how these 'contrasts or reconciliations' are worked out in different ways by many of the major thinkers of the late nineteenth and early twentieth centuries, including Nietzsche, Bergson, Husserl and William James.[49] Chris Stephens has argued for the influence of Bergson's theories of flux and duration on some of Graham's St Ives artist friends in the early 1950s, and suggests that Heidegger was also a factor.[50] Certainly T.E. Hulme's description of Bergsonism could not be more relevant to the rhetoric of 'Notes':

> I always figure the main Bergsonian position in this way: conceiving the constructs of logic as geometrical wire models and the flux of reality as a turbulent river such that it is impossible with any combination of these wire models, however elaborate, to make a model of the moving stream. [. . .] You cannot hold water in a wire cage, however minute the mesh.[51]

While it is tempting to infer at least an indirect influence of Bergson from this striking parallel, the use of the image of the stream to represent either consciousness or time, subjective or objective reality, was, as Schwartz remarks, 'remarkably widespread' and it is probably not possible to trace a single philosophical source for Graham's use of it.[52] (I shall consider the implications of the concept further in Chapter 4.)

Whatever the origins of this opposition may have been, Graham interpreted it in the light of his own concerns. He seems to have associated flux primarily with community because a community is an uncontrollable body of living, changing people; furthermore, the conduit metaphor depicts communication as a channelling of flux between self and others. The poem, on the other hand, was to him a textual object, an unchanging goal towards which he could direct his efforts – the making of tables is a controllable process. Or, to switch to a closely related metaphor, the cage was a static boundary protecting him from the world's flux. All the ambivalence which he felt about the relationship of community to the text, uncontrollable love versus unlovable control, is therefore manifested in his attitude to this theme. In Chapter 2 I argued that he sought out the mythic text for the protection it might provide from the will of others, but was then compelled to prove rhetorically that this action was in some sense a surrender to that will as embodied in language. To do this it was necessary to show that the stasis of text was charged with the flux of the lifeworld.

This theme of flux generates one of the most important strands of imagery in Graham's work, that of water and, above all, of the sea. His sea symbolism is most thoroughly worked out in the two volumes of what I have called his middle period, *The White Threshold* and *The Nightfishing*, but water imagery is already prominent in the early work. In 'The Third Journey', for example, he describes himself as 'a genius of rivers' and later as 'a scholar of seas', a phrase which was to recur in 'The Nightfishing' as 'sea-scholar' (*NCP*, p. 7, p. 115). The 'scholar of seas' is one who can deal with the flux by writing it down, since he knows 'the grammars of tide' (*NCP*, p. 6). *2ND Poems* explores in some detail the Biblical theme of the Flood. 'My Glass Word Tells Of Itself', for example, contrasts the fate of a 'drowning Noah' with the self-reflexive work of a writer who must work in sand and glass rather than in the watery material of reality: 'I pour round glass the sand my rivers have' (*NCP*, p. 43). It is understandable that the lifeworld to which text has such a problematic relationship should be associated with catastrophe at the time of this volume, which was published in 1945, and that the flux should therefore be depicted as a flood. The drowning theme, his own adaptation of a widespread poetic response to the Second World War, which was to become still more prominent in *The White Threshold*, is already well-defined in 'Continual Sea and Air' (*NCP*, p. 45–6). The writer insists that he has a role in these perilous circumstances, and his insistence takes the form of a surreal juxtaposition of Flood and writing imagery:

> So I everywhere, where winter meets the ark
> Float my table, my books, my precious object
> Towards shore
>
> (*NCP*, p. 41)

In these poems, as throughout his career, Graham is trying to work out how to use a static, controllable text to demonstrate his continuing allegiance to the changing, uncontrollable community in which he grew up, with its flux of love and reality. The cage of the poem must be made to contain a river.

The catachresis of the early poems is both the boldest and simplest of these attempts. The notion of poetry he inherited from Thomas and others, the fusion of apparently incompatible entities, implied that stasis and flux could coexist in it, at least as images. 'The First Journey' is full of such fusions: 'spittle of glass', a birth that takes place 'in a diamond', 'seas tasselled and trellised in emerald'. Another example, this time from *Cage Without Grievance*, is 'Say That In Lovers With Stones For Family' (*NCP*, p. 23). Instead of families, the lovers have stones; the liquid humanity of blood and tears is transformed into unyielding iron and 'metal law', 'bridal rivers' become a 'prison's plain' and the fluidity of fertility ('a seedway' which 'streams') is channelled through 'rocky viaducts'. The poet-husband is trapped in a tor and becomes 'a crop of peaks'.

As well as stasis and flux, there are many other opposed qualities generated by Graham's mythic opposition of text and community: hardness and softness, death and life, cold and heat, and so on. The myth serves him as a powerful generator of catachreses and hence of the kind of poems he was writing at this stage of his career. In the remainder of this chapter, I shall consider the aesthetic implications of one such opposition whose social significance I have already discussed, that between the organic and the mechanical.

Mechanical Pastoral

The world of many of the early poems, and in particular that of *Cage Without Grievance*, is a pastoral one. 'God will hear all that pastoral can tell', Graham writes in 'Let Me Measure My Prayer With Sleep', which concludes with an evocation of the poet 'hubbed in harebells / Where planets in pasture multiply my face' (*NCP*, pp. 24–5). The words 'pasture(s)' (*NCP*, p. 8, p. 39), 'meads' (*NCP*, p. 17), 'meadow' (*NCP*, p. 13) or 'orchard(s)' (*NCP*, p. 7, p. 47) suggest a landscape that harmoniously accommodates human beings and their needs. It is usually spring (*NCP*, p. 17, p. 18, p. 19, p. 22, p. 24) – occasionally March (*NCP*, p. 21, p. 53) or May (*NCP*, p. 11, p. 24), but more often April (*NCP*, p. 6, p. 18, p. 23, p. 24, p. 25). The image implicit in much of this pastoral writing is of the poet lying among the weeds and flowers of a field on a spring day, watching insects and small animals, listening to the song of birds, at peace with the world. In 'Over the Apparatus of the Spring Is Drawn', the imagery includes bluebells, a daisy, a dormouse, the 'choral vagaries' of birds, the song of a beetle, a cuckoo and a scarecrow (*NCP*, p. 17). In 'Of the Resonant Rumour of Sun, Impulse of Summer', there are thistles which 'blow the time' with their 'silken floaters' ('April' and summer coexist in this poem with a disdain for consistency typical of the early Graham), myrtle, nettles and docks and the mention of picnics (*NCP*, p. 18). In 'Let Me Measure My Prayer With Sleep', there are a hedge, campions, rowan, sorrel, silverweed, harebells, moles and rooks (*NCP*, pp. 24–5). That Graham was well aware of the literary history of pastoral is shown by his self-conscious and often anachronistic use of many of its conventional terms and trappings: shepherds, (*NCP*, p. 3, p. 35), the nightingale (*NCP*, p. 10), ploughmen (*NCP*, p. 23) and words like 'groves', 'bower', 'dells', and the ambiguous 'margins' (*NCP*, p. 23, p. 39, p. 5, p. 6). In 'The Fourth Journey', this imagery is associated with Elizabethan poetry and song. The phrase 'the chimes of sweet Elizabethan turtled air' alludes to the turtle-doves often mentioned in Elizabethan poems, the nightingale appears in her conventional guise as Philomel, and there are 'madrigals' and a 'swain' (*NCP*, pp. 7–8).

Graham is attracted to this language and imagery by its literariness, its artificiality. Instead of a straightforward celebration of spring as a natural manifestation, we are presented with 'the apparatus of the Spring' and 'a constructed festival' or a 'lyrical contrivance' (*NCP*, p. 17, p. 19). This is an unusual mechanical form of pastoral with all its machinery visible, pulleys, 'a derrick in flower', 'an ephemeral mechanism' erected by birches (*NCP*, p. 17). An architectural diction is combined with natural images: plants form 'parapets', heaven has a 'joist' and the poet waits with 'the promise of primrose' in a 'rare scaffolding' (*NCP*, pp. 19). Lopez suggests that this language may be a consequence of Graham's background, a 'peculiar combination of shipbuilding superstructure (cranes, derricks, pulleys and scaffolding) with the surrounding natural features (the Renfrew hills, Loch Thom, the southern highlands just in view across the Clyde)'.[53] There is no doubt that Clydeside is present in these poems, but it is a Clydeside transformed into the magical landscape of text, 'a Mayscape' (*NCP*, p. 11).

In linking pastoral with machinery, Graham was in an obvious sense demonstrating his flair for incongruous juxtapositions: one does not expect the sky to have pulleys or a derrick to be in flower. But these images are also transgressive in a subtler sense which is more fundamental to his thought. They imply that text is a mechanical equivalent of landscape, and in so doing establish a contrast between *mechanical* text and *organic* reality. This is the personal twist he applies to an opposition between the two adjectives which was as common in the aesthetics of his time as it was in the social theory.

'Organic' is a word used of a unified and autonomous work of art as well as of a unified and autonomous community. The *locus classicus* of this use in English literary criticism is Coleridge's lecture notes on Shakespeare, in which he defends Shakespeare's plays from the accusation that they do not fit the rules of classical drama by claiming that such demands confuse 'mechanical regularity with organic form':

> The form is mechanic when on any given material we impress a predetermined form, not necessarily arising out of the properties of the material, as when to a mass of wet clay we give whatever shape we wish it to retain when hardened. The organic form, on the other hand, is innate; it shapes as it develops itself from within, and the fullness of its development is one and the same with the perfection of its outward form.[54]

Like a living body, the work has a form of its own, independent of external rules or standards. According to *The New Princeton Encyclopedia*:

> In 20th-century poetics, the organic analogy has been particularly attractive to theorists who argue that a poem must be experienced in isolation from other objects for the sake of its intrinsic values. A poem is an autonomous, autotelic object which, properly apprehended, produces in the reader a unique kind of 'aesthetic' experience.[55]

Peter Bürger has identified this theory with the nineteenth-century aestheticism which represents both the apogee of the bourgeois institution of art and the origin of the avant-garde attempt to undermine this.[56] The concept of autonomous art remained deeply entrenched in the twentieth century, however, even among some of those who considered themselves avant-garde; Graham, as we shall see in Chapter 6, experimented later in his career with modes of writing which, carried to their logical conclusion, would have represented an attack on institutional art, but used these merely as rehearsals for his more formal, public work. British aesthetic theorists of the 1940s, despite their interest in Surrealism, remained generally committed to the principle of artistic autonomy. This commitment cannot be clearly separated in many cases from the commitment to an organic community with all that that entails. In the United States, the New Criticism had connections with the conservative, anti-industrial Agrarian movement; in Britain, the writers associated with the New Apocalypse saw their work as an organic response to 'mechanistic ideology', a concept which linked industrialization with Marxism and Fascism.[57] G.S. Fraser, explaining the movement from a detached but sympathetic position, wrote in the second New Apocalypse anthology:

> As a person, then, the New Apocalyptic will be on the side of [. . .] the living and organic expression of human need, against the 'object-machine' – the attempt by newspapers, government rhetoric and systematic organization to manipulate men as mere parts of a huge (but quite silly and non-productive) State Machine.[58]

In a book on Dylan Thomas, Henry Treece, one of the founders of the New Apocalypse, explained this connection between machine, object and certain political and literary practices. His chapter 'The Poet and Mechanistic Ideology' attacks 'a cult of the machine in writing' which is identified with the Auden generation: 'these machine-state enthusiasts [who] opened their gold-filled mouths to roar a Hymn to Lenin in public-school telegraphese.'[59] Marxism is accused of being like a machine, that is, of imposing inflexible patterns of thought on its adherents, but also of being dependent on industrialization. Marxist-influenced writers like Auden are criticized for their interest in such images as a 'disused pitshaft'.[60]

The term 'organic' in the rhetoric of Treece and others has several implications: an autonomous community free from imposed rules, an autonomous art free from imposed rules, and a 'natural' community and art free from the contamination of industry. The point about the organic community, as I explained in Chapter 2, is that is mythical – it exists only in the past or the future; the organic work of art, on the other hand, exists here and now, in the context of the unsatisfactory 'organized' or 'mechanistic' society of the present, which is all the more reason why the aesthetic use of 'organic' should come to be almost a synonym of 'autonomous'. The work, by remaining separate from society, becomes an image of the organic community; it bypasses technological and political modes of communication and offers a humane and personal form of knowledge. (The metaphor's network of implications is complicated by Bergson's alternative term 'vital', which T.E. Hulme erroneously attributed to Coleridge in his essay 'Romanticism and Classicism'.[61] Bergson emphasized the special role of the aesthetic and intuitive faculties, which explains his appeal to artists. According to him, intuition could capture the vitality of experience, pictured as flux, in a way that was denied to rational, 'mechanistic' modes of thought.[62])

One aspect of Graham's response to this intellectual complex is straightforward enough: he rejected its anti-industrial bias. Like Raymond Williams, he grew up in a community where the importance of machines to the economy was well appreciated. Treece could write sarcastically about the kind of poetry which mentioned disused pitshafts, but Graham's future wife, Nessie Dunsmuir, came from the mining district of Lanarkshire, and her own poems, such as 'Stanis Pit', 'Raith Pit' and 'The Night-Walking Men Taken Into the Dark', rely heavily on the imagery of the industry. Dunsmuir's 'cage' is the one in which the miners descend to their work, and it is seen as sinister because it takes them away from light and family life: in 'Stanis Pit', it 'falls like a guillotine'.[63] However it cannot be simply be dismissed, as Treece would propose. At the time of which she wrote, machinery was central to her life, and it is not surprising, therefore, that it became central to her poetry. For Graham, too, machinery was a significant feature of his childhood, but he does not seem to share Dunsmuir's negative feelings about it. In his later poems, such as 'Greenock at Night I Find You', the vividness of the industrial imagery is associated with a lost world of love and community (*NCP*, pp. 219–20).

Nevertheless, he could not be untouched by the prevailing rhetoric of his period. In particular, its talk of the vital, the organic and the personal was very appealing to him. When Treece writes: 'We are, or should be, concerned with the personal reactions of man to man, where those reactions are honest and individual', one can imagine the man who was to write 'we want to be telling // Each other alive about each other / Alive' applauding (*NCP*, p. 200).[64] The images of flux in 'Notes on a Poetry of Release' are reminiscent of Bergson, and so, too, is some of the vocabulary:

> Shapes of language (right out of the gasp and gesture of speech) spill round our ears and I am at once the man of technique who books the phrases of drinking and affection so that later I might explore the mechanics of their memorableness and vitality.
>
> (*NFM*, p. 381)

Given all I have said, the phrase 'mechanics of [. . .] vitality' is not so much a catachresis as an oxymoron. In another passage, he writes:

> He [the poet] has to explore the imagination by using the language as his pitch. On it he must construct (intuitively to an organic as true as a tree) an apparatus which will work and to a special purpose.
>
> (*NFM*, p. 381)

The verb 'construct' reminds us that Graham was a contemporary of the artistic school known as 'Constructivism'.[65] But he does not simply compare the poem to an 'apparatus', that is, a machine. He also states that the building of this apparatus must be performed 'to an organic as true as a tree'. Quite what 'an organic' is, I am not sure.[66] But if an apparatus has 'an organic', it is clear enough that it is not just a machine but also at least resembles something living such as a tree. At a guess, I would say that Graham himself does not know what an organic is, but is merely using the word to bridge the troublesome gap between two opposed metaphors, to insist that the poem resembles both a machine and a tree. Similarly, when he writes notes on the phrases he hears in the Atholl Arms: 'An organic rhetoric is built up which charges and maintains the formal mechanics of poetry.' (*NFM*, p. 382.) We have already looked at the electrical image here. Whereas he was saying a moment ago that by writing words in his notebook he discovered the mechanics of speech, now he is reversing the emphasis: the speech he records 'charges' the mechanical structure of poetry, vitalizing what would otherwise be a formal machine. Confirmation of this analysis is to be found in the 1949 notebook in the National Library of Canada. Graham writes: 'mechanics [. . .] – any versification – but must remain organic to spoken conversation'. (In letters, where the maintenance of a consistent position is less important, he moves easily between the two sets of terms. Discussing his writing of 'The Nightfishing' in a letter to Sven Berlin, he complains: 'So often I feel lost in the middle of it not able to get out and back from it to see it as *one object*. But the bugger shall be fucked into an organic whole all the same.')[67]

This complex of metaphors demonstrates how committed Graham was to the opposition between a living community, a lifeworld, and a reified, mechanical text. When the fashionable aesthetics of his day insisted that text could be organic and hence an equivalent of the only community worth having (a mythical one), he absorbed this rhetoric into his own and tried to force the two schemas to coexist. Although he was every bit as committed as the Apocalyptics were to the autonomy of the text, he continued to imagine this not as the wholeness of an organism but as the hard, clean lines of a machine. To abandon his version of the distinction would be to give up the control that attracted him to writing in the first place, as well as the masculine connotations of the text as a place of industrial labour or construction. Nevertheless, for this labour to be meaningful, there had to be some truth in the arguments of the organicists. The catachresis of the early poems allowed him to satisfy both sides, to make a mechanical pastoral out of the juxtaposition of organic and mechanical imagery. But this strategy was a very limited one; it allowed for verbal pyrotechnics, but not for a sustained argument, and Graham needed an argument to maintain his position, even if only against the criticism of his own internalized communal values. To do this, he had to develop in detail his metaphor of language as a community, and this was the achievement of the next phase of his career.

CHAPTER 4

Drowning in Words:
The Middle Period

The Drowning Poems

The White Threshold, like its predecessor *2ND Poems*, pursues a central image with extraordinary persistence: the image of the sea, and, in particular, drowning at sea. The drowning theme was to persist into Graham's later work: in *The Nightfishing*, it is present at a lower level, absorbed into the metaphorical language of the verse, and it also recurs in Sections 49 and 50 of 'Implements', 'Falling Into the Sea' and some of the versions of 'A Dream of Crete' (*NCP*, p. 251, pp. 272–3, p. 307, p. 343). In *The White Threshold*, drowning is the main theme of seven poems ('Shian Bay', 'Gigha', 'Men Sign the Sea', 'Night's Fall Unlocks the Dirge of the Sea', 'At Whose Sheltering Shall the Day Sea', 'Three Poems of Drowning' and 'Michael's Sea-Lamb Before My Breath This Day'), a principal theme in 'The White Threshold', and part of the imagery of several others (*NCP*, pp. 81–6, pp. 92–8).

Nearly all the major images of Graham's poetry are drawn from the conventional literary stock of the 1930s and 1940s, and drowning is no exception. A glance at any anthology of poetry of the period reveals a number of laments for the drowned. John Heath-Stubbs asks of one victim:

> What peace has he, when jewelled fishes come
> To strip the flesh from his well-moulded bones?
> Only unending pain, while the tides roll
> Him round and round among the glittering stones.

(This answer, as we shall see, is very different from the one Graham would give.) Vernon Watkins asserts that 'it is fitting to mourn the drowned' / To imagine them clearly for whom the sea no longer cares' – again an un-Grahamlike conclusion, since Graham's sea has its own special mode of caring. In Tom Scott's 'Sea-Dirge', a woman finds her drowned lover:

> Bare he was as the sea and the rock on either side,
> With a rag of silk in his hand
> And sand in his nose[1]

Linda M. Shires has referred to drowning as 'one of the major mythic leitmotivs that plays throughout Second World War literature', and of course the war itself focused people's attention on the dangers faced by sailors.[2] No doubt also there was something subtly consoling about the thought that some of those dangers were the same ones that human beings had faced ever since they first went to sea. By using drowning as a synecdoche for all the deaths suffered in war, poets were able to disperse some of the attendant terrors, such as deadly new technology or attacks on civilian populations. Danger became natural and impersonal. The fact that drowning is, as Shires points out, a recurring theme in literature, made this strategy easier; the writers had the rhetorical tools ready to hand, and soon found out how effective they were in the new situation.

Graham had many contemporary models to draw on, then, in writing of drowning. Nevertheless, although the theme became prominent during the war and his own exploration of it was most intensive immediately after that period, its importance for him goes beyond the wartime fashion, which explains why he was still writing of it years later. Drowning dramatized the relationship between the individual and the community in a way he found very powerful. This dramatic tension is exemplified in two twentieth-century texts which, in my opinion, strongly influenced his own approach to the image: J.M Synge's *Riders to the Sea* and the 'Death By Water' section of 'The Waste Land'.

While studying at Newbattle Abbey, Graham took part in a production of *Riders to the Sea*, already a classic work.[3] This one-act play is set in an island off the west of Ireland where many of the young men have been lost at sea. The focus of Synge's interest is the character of a community in which a particular form of death is so bound into the texture of communal life. It is always the young men who die and the women who mourn them, expressing their grief in the traditional way by keening.[4] When one of the men, Michael, is lost at sea, his sister

Cathleen cries:

> Ah, Nora, isn't it a bitter thing to think of him floating that way to the far
> north, and no one to keen for him but the black hags that do be flying on
> the sea?[5]

Her lament is an image of total alienation, an absorption into a foreign
element, and the phrase, 'the far north', which she uses to describe this
place must have made an instant appeal to Graham with his fascination
with the Arctic. The men go to encounter the sublime, rather than
simply death.[6] But the play does not show that encounter – instead it
concentrates on the women who stay behind and suffer. This suffering
is a communal activity: it brings with it the practical obligations of
making coffins and burying those of the dead who have been retrieved
from the sea. The grief is shared, vocalized in conversation as well as in
keening. The main duty of the women and the village priest who
between them represent the permanent basis of this continually eroded
community is to defend its values against the damage caused by the
repetitive encounter between it and the sublime. The priest is the
official medium by which this process is to take place; the sublime is to
be tamed by absorbing it into Christianity, a religion which insists on
the continuity, the family relationship, between the human and the
superhuman. But the priest does not appear in the play, and his author-
ity is slightingly referred to. He is proved wrong in his claim that God
will not deprive Maurya of her last remaining son, and her daughter
Nora remarks, 'It's little the like of him knows of the sea.' In the play's
construction of sexual difference, the priest, a man who does not risk
his life by going to sea, falls outside the traditional gender roles. The
spiritual focus is provided instead by Maurya's vision of her recently
dead son, and by her account of the deaths of her husband and six sons.
This litany of masculine encounters with the sublime recited by a
woman is an affirmation of sexual roles, of the survival of love in the
form of grief, and of the unbroken line connecting the present with the
past (Bartley, the son Maurya sees riding to his death, and Michael, his
dead brother, ride in single file, and Maurya's recital of the deaths of the
men in her family gains its ritualistic power from its consecutive struc-
ture). The community has met the challenge of the sublime again and
again; the 'young priest', with no role to play in family life, is an
outsider who can never understand this.[7]

Riders to the Sea affirms the self-containedness of a community and a
tradition. It offers a potent myth, that of a community that has

absorbed the sublime within its boundaries and recuperated alienation for social purposes. The image of an island – land surrounded by sea – is in effect reversed: the sea is surrounded by land. (Patch, for example, is brought back for burial wrapped in a sail with water dripping out of it.)[8] In seafaring communities, people regularly risk their lives to earn a living. Their relationship with the sea can be seen as a kind of contract: the risk of drowning is the price people pay for their attempts to use it to their advantage in voyaging and fishing. Those who try to exploit nature run the risk of being destroyed, but without this contract the community could not survive. The drowned men have willingly sacrificed themselves for the sake of their fellows.

Like *Riders to the Sea*, 'The Waste Land' uses the theme of drowning to explore the nature of community. The death of Phlebas, like those of the sons of Maurya, confirms his role in life. He is a Phoenician, a member of a trading nation, and one of the things he forgets as he lies under the sea is 'the profit and loss'.[9] He has suffered the fate of those who 'do business in great waters'. According to the Psalm, 'these see the works of the Lord, / And his wonders in the deep.' His rising and falling motion suggests the same Psalm: 'They mount up to the heaven, they go down again to the depths.'[10] 'Death by Water' is a *memento mori*, a reminder to the living that they must die. Traditionally, such statements are designed to point out the futility of earthly values, and such is the superficial meaning of the exhortation 'Consider Phlebas who was once handsome and tall as you.' Good looks, like the profit and loss, no longer matter now he is dead. But in other ways Phlebas's fate is a repetition of his life rather than a refutation of it. He has assumed an underwater existence which mirrors his career as a merchant and sailor. Instead of profit and loss he has rising and falling, instead of the wind 'a current under seas', instead of the turning wheel a whirlpool. Ariel's song 'Full fadom five' in *The Tempest* lies behind this description, and we are therefore to assume that Phlebas has been transformed 'into something rich and strange'. The reminiscence elsewhere in the poem of the line 'Those are pearls that were his eyes' encourages us to take the word 'rich' literally.[11] What goes on under the sea is not very different from what goes on above it or beside it.

The sea has a special significance for the communities which live by it and which seem, indeed, to depend for their collective livelihood on the drowning of individual members. At the end of *Riders to the Sea*, the community may be on the brink of extinction because of this dependence, while in 'The Waste Land' it is already destroyed, but in each case the sea seems to have taken its place. The sea is the apotheosis of community, a power both loved and feared. But it also provides a means of escape from it; a community that lives by the sea sanctions the departure of its members, and its acceptance of the possibility that they might drown demonstrates that this escape may be permanent. For Synge and Eliot, I suggest, this symbolism must have had a powerful personal appeal. Both writers were renegades from their Protestant backgrounds, and for both drowning combined a fantasy of departure with a fantasy of ultimate acceptance, the absorption into the greater community of the sea.[12]

We have seen, then, that the theme of drowning is not merely a way of marking and mastering the sense of catastrophe induced by the war. For two writers familiar to Graham, it represented an attempt to resolve the authors' sense of having betrayed or deserted the community in which they were brought up by implying, firstly, that desertion was already inscribed in the ideals of that community (the sea is part of the land), and secondly, that the community continues to enclose even those who have apparently abandoned it (the drowned take their values with them to the bottom of the sea). Drowning is, on the one hand, the ultimate alienation, a giving of oneself to the sublime, which is by definition inhuman. On the other, it is an immersion in that which transcends the individual and therefore a metaphor for community itself, which always insists that its members sacrifice something of their individuality. This immersion is a hyperbolic image of baptism in which the ritual associated with birth becomes the means of death and the way out of communal life reflects the way in. These celebrators of the drowned are using the theme to claim that, far from abandoning home and family, they are seeking better ones, ones which more perfectly obliterate individuality. Whether we believe them or not is another matter.

In the examples I have considered it is men rather than women who leave and rediscover home in this way. To read Synge and Eliot – and, indeed, most of the British drowning poems of the Second World War – one might think women and children never drowned.[13] They are telling us something about the destiny of men, whose hard fate it is to leave their comfortable homes in order to create new ones elsewhere. By tapping into this ideological preconception, they hope to normalize a departure which they fear may have gone beyond masculine duty to delinquency. That, they claim, is what men do, and if this particular man has apparently done it too enthusiastically, it makes him, not a deserter but a hero – a superman, in fact.

Graham, like Synge and Eliot, was brought up in a Protestant commu-
nity with links to the sea, and when he left Presbyterian Clydeside it was
only to take up residence in Methodist Cornwall. He told Lopez that he
was 'never a member of any religious group or sect'. He did, however,
sing in a Church of Scotland church choir as a boy, and his poems
contain many references to the Bible.[14] Whatever his personal convic-
tions, religion must have coloured his environment both in childhood
and adult life. As he puts it in one poem, 'men sign the sea', and in the
case of Cornwall, it is a 'Methodist sea' (*NCP*, p. 82, p. 164). This sea pene-
trates the land in the same way that it did for Synge. In 'Night's Fall
Unlocks the Dirge of the Sea', the poet hears the sea from his safe haven
on land. The sound becomes more intrusive as it grows dark (*NCP*, p. 83).
The sea's release allows it 'to pour up from the shore'. Later it is heard
'wading the land away', and the poet breathes not only air but also,
though the enjambment defers and camouflages the zeugma, 'the
friendly thief sea'. The paradoxical adjective echoes the 'befriending /
Gestures' of the waves in the opening stanza; in a poem about death and
loss, one would not expect such cosiness. But cosiness, though of a tran-
scendent kind, is precisely what characterizes the sea in Graham's
drowning poems.

In a world where sea and land interpenetrate, where is shelter to be
found? The answer is obviously in both places, just as storms and danger
are to be found in both. In 'Shian Bay', the dead are 'washed [. . .] into
the bay's stretched arms' and 'drowned into shelter', while the stones go
in the other direction to find the same paradoxical destiny: 'The stones
roll out to shelter in the sea' (*NCP*, p. 82). 'At Whose Sheltering Shall the
Day Sea' shows the drowning man asking for shelter with 'land-dry
prayers' and finding it because of the land community which remem-
bers him. The sea protects him with its 'stretched whitefingered / Hand'
and its maternal 'spilling aprons', and he becomes a memory:
'Sheltering / In sea he breathes dry land, dry grave and dwelling'. But if
this is a form of rescue for the sailor, it is equally a form of catastrophe
for the land-dwellers: 'Grief fills the voice with water, building / Ruin on
the ruining land.' (*NCP*, p. 84) The image used here, tears as a miniature
sea invading the mourners' throats, is also present in 'Night's Fall',
where the poet complains:

> [. . .] I can't
> Sleep one word away on my own for that
> Grief sea with a purse of pearls and debt
> Wading the land away with salt in his throat.

Literally, the salt is in the throat of the sea, but the sea in this case is only grief writ large. The idea that the poet is so upset at the thought of all those (none of them close friends or relatives) who have died at sea that he cannot sleep is itself a little hard to swallow. The drowning seems to be a metaphor for his emotion rather than the cause of it. There are only hints to suggest the real cause of the speaker's grief: he is on his own, tormented by the thought of 'debt', trying to sleep away not his troubles but his words. Used as we are by now to the idea of drowning as a mystical consolation for those who fear they have betrayed their birthright, these hints are surely enough. Poetry, with its consequent estrangement from community, has made him unhappy. For readers unfamiliar with his themes, however, the origin of all this distress is likely to be obscure, and this is because Graham is unable to explain it, even to himself. He is pining for something that he does not want, to go home; what he does want is the emotion that both connects him to that home and marks his separation from it, the sea of tears through which it is still visible. To specify his object would be to run the risk of attaining it, or at least to invite the question why he does not try to. However, the object is not concealed, only disguised. Just as the ostensible object of the drowning poems turns out on closer inspection to be a metaphor, so an ostensible metaphor, home, is the real object.

The drowning poems are full of references to home. In 'Continual Sea and Air', 'the long outline' of the sea 'leans over waving houses' of the drowned (*NCP*, p. 46). (The verb is interesting, suggesting maternal protection, perhaps. It appears also in 'The Nightfishing' – see, for example, Section 4, *NCP*, p. 116) In 'Men Sign the Sea', the sea is a 'loudraftered foamfloored house' (*NCP*, p. 82). The phrase 'the white threshold', used in 'Three Poems of Drowning' as well as in the poem of that name is ambiguous – do the drowning men cross from home to outside or the other way about? In Graham's paradoxical rhetoric, the threshold is crossed both ways, so that home is another kind of absence and absence another kind of home. The sea has a 'lintel of foam and door of breath'. It also has 'floors', (though these 'drowning floors' are the scene of active, violent transformation, and resemble the threshing floor of a barn rather than the floor of a house), a 'ceiling', 'gardens', and a 'sill'; the victim is said to 'inhabit' it, and the speaker is invited in: 'You'll likely wake [. . .] and lean from the sill [. . .] to ask me down.' The destructive waves are transformed into babies: 'screaming bundles of foam'. (*NCP*, pp. 84–6). The poem 'The White Threshold' continues this idea of a domestic undersea existence. The sea's 'welcome-roaring threshold' insists on being taken as a way in rather than a way out. The undersea house has 'foamthatch' and is inhabited by 'sea-families' so numerous they are described as 'swimming crowds' (*NCP*, pp. 92–3).

The sea is not merely a domestic environment – it is a complete replica of the land with an economy of its own: 'wrecked seagrain'('Many Without Elegy' *NCP*, p. 40) 'herds' ('Gigha' *NCP*, p. 82) and 'workmen' ('Three Poems' *NCP*, p. 84). Most of all, it has trade. The vocabulary of commerce is everywhere: 'employ', 'profit', 'loss' ('Many Without Elegy'), 'trade' ('Continual Sea and Air' *NCP*, p. 45), 'debt', 'traded' ('Night's Fall' *NCP*, p. 83), 'moneychanging', 'pay', and 'exchange' ('Three Poems' *NCP*, p. 85–6). This vocabulary is consistently combined with religious imagery in a way that suggests Max Weber's equation of trade and the Protestant tradition.[15] In 'Night's Fall', the sea sound is 'traded into evidence / Of a dark church of voices'. In the second of the 'Three Poems of Drowning', the victim:

> Now endured sea-martyrdom crucified by the soldier sea,
> Hoisted high to nails, crowned over the inventing host
> And struck through hammering, his all grief well over
> The moneychanging, manfed water;
>
> (*NCP*, p. 85)

The same combination of religion and trade can be found in the third of the 'Three Poems':

> Now in these seas, my task of the foam-holy voyages
> Charted in a bead of blood, I work. I answer
> Across the dark sea's raging bridges of exchange   (*NCP*, p. 86)

The exchange the sea deals in is that of life and death, but the wordplay has a basis in the Protestant tradition which puts the afterlife on a sound commercial basis. Business and work are holy to Graham because they are communal and therefore involve a sacrifice of individuality. There are many words in the drowning poems which relate to this sacrifice: 'saviour', 'saint', 'offering' (*NCP*, p. 40), 'hero' (*NCP*, p. 82), 'sea-martyrdom' (*NCP*, p. 85) and 'lamblood-reddened' [*sic*] (*NCP*, p. 92). Trade, work, heroism – they are all the duties of men, the particular contribution expected of males by the community. The sailors die in order that their community may live. In so doing, they join a transcendent community, one to which their masculinity had already predestined them, in which they are united with the sublime femininity of the sea with its spilling aprons and screaming bundles of foam. Such, Graham insists, is his own destiny as a writer, abandoning his birthplace in order to return to it in the imagination:

> All arriving seas drift me, at each heartbreak, home.
>
> (*NCP*, p. 86)

In the early poems, Graham explored a playground protected by the autonomy of text. The poem, isolated from the flux of the world, was a miraculous machine over which he could have total control. In *The Seven Journeys* and *Cage Without Grievance*, flux is absorbed into and transformed by the poem, so that spittle turns to glass and spring to an apparatus. However, as we have seen, the essay 'Notes on a Poetry of Release', which was probably written at about the same time as *The White Threshold*, shows him becoming dissatisfied with this simple formula. Its rhetoric attempts to satisfy the demands of flux as well as stasis, the organic as well as the mechanical, to prove that the poet's construction of a static, controllable object is his own subtle form of self-sacrifice for the sake of love and community. In *2ND Poems*, the 'precious object' is already bobbing precariously on the flood of history as the poet tries to navigate it to land. Another combination of object and flood is offered by 'Continual Sea and Air': 'Catastrophe / Slapped tinbox on my element', (*NCP*, p. 45). By the time of *The White Threshold*, the imagery of flux has temporarily taken over from that of stasis. No doubt partly because of the continuing effect of the war on life and culture and partly because of his own intellectual and emotional development (he was past thirty when the book was published), the justification of his work in terms of the communal values which he associated with flux had become his chief priority. In the theme of drowning in Synge, Eliot and many of his contemporaries he found a symbol which could accommodate his own ambivalent feelings towards community. His drowned sailors have both run away from home and fulfilled its demands; in dying they have accepted and been accepted by a home whose authority transcends that of the real one, and which is thus able to excuse their delinquency.

All this would seem to imply that the drowning poems are about community *as opposed to* language, and that they constitute a radical rejection of the mechanical pastoral, the playground of the text, celebrated in the early poems. But Graham's career contains no such reversals, and, as I remarked in Chapter 3, he was still defending his early books towards the end of his life. As the shifting rhetoric of 'Notes' shows, the autonomy of the text, which seems to have been his primary motive for becoming a writer, was hard to defend in terms of his new priorities, and the imagery of stasis and separation therefore becomes less prominent at this time. However, the metaphor of the sea offers metapoetic possibilities of another kind because it shares some of the qualities I described in Chapter 2 as linking language and community. It rebukes the individual will by its superior size and power, it has the unpredictability of constant change and at times, though its gender is as changeable as its other characteristics, it also possesses a feminine voluptuousness which demands a response from males. In a poem like 'Night's Fall' or the first of the 'Three Poems', the poet's role seems to be merely to lament the fate of others; by the third of the 'Three Poems', however, it is clear that he himself, having witnessed their deaths, must now engage in a struggle with the sea, 'my own fought drowning' (*NCP*, p. 86). This can only be a reference to his writing career, and if this is not made explicit in the drowning poems, it is, I think, because the symbolism was so natural to him that he did not realize it needed explaining. As we shall see, it becomes clearer in 'The White Threshold' and even more so in 'The Nightfishing', though both these poems are complicated by other themes. The established analogy between the sea and community suggested to him a further analogy between the sea and language, and these together were enough to compel his interest in this fashionable theme of the day. The sea represented a transcendent community and the only such community he would acknowledge was language.

Walking on Water

The first poem in *The White Threshold*, 'Since All My Steps Taken', deals not with drowning but with another characteristic theme, walking, and the prominent position it occupies suggests that Graham may have regarded it as a particularly important statement (*NCP*, p. 59). In 'The First Journey', he presented his narrative persona as a walker, striding vigorously through the countryside. That persona was self-born, and the landscape he walked through was deprived of human and, in particular, maternal comforts. The walker in 'Since All My Steps', on the other hand, has travelled from his flesh-and-blood parents into the textual landscape:

> All journey, since the first
> Step from my father and mother
> Towards the word's crest

Whereas 'The First Journey' was autonomous, this one has a connectedness. It can be traced back all the way from 'the word's crest' to Greenock. The drowning poems suggested Graham's increased need to justify his activities in terms of communal values, and this adaptation of his walking imagery confirms that impression. His childhood community was a freely traversible space: no matter how much walking he did, either with his parents or with their approval, he always returned home. This being the case, to walk away is impossible, since every step is connected to the one before so that all walking remains only an outing, a perambulation of the outlying regions of Greenock. Even the poem itself travels a circular route, ending with the same lines that began it.[16]

Nevertheless, the line connecting him to home is not unbroken – it consists of a series of individual 'steps'. Furthermore, while the scene of this walk shifts from 'the kyleside shingle' to 'Ben Narnain', the phrase 'the word's crest' itself suggests ridge walking, a discontinuous form of exercise in which each successive ridge or crest offers first a goal and then a new view and an opportunity to rest; this too implies a journey broken into distinct stages. It is not home to which the poem returns at the end but the 'word's crest'. It insists on autonomy as well as continuity, on the separateness of the footsteps as well as the line leading back to Greenock. It is interesting that they are footsteps rather than footprints. A series of visible impressions would indeed be traceable back to their point of origin, but sounds are temporary, each one 'dying from [the poet's] heel'. He does not have to give 'a hark back' because the personified steps remain behind him to do so, but since their own sound has died their presence is ghostly. This is the 'dead horde' that listens to his progress, bearing witness to his loyalty but unable to interfere with what remains a solitary and hence controllable mission.

The point of intersection between this walking theme and the sea imagery of the drowning poems is 'The White Threshold' itself (*NCP*, pp. 92–8). The basic image is a fusion of Christ walking on the water, which Graham probably took from a poem by W.R. Rodgers, with the Resurrection and the closely related idea of the speaker as ghost.[17] Instead of finding rest in a transcendent home at the bottom of the sea, the drowned poet rises up and returns to his home over the waves: 'I walk towards you and you may not walk away.' (*NCP*, p. 92). The image of the speaker walking pervades the poem:

I look well out to land and walk as
Watermaster towards the flecked rhinns

(*NCP*, p. 93)

I walk the midnight waters of the heart.
They walk towards me too well suffered from

(*NCP*, p. 96)

I move towards you across
The strange sea borne in a gesture

(*NCP*, p. 96)

Good voice towards me all ways let me move
Advanced across the kiss filled with a thousand
Crowded seas.

(*NCP*, p. 98)

This constant movement is an uncanny one, for three reasons. Firstly, and most obviously, it is a movement over a surface that cannot sustain it. (Even an apparently realistic scenario in Section 4 echoes this walking on water: 'We've met when on a time / We walked the foggy dew' – *NCP*, p. 96.) Secondly, it never arrives at its object; the poet is still advancing at the end of the poem and expects to do so 'all ways' (always). Thirdly, it has a psychological power over the unspecified addressee, who is paralysed by the sight.

Walking is the defining activity of ghosts (one speaks of a ghost 'walking' almost as though 'to walk' were the ghost equivalent of 'to exist'), and it is characteristic of them that they walk independently of the material world, through walls, on air or, as in this case, on water. Similarly, the failure to arrive emphasizes the ghost's separation from reality; ghosts are essentially symbolic beings, which exist to be seen and understood rather than to act. They are usually observed in the grip of a repetition-compulsion, carrying out the same actions or travelling the same route night after night. The ghost that walks down the passage at midnight has never really arrived because tomorrow night it will make exactly the same journey. The linear structure of attempt and achievement, journey and arrival, is replaced by a cyclical one. Finally, the power of the ghost is its ability to frighten, and it owes this power to the beholder's sense of what it is.

Freud assigns the uncanny to ghosts and the resurrected dead in particular.[18] The German word he discusses is *unheimlich*, literally translated as 'unhomely', and he emphasizes that '*Unheimlich* is in some way or another a sub-species of *heimlich*.'[19] The uncanny is a feeling about home. A haunted (*unheimlich*) house is a home defamiliarized, revealed in the eerie light of the unconscious. By transforming himself into a ghost (or resurrecting himself as Christ), Graham is able to revisit his home. He emerges 'five fathoms up / Into nightair' to see the lights of the shore (*NCP*, p. 93). He approaches the land, 'looking back' fearfully at the aquatic underworld he has escaped with its 'waterdead', a Eurydice without the same fatal prohibition (*NCP*, p. 94). In Section 3, he visits first the Lanarkshire of Nessie Dunsmuir, then the Clydeside of his own childhood. Just as he is a ghost to this world, so its inhabitants are ghosts to him, the uncanny cutting both ways:

> They walk towards me kindly as I hold
> Well into memory drowned in the crowded seanight.
> Drowned in my crowded head and singled out
> I walk the midnight waters of the heart.
> They walk towards me too well suffered from,
> Bright opposites in imagination's room,
> Voiced on my seachanged lifetime from their home.

> (*NCP*, pp. 95–6)

The contrast here is between the internalized 'crowded' home and the poet 'singled out' by the solipsism of art. These crowds were in the sea in the earlier sections of the poem, the 'swimming crowds' also evoked in phrases like 'waters millionshared' and 'humancrowded inhuman sea' (*NCP*, p. 92, p. 94). At this stage of his career, Graham is seldom content with one metaphorical schema – both he and the people from his past are ghosts; both sea and land stand for a ghostly community; ghosts, quasi-divine resurrection and dreams (the 'bed') compete to account for the uncanny content of the poem (*NCP*, p. 96).

This meeting with the communities of Clydeside and Lanarkshire, then, takes place in the sea, in the places concerned, in sleep and, of course, in language, 'the breath of the dead' on which he is 'cried out loud' (*NCP*, p. 96). The imagery of death and the uncanny is enlisted to protect him from the consequences of a real meeting, to ensure that a safe distance remains between himself and the world he has guiltily rejected. This world is defined by collectivity, belonging and work. The imagery of crowds thunders through the poem, reaching a climax in Section 5:

> I see the crowds. I stand beneath the fires
> Wound into the cheering air and furious roof.

> (*NCP*, pp. 97–8)

His separation from this collective environment is an 'exile' and his return to it is the crossing of a 'threshold', and a 'homecoming' (*NCP*, p. 92, p. 96). Home is industrial, urban and working-class, with 'derricks donkeymen / Caulkers platers from the blacksoap timbered cradles' and noisy 'arkyard hammers', a 'furnaced city' where 'Endeavour burns its gases' (*NCP*, p. 95, p.98). In a literal sense, 'the first fires of [Graham's] past' are the fires of the Clydeside docks, which burn so brightly in his imagination that he can even see them from far out at sea (*NCP*, p. 98, p. 93).

'Since All My Steps' and 'The White Threshold' both use the imagery of walking to define a highly problematic relationship between the poet and his home. In so far as the walking is away from home, it must contrive to remain somehow connected to it; in so far as it is towards home, it must never entirely arrive. The ghostliness of the poems is a way of ensuring that the poet and his family are never fully present to one another. Graham cannot be satisfied any more with the idea of the autonomous text; now he must be connected to his community by a chain of footsteps, but it is a chain in which each element preserves a virtual autonomy. The walking image allows him to imagine such a chain – after all, each step starts from the one before it and at the same time separates the walker from the one before that. It is possible to visualize walking as both continuity and discontinuity.

We have seen that the imagery of flux takes over during the middle period from that of stasis, but Graham had not abandoned his commitment to autonomy. Instead, he was trying to find a way of preserving the independence which he valued in textuality while enjoying the sense of community associated with the imagery of flux. Most of his poetic energy at this time was devoted to exploring the implications of this flux. Flux is continuity, the spatial connectedness between the molecules of the Heraclitean river and the temporal connectedness between the present state of the river and all its past and future states. But what Heraclitus is supposed to have said was that no one stepped into the same river twice; he thus opened up the possibility, at least in philosophical speculation, of breaking up the river into its constituent molecules and temporal states, all of which are different from each other. The attempt to understand flux turns it into its opposite, a state of discontinuity rather than continuity. According to Charles H. Kahn:

> The notion of periodicity, of measure and equality preserved by regular recurrence over time – whether a single day, a lifetime, or a Great Year – is a central theme in the fragments.[20]

This polarity, as I have stated, was widespread in modernist thought, and Graham must have been encountering it in various forms in his reading and conversation. Bergson, for example, had argued that:

> Not only do we shut our eyes to the unity of the impulse which, passing through generations, links individuals with individuals, species with species, and makes the whole series of the living one single immense wave flowing over matter, but each individual itself seems to us an aggregate, aggregate of molecules and aggregate of facts. The reason of this lies in the structure of our intellect, which is formed to act on matter from without, and which succeeds by making, in the flux of the real, instantaneous cuts, each of which becomes, in its fixity, endlessly decomposable.[21]

The attraction of the opposition for Graham in particular, I suggest, was that these impossible attempts to apprehend flux by measuring it or, as we shall see, even by remembering it, create autonomous areas within it, and are thus themselves analogous to writing as he understood it.

One of his major themes, he stated, was 'the difficulty of speaking from a fluid identity' but his work of the middle period juxtaposes such an identity with an intermittent model of time made up of separate moments, with the result that the 'fluid identity' is explained paradoxically by its discontinuity.[22] As Graham put it in a letter to Sven Berlin: 'I am a river flowing past a certain point, not the man I was a second ago'.[23] (He may well have known that the later philosopher Cratylus capped Heraclitus by denying 'that you could even step into the same river *once*, since you are changing too'.)[24] Clearly there must have been some connection between the present Graham and the man he was a second ago, but this connection remains mysterious and insubstantial; he describes it to Berlin as a 'ghostly constant', a phrase he was to use in 'The Nightfishing' (*NCP*, p. 111). The essence of flux cannot be pinned down: it is a mysterious continuity which disappears on examination to leave a series of discontinuities or autonomous states. This autonomy is a useful alibi for a man suffering from guilt: any connection between the walker of 'Since All My Steps' or the sailor / walker of 'The White Threshold' and what they may have done in the past or may plan to do in the future is impossible to identify.

In 'To My Mother', the poet is separated from his mother not merely by her physical death but by the discontinuities of time and text. His fluid identity changes with the intermittent measurement of time:

Suddenly some man I am
So finds himself endless stream

> Of stepping away from his
> Last home, I crave my ease
> Stopped for a second dead
> Out of the speaking flood.

(NCP, p. 101)

The stream here is understood in the context of a time that allows itself to be stopped 'suddenly' and 'for a second'. Similarly, the changes of memory earlier in the poem take place to the staccato rhythm of a 'heartbeat'. The image of the stream in the poem is provided by the River Clyde, 'flowing [. . .] towards the sea' but this flow is balanced by images of stasis and autonomy. The poet's memory is a 'flowing strong-hold' and the Clyde itself is also 'strongheld', presumably by the machinery of its 'ship-cradles and derricks'. The mother has been traduced even before she is written about simply by being remembered; her living image is confined in the autonomous stronghold of the poet's brain, just as her dead body is confined in the tomb. This discontinuity is brought about not by her death as such, but by the distance between her and her son, which is simultaneously created by the smooth invol-untary flow of a river (the natural passage of time) and his discrete and deliberate steps which take him away not only 'from his / Last home' but from all its predecessors. In this condition of discontinuity, Graham can hardly claim to be the son his mother gave birth to; instead, each of his changing personas becomes in turn a new son to her, so that he is able to ask 'What son did you inherit?'

Writing is only the latest of the changes which have intervened in the natural relationship between mother and son, each one taking him further 'away from the parent fire'. The son's walking away was the orig-inal crime, but memory itself, the 'daily aloneness' where she rests 'Under (not ground but the mind's) / Thunder' would have done the same (*NCP*, p. 100). Writing merely selects one of the many discrete moments isolated by memory and makes it permanent, consigning it to 'a perfection's / Deadly still anatomies' (*NCP*, p. 101). Memory is occupied not by people but by their images, ghostly imitations of people. For this reason it is both lonely and crowded: 'Sometimes like loneliness / Memory's crowds increase'. To write about the mother can at least do no further harm. It may even restore her to the community of language, 'the speaking flood'. At the end of the poem, she is no longer trapped in the 'aloneness' of memory but rests 'under [. . .] the words' with the 'speaking hordes' of language. Writing is justified because, in contrast to the purely solipsistic writing of memory, it submits itself to the communal will of language.

In the drowning poems we saw Graham preoccupied with community apparently to the exclusion of his interest in language, which was only present as an implicit metaphor and an otherwise unexplained sense of guilt. The theme of walking throws some light on this guilt, since, like seafaring, it is a mode of departure. Unlike seafaring, though, walking is analysable into discrete steps. The image of walking on water which he found in Rodgers's poem and which dominates 'The White Threshold' combined these two forms of motion, offering simultaneously a continuity that could link him to his past and an autonomy that could protect him from it. At the same time, he explored the nature of flux and came to believe that measurement and memory, like writing itself, transformed it into a series of virtually autonomous moments.[25] To one who suffered from a guilty sense of exile from a community he associated with the flux of the lifeworld, this provided a motive for writing: since memory had already transformed that flux into a static text, the shifting seas of language were his only hope of restoring it to something like its former condition. Of course the linguistic community was not a real one; its 'speaking hordes' were uncanny figures, the ghosts of all those who had used the language before. But a 'ghostly constant' was precisely what needed to be restored to his discontinuous memories in order to bring them back to life. This extraordinary shamanistic project culminated in the most ambitious task he ever undertook. 'The Nightfishing' is the climax of Graham's attempt to resurrect the dead.

The Ghost Ship

The theme of flux in 'The Nightfishing' was first noted by G.S. Fraser, and forms the basis of Lopez's analysis of the poem.[26] The combination of that flux with the discontinuity created by measuring it is announced on the poem's first page: 'This staring second / Breaks my home away' (*NCP*, p. 105). As the narrator leaves his house to go fishing, he is already turning into someone else:

> I bent to the lamp. I cupped
> My hand to the glass chimney.
> Yet it was a stranger's breath

From out of my mouth that
Shed the light.

(*NCP*, p. 106)

This process of transformation continues all the way through the poem. As the boat sails out of the harbour, the poet tells us: 'He drowns who but ill / Resembled me' (*NCP*, p. 108). Later, the water that is shipped during the storm is temporarily trapped in the vessel, 'like an early self' separated from the continuity of identity (*NCP*, p. 114). As he arrives back in harbour, the narrator is once again replaced by him 'who takes my place continually anew', and 'he that / I'm not lies down' (*NCP*, p. 116).

This succession of discontinuities gives rise to the poem's frequent shifts between present and past tense. The first sentence of all has no main verb, only a past participle which does duty for it: the effect is to suggest that the striking of the bell is so much anterior to the action as to be in a different time frame altogether, or even that it somehow marks the boundary of time itself and is thus not properly an event at all:

Very gently struck
The quay night bell.

(*NCP*, p. 105)

The next word, significantly, is 'Now' and the story continues in the present tense. The shift into the future, however, brings a change of identity:

[. . .] I'll not pass
Though one shall pass
Wearing seemingly
This look I move as.

(*NCP*, p. 105)

The next striking of the bell, punctuating time like the chime of a clock, heralds the change to the past tense a few lines further on and another change of identity, to be followed by another 'and now'. Later, following the calling of 'the continual sea' there is a further 'now' (*NCP*, p. 106). Finally, the presentness of the moment is announced as if for the first time: 'The present opens its arms' (*NCP*, p. 107). The narrative of the voyage itself undergoes similar shifts. It begins in the present:

I, in Time's grace, the grace of change sail surely
Moved off the land

(*NCP*, p. 107)

The first switch into the past takes place as the crew prepare 'to shoot the nets':

> [. . .] We dropped to the single motor.
> The uneasy and roused gulls slid across us with
> Swelled throats screeching.

> (*NCP*, p. 109)

A few sentences later, we are back in the present: 'The bow wakes hardly a spark at the black hull.' (*NCP*, p. 110) After the hauling in of the nets is completed, the alternation between present and past becomes more rapid:

> [. . .] And then was the first
> Hand at last lifted getting us swung against
> Into the homing quarter, running that white grace
> That sails me surely ever away from home.

> (*NCP*, p. 113)

As the boat re-enters the harbour, the alternation of the two tenses combines with that of personal pronouns:

> Now he who takes my place continually anew
> Speaks me thoroughly perished into another.
> And the quay opened its arms. I heard the sea
> Close on him gently swinging on oiled hinges.
> Moored here, we cut the motor quiet. He that
> I'm not lies down. Men shout. Words break. I am
> My fruitful share.

> (*NCP*, p. 116)

The speaker has not only arrived in harbour but in the present and in his new identity too – but these arrivals have in fact been going on throughout the journey.

The discontinuities of time and identity are seen as a series of deaths and rebirths.[27] The tolling of the bell at the beginning is a kind of knell, for the speaker continues: 'Now within the dead / Of night and the dead / Of all my life' (*NCP*, p. 105). Similarly in Section 2, when the speaker is apparently getting ready for his voyage, he tells us: 'My death / Already has me clad anew' and 'Here we dress up in a new grave'. On the other hand, this death is matched by a birth in which the speaker falls 'from the hot' of his mother's body 'to the cold' of the world, and the midwife throws away 'the bundle' of the placenta (*NCP*, p. 107). On the voyage itself, as we have already seen, the narrator describes himself, or rather one of his selves, as drowning, but a few lines later, he reverses the image: 'I am [. . .] burnt by salt / To life' (*NCP*, p. 109). Later, the narrator attempts to distinguish between his writing self, 'the poor sea-scholar' and the poem's 'hero', but both seem to be referred to by the phrase 'So he who died is announced'. These multiple identities suffer an appropriately 'intricate death' (*NCP*, p. 115). At the arrival in harbour, too, the speaker is 'perished into another' (*NCP*, p. 116). Similarly, at the very end of the poem, he tells us 'So I spoke and died' (*NCP*, p. 120).

These discontinuities are the consequence of the poet's attempts to measure flux. The sea is constantly transformed by these attempts; it is 'formal and struck into a dead stillness [. . .] And on its wrought epitaph fathers itself' (*NCP*, p. 108) In the scene where the narrator dreamily watches the nets in the dark water and waits for the sun to rise, the vocabulary of craft and even of science is applied to the natural world: 'measurement', 'proportions', 'the iron sea engraved', 'fretted and fixed at a high temper, 'fixed in this metal and its cutting salts' and 'exact degree' (*NCP*, p. 111). (Another such phrase "tensile light" is almost certainly a borrowing from Pound.)[28] The key notion here is fixity, the transformation of the flowing sea into something 'still', a word that also recurs several times. The stillness is caused by measurement which creates a discrete 'instant, / Bounded by its own grace and all Time's grace'.

In 'To My Mother', as we saw, there were two distinct measurements, the first performed by memory and the second by writing. This is not the case here. There are references to the transforming effect of memory on action, but these are never clearly separated from the poem's pervasive interest in itself: 'The eye reads forward as the memory reads back' (*NCP*, p. 117). Phrases like 'now' and 'this place' refer not merely to the time and place of the narrated events but also to those of the narrative itself (*NCP*, p. 105). Similarly, the splitting of the narrator into separate selves is a consequence of narrative. In effect, there are two stories happening simultaneously: in one, a group of men work together on the sea to gather a harvest of fish; in the other a solitary man works at his table to produce a poem which a solitary reader reads. As the boat sets sail, the narrator is 'merged / In this and in a like event', and 'the keel . . . / Goes through each word' (*NCP*, p. 108). Later, in a phrase I have already cited as a classic example of self-reference, he states simply 'These words take place' (*NCP*, p. 110). The craftsmanlike diction is determined by this metapoetic theme. When he asks 'What measures gently // Cross in the air', it is lines of poetry he has in mind (*NCP*, p. 111). If the sea appears like iron, it is because he has 'wrought' it into a poem (*NCP*,

p. 111, p. 108). The poem is praised in Section 4 as:

> [. . .] the place fastened still with movement,
> Movement as calligraphic and formal as
> A music burned on copper.
>
> (*NCP*, p. 117)

The birth in Section 2 is the equivalent of that in 'The First Journey', an entry into text. The fall 'from the hot to the cold' is more than just a striking way of describing physical birth; it is also one of Graham's many accounts of textuality as a fall from 'the hot' of the lifeworld to 'the cold' of this place, that is, the page, which is 'a new grave' as well as a place to live. The death imagery of the poem is bound up with textuality; as Lopez points out, the reference to engraving, as well as referring to craftsmanlike writing, is a pun on 'grave' (*NCP*, p. 111).[29] The instant 'bounded by its own grace and all Time's grace' is so because it has been 'written dead'. Language is blamed for the death of its speakers: 'Each word speaks its own speaker to his death' (*NCP*, p. 115). Caught in the stasis of text, the boat becomes a 'rigged ship in its walls of glass' – that is, in a bottle – and the speaker, whose 'death is past' sits 'at the grave's table' to work (*NCP*, pp. 118–9). At the end of the poem, 'this present place' becomes a 'breathless still place / Unrolled on a scroll' and we are told, fittingly in the past tense since all text is already written when we come to read it, that 'within the dead [. . .] / Of all my life those / Words died and awoke' (*NCP*, p. 120).

Like earlier poems, then, 'The Nightfishing' is a journey into text and combines the imagery of flux with that of stasis. Like other poems of the middle period, it is more concerned with the former than the latter. Instead of bringing liquid imagery into the poem and freezing it into static emblems, the poet takes us on a journey through flux itself, exposing us to the changeability, power and sensuousness of a vividly described sea:

> [. . .] The long rollers,
> Quick on the crests and shirred with fine foam,
> Surge down then sledge their green tons weighing dead
> Down on the shuddered deck boards.
>
> (*NCP*, pp. 113–4)

At every stage of this journey, in the imagery of artifice and measurement, in the changes of tense and person, in the assertions of death and rebirth which punctuate the narrative, the flux of this sea is transformed into stasis. These transformations are part of the texture of the verse, so pervasive as to be easily missed, like the punning use of the word 'still' in the contradictory senses of temporal continuity and motionlessness, in the phrase 'Still where it lies struck in express proportion' (*NCP*, p. 112). The word 'struck' here is interesting, too – a few lines earlier, the dawn is described in the words: 'suddenly like struck rock all points unfix' (*NCP*, p. 111). The reference is to the striking of water from the rock by Moses, suggesting that the dawn is liquid.[30] But 'struck in expressed proportion' changes the meaning of the word – it now seems to imply something like the striking of a coin or perhaps the transfixion of someone under a spell. The fluidity of the earlier use is magically arrested.

Flux is continuous change, but Graham, as we have seen, had come to believe that the attempt to measure it and above all to capture it in writing, would inevitably transform it into discontinuous change. In 'The Nightfishing', he tries to demonstrate his commitment to the lifeworld by tracking 'Time's grace, the grace of change' in the minutest detail possible (*NCP*, p. 107). This process must always be retrospective and can never quite do justice to the action it deals with, both because retrospective narration adds a separate time-frame, in effect doubling the story so that every event becomes paired with the 'like event' of its mimesis, and because no such mimesis can match the smooth transitions of reality:

> I, in Time's grace,
> The grace of change, am
> Cast into memory.
> What a restless grace
> To trace stillness on.

> (*NCP*, p. 119)

The attempt to participate in 'the grace of change' matters because it is a condition of community, without which the poem could only be 'that loneliness / Bragged into a voyage' (*NCP*, p. 117). 'The Nightfishing' is about being a member of a boat's crew, and the camaraderie this implies is, I suggest, much more important to the poem than the voyage itself. After all, as literary voyages go, this one is unusual. Nansen's voyage in the *Fram* (which, Graham told Lopez, 'helped me to steer', and which I shall discuss in my next chapter) took him across the frozen Arctic ocean; the Ancient Mariner, another model, journeyed both to the tropics and the South Pole.[31] The essence of such voyages, surely, is distance. Without the sense of a remote (or even unknown) destination some of the heroism is lost. The extreme case is that of Rimbaud's hero, who ventures into the ocean on his own with no idea of his destination or control over his vessel. Without wishing to play down the courage of fishermen, we should note that an expedition to catch fish is not the obvious example of a heroic voyage. It does not cover great distances or enter unknown waters; it has a commercial purpose rather than a quixotic goal of exploration or danger for its own sake; and, above all, it is routine. The very title 'The Nightfishing' emphasizes both the limited duration and the quotidian nature of this particular voyage. However, the poem is not only about voyaging, but also about work and the communities which are formed round it.

The speaker is a member of the crew, and as such he has to share in their work. Often we see him doing nothing in particular, and at such times he seems most the isolated artist, meditating on nature. Even at these moments, though he is still doing his duty. Early in the section, he reproaches himself:

> Here, braced, announced on to the slow
> Heaving seaboards, almost I am now too
> Lulled. And my watch is blear.

> (*NCP*, p. 109)

Gazing at the sea is one of his legitimate tasks, his watch, but he must not allow himself to become 'too / Lulled'. Later, it appears that he has taken the helm:

> The undertow, come hard round,
> Now leans the tiller strongly jammed over
> On my hip-bone.

> (*NCP*, p. 109)

During the descriptions of work, 'we' is the dominant pronoun, reflecting the fact that the narrator feels himself part of a community when they are all working together. The lines just quoted, for example, lead into an account of the crew's preparations for casting the nets. The statement 'it is us at last' sounds almost like a sigh of relief. Now, when there is work to be done, he is no longer lonely. The fetishistic naming of the tools of the men's trade is another aspect of the security he finds in work:

> [. . .] Our mended newtanned nets, all ropes
> Loose and unkinked, tethers and springropes fast,

The tethers generous with floats to ride high,
And the big white bladder floats at hand to heave.

                                                    (*NCP*, p. 109–10)

But this community is an uncanny one. None of the crew is described, and they are present only in the pronouns 'we' and us'. The *TLS* reviewer of *The Nightfishing* complaining about this depersonalized condition, remarked 'Coleridge at least had the tact to man his ship with ghosts'.[32] But in effect this is what Graham has done, and the allusion to the Ancient Mariner is surely to the point. [33] Alfred Wallis's journey to death, as depicted in the so-called 'Death Paintings' and described by Sven Berlin, is perhaps a still closer analogy:

> In earlier years Wallis had sailed in a metal steamer through slushy brown seas to Labrador. Looming under a dark green, brooding sky, icebergs had towered over him – immaculate, inviolate, remote, passing silently in the night. Arctic winds had formed ice on the rigging, had cut his face and hands [. . .] Half a century after Wallis had sailed to Labrador he took the bridge once more on the Iron Boat, steering it out to sea; but a sea that was no longer of this world, thinned to a transparent fluid, ghastly and cold, that broke on the rocks skirting the edges of life [. . .] So they had left their useless bodies lined up in a row of iron beds in a room painted green and brown [. . .] Left them and went down to the sea. Left them and sailed on an Unknown Ocean.[34]

As Barthes pointed out, the ship in literature is a symbol of home, and the only way to negate this symbolism is 'to eliminate the man and leave the ship on its own'.[35] To depopulate a ship, then, to transform it into the equivalent of the Drunken Boat or the Flying Dutchman or the Mary Céleste, is to change it from *heimlich* to *unheimlich*. In the very first section of the poem, the narrator's 'home' is broken away as he finds himself in 'this place', and again at the very end he tells us 'Home becomes this place' (*NCP*, p. 105, p. 119). The departure of the boat is a transition from one sort of home to the other – he is 'waved from home to out' but at the same time 'nursed [. . .] on movement' (*NCP*, p. 108). The casual references to hauling the nets 'home' are juxtaposed with the 'home' on dry land to which the boat must return. At the same time, however, the poet is being carried in the opposite direction by 'that white grace / That sails me surely ever away from home' (*NCP*, p. 113). Home is a mysteriously inaccessible place somewhere beyond the ship which is nevertheless the object of the narrator's love and loyalty:

[. . .] Each word is but a longing

Set out to break from a difficult home.

(*NCP*, p. 108)

As this last example suggests, the narrator's equivalent of home is language. The ghost crew to which he belongs is the community of all those who have used the language before him. For this reason, like the Ancient Mariner surrounded by his ghostly shipmates, he is a lonely and alienated figure, but at the same time not alone. Language is both the ghost crew and the sea itself, 'the all common ocean' whose 'lonely behaviour' causes him to cry 'headlong from my dead' (*NCP*, p. 113). It is a 'mingling flood' with the fluidity of community which the narrator has to transform into the stillness of a poem 'formed in exact degree and set dead' (*NCP*, p. 109). The deadness of the poem, an inevitable consequence of the attempt to incorporate flux into the stasis of either text or memory, also reflects the deadness of the community who inspire it, for language is the property of the dead.

The opening of the poem shows the narrator being summoned by this ghostly community, first by the tolling of the bell and then by the calling of his name. Names and naming, as I shall show in Chapter 5, are one of Graham's obsessions. The name represents the identity which one receives from community – it is how community recognizes and controls the individual. In this case, significantly, he is called by his name but the name does not appear in the poem. The identity he receives is not for us to know, since we are the living. He is the 'I' of a text now, the 'narrator', 'speaker' or 'poet' I have referred to in my reading of the poem rather than the flesh-and-blood Sydney Graham. From the moment the name is called, he is a ghost. Now he fulfills the destiny prefigured by this primal naming and becomes a ghost watched by 'the dead' who, through his words, 'speak out on silence' (*NCP*, p. 106). This speech of the dead is in fact writing – as I remarked in Chapter 1, Graham tends to depict writing as a mode of speech and in comparison finds it inadequate or even, as here, uncanny. The dead not only speak 'on' silence but in it, as a later passage makes clear: 'So I have been called by name and / It was not sound' (*NCP*, p. 111). This is the silence that the sea-scholar both travels through and is fixed on:

[. . .] Here, in this intricate death,
He goes as fixed on silence as ever he'll be.

(*NCP*, p. 115)

'The Nightfishing' is a poem about the flux of language, the 'mingling element' in which the poet has to work (*NCP*, p. 115). The work is hard and dangerous because language is big, powerful, constantly changing and belongs to others, but these are all features it shares with community. It shares them with the sea, too, and the crew of a fishing-boat can be regarded as a sort of makeshift community stranded between two larger communities – the home they have left behind and the sea which represents the most intimidating and unappeasable demands of that home. The fishermen bring home a harvest of fish; the writer brings home a poem. Working with words, then, is working in and for community in much the same way as fishermen do, but there is an important difference: the writer works alone. As Graham wrote at about this time: 'I wish that writing was not such a lonely labour (lonely of human sympathy) or, I suppose, that making art was not such a one-way contact.'[36] To the extent that any company is available in this labour, it is the company of the dead, whose creation language is. The only companions he can have on this particular voyage are ghosts. This is appropriate, because to write about flux is inevitably to kill it, to turn it into its opposite, stasis. Even something as flowing and shapeless as the sea, once described, becomes as solid and still as wrought iron. In this situation, he apparently has no choice but to try to reconstitute both community and himself in words, to match the flux of the life-world with the discontinuities of narrative. It is no substitute for the flesh-and-blood comforts of a real family and a real workplace, but it is what the community has demanded of him, and he willingly – indeed, heroically – accepts. An uncanny home, one full of ghosts, is better than no home at all.

These transformations began even before he started to write the poem. Change, when recorded, measured or merely remembered, develops discontinuities, breaks into instants, each separated by its own autonomy. So staccato is this process that it becomes hard to imagine in retrospect any continuity at all. The identity that connects Graham to the man he was a second ago is tenuous and impossible to define. Identity itself, then, is ghostly when one tries to measure or define it, and so his exposure to the fixity and deathliness of language was already prefigured even before he became a writer. The responsibility for this 'stumble', as I argued in Chapter 2, is a matter he is determined to leave ambiguous, and in this case the ambiguity is concentrated in a single crucial phrase. The calling that transforms him into a linguistic entity is only the latest of many: 'from the first that once / Named me to the bone' (*NCP*, p. 105). On the one hand, this can mean that naming is the only kind of writing that truly penetrates and signifies the self, and in this sense his father and mother, by baptizing him, have given him the only real identity he will ever have. On the other, this naming by his parents was the moment when he was originally transformed into a ghost, a linguistic fixing of the flux of identity which began his endless sequence of momentary deaths. In the first case, community retains its innocence and it is Graham who is at fault for exchanging his true name for a temporary and inadequate one. In the second, community, which gave him his identity, is also responsible for simultaneously taking it away from him.

The problem Graham had with 'The Nightfishing', I suspect, was that it succeeded too well. For one thing, it has an extraordinary vividness and controlled complexity that any poet would find great difficulty in surpassing, and for this reason alone the long silence that followed the publication of the volume containing this poem and the closely related 'Seven Letters' and 'Two Ballads' would be understandable. But more importantly, the rhetorical case it made was so convincing as almost to bring his self-imposed poetic mission to a close. His attempt to justify writing in terms of the values of community comes close to abolishing the distinction between them. Text may be static, but memory produces the same stasis. Writing may provide only a ghostly identity as part of a ghostly community, but the ambiguity of 'named me to the bone' threatens his belief in a living community with the power to confer a stable identity by suggesting that the turning of human beings into ghosts begins long before the adoption of a literary career, with baptism and the entry into language. He is thus faced with the prospect of absolution at the price of one of his cherished myths. It is at this point in his career rather than in the late poems that Graham sounds most like a post-structuralist theorist, tentatively reading the absences of language into life in general rather than contrasting them with it as was his habit.[37] As we shall see in the next chapter, the later poems acknowledge only one possible interpretation of naming, the perfect identity conferred by the mythic community. 'The Nightfishing' had risked returning him to community on the same flawed terms as everybody else, leaving him with nothing to long for. If he was to retain his dreams of Greenock, he was going to have to do worse than that. His future attempts to communicate must be sure to fail.

CHAPTER 5

Voices in the Snow:
The Late Poems

For God's Sake Look After Our People

'Malcolm Mooney's Land' is a poem of retrospection summarizing Graham's career so far. Its opening line can be seen as the statement of a new direction: 'Today, Tuesday, I decided to move on'. The veering wind suggests a change in literary fashion. The 'poor friends' he 'buried earlier under the printed snow' are his earlier poems, significantly represented as living beings whose publication has killed them. In case we miss the pun on 'print', it is repeated with a clarifying enjambment and an explicit translation a few lines later: 'Footprint on foot / Print, word on word and each on a fool's errand.' Other puns on the first page are 'cranes', a reference to Hart Crane's poem 'North Labrador', which I shall discuss shortly, and 'rimed' (*NCP*, p. 153).[1] The 'landlice' which irritate him are words themselves, insect-like in their black intricacy against the whiteness of the page, and this is confirmed by a favourite joke when he calls them 'brother / To the grammarsow and the word-louse' (*NCP*, p. 154). 'Grammersow' (so spelt) is a Cornish word meaning 'wood-louse', so by changing a single letter in the Cornish word and its English equivalent, Graham is able to make the connection between insects and words twice over.[2]

From his new position as an experienced and disillusioned explorer of language, Mooney is able to observe younger poets starting out with the same optimism that he had shown in *The Seven Journeys*:

[. . .] Here
In Malcolm Mooney's Land

I have heard many
Approachers in the distance
Shouting. Early hunters
Skittering across the ice
Full of enthusiasm
And making fly and,
Within the ear, the yelling
Spear steepening to
The real prey, the right
Prey of the moment.

(*NCP*, pp. 155–6)

Graham may have been influenced in this analogy by the comparison of English poets to sportsmen shooting birds made by W.H. Auden in an article published in *New Verse* in 1938.[3] Another hint as to its meaning is provided by the phrase 'making fly'. a variant of the more familiar phrase 'letting fly'. By changing 'letting' to 'making', Graham reminds the reader of the old Scots terminology of 'making' for 'poetry' and 'maker' or 'makar' for 'poet', of which he was fond. (See, for example, 'Sgurr Na Gillean MacLeod' with its epigraph 'For the Makar and Childer' – *NCP*, p. 223.)[4] The young poets believe they can catch their prey, 'the real prey, the right / Prey of the moment', as Graham himself had believed he was capturing a harvest of static moments of perfection from the flux of reality in 'The Nightfishing'. They fail, however, for their prey, 'the honking choir' of geese:

Leave the tilting floe
And enter the sliding water.

(*NCP*, p. 156)

One issue that must have concerned Graham at the time he was writing 'Malcolm Mooney's Land' was the relationship of poetry to politics and history. It was a period dominated by the Vietnam war, to which he later referred in the unpublished poem 'Five Verses Beginning with the Word Language' (*NCP*, pp. 331–3). As I suggested in Chapter 1, his attempt to deal with the war there must have dissatisfied him, since all references to it have disappeared in the poem's published version, 'Language Ah Now You Have Me' (*NCP*, pp. 207–9). It seems possible that the pressure on writers to take such political developments into account was the 'veering' wind he referred to at the beginning of 'Malcolm Mooney's Land'. Although there is no direct reference to contemporary politics in the latter, it does contain an allusion to an inescapable event of modern history, the Holocaust:

Come and sit. Or is
It right to stay here
While, outside the tent
The bearded blinded go
Calming their children
Into the ovens of frost?
And what's the news?

(*NCP*, p. 156)

To explain why Graham felt under pressure to mention the Holocaust in a poem written many years after it took place, one must remember the symbolic significance of this event in an era haunted by the fear of nuclear mass-destruction and increasingly aware of similar atrocities being perpetrated throughout the world. The poetry of Sylvia Plath and John Berryman, for example, struggles similarly to adapt the imagery of international violence and oppression to their more personal themes, as Graham himself was to do in 'Ten Shots of Mister Simpson' and 'Clusters Travelling Out'. Contemplating his future career, Mooney asks himself, with sly ambiguity, what he is to make of the news. The 'bearded blinded' outside his tent of language are both snowblind, haggard explorers and tortured prisoners. The 'ovens of frost' make the allusion clear.

In 'Malcolm Mooney's Land', then, Graham is assessing his career so far and looking to the future. His old poems are behind him. The enthusiasm of young poets, reminding him of his own early days, seems to him ridiculous. He asks himself if he can effectively respond to the perceived pressure to write about history and politics, and does not come up with an answer. Nevertheless, he has 'decided to move on', and this poem is to show the way. Since the way he has chosen is the writing of poems which explore their own textuality, and since, as I have argued, this was the major theme of his verse all along, it might be thought that the way forward was not too different from the way back. Nevertheless, there are considerable differences in Graham's later output, both in style and attitude. In style, a simpler diction and the increased use of direct addresses to the reader make the theme explicit where it was previously often hidden. In attitude, an ambivalence which balanced the joy and the loneliness of creation is replaced by pessimism – a pessimism often lightened by wit, but all-pervasive nevertheless. The images that embody this new attitude are ice and snow. Their whiteness resembles the whiteness of the page, their coldness is a reminder of its impersonality, their crystalline hardness suggests the intricacy and permanence of print, and the fact that nothing grows in them makes them an appropriate image for the deadness Graham associates with textuality. The seas of the middle period have frozen over permanently, leaving a stasis reminiscent of the early poems but without the virile self-celebration that the catachresis of those poems made possible.

In choosing the setting for his poem, Graham was following a fashion of his youth. As Cunningham has noted, the expedition to the North was a favourite theme of writers in the 1930s, the period when Graham was learning his trade.[5] The comparison with language was not new either. In Stephen Spender's 1939 poem 'Polar Exploration', the snow is compared to 'virgin paper', and the explorers' footprints are seen as a kind of text.[6] In 1955, many years after Spender's poem but still well before Graham's, Hugh MacDiarmid parodied polar exploration stories with a description of an expedition 'to the ice cap a little south of Cape Bismarck / And keeping the nunataks of Dronning Louise's Land on our left'. MacDiarmid's polar journey also turns out to be a metaphor for language. After describing such features as 'bergs' and 'crevasses' and 'a wind of 120 miles an hour' which assaults the explorers, he concludes 'This is what adventuring in dictionaries means'.[7]

Malcolm Mooney's Land is not a place one conquers or passes through, but the sublime in its most negative manifestation.[8] It is this Arctic that Crane evokes in his poem 'North Labrador':

> A land of leaning ice
> Hugged by plaster-grey arches of sky,
> Flings itself silently
> Into eternity.
>
> 'Has no one come here to win you,
> Or left you with the faintest blush
> Upon your glittering breasts?
> Have you no memories, O Darkly Bright?'
>
> Cold-hushed, there is only the shifting of moments
> That journey toward no Spring –
> No birth, death, no time nor sun
> In answer.[9]

This poem presents the Arctic as a series of negatives, an expansion of the straightforward denials of the penultimate line. The 'shifting of moments' is reminiscent of the staccato movement of recorded time in Graham's poems of the middle period, but here it replaces the temporal flux instead of being juxtaposed with it. (The sailor in Crane's 'The Bridge' has also experienced the negation of time in the Arctic: '"I don't want to know what time it is – that / damned white Arctic killed my time. . .." '.)[10] This shifting, negative time goes nowhere, 'a journey toward no Spring', like Mooney's wandering. Crane's Arctic is the apotheosis of purposelessness, rather than a place that can be appropriated for purposes. Such a 'reversal' or 'counter-attack on the everyday scheme of the world' is characteristic of the polar sublime according to Francis Spufford.[11] The references to plaster and arches depict the landscape as a parody of home. (The analogy between ice-formations and architecture was conventional.)[12] Crane's address to it is in inverted commas, as if to emphasize the fact that he actually speaks to it and expects, though he does not receive, an answer. It is a negative woman, refusing sex, speech and memory. Spufford remarks that 'personifications of the poles were comparatively rare' in the nineteenth century because their apparent sterility contrasted with the fertility normally associated with nature, which lent itself to visions of goddesses and nymphs. Nevertheless, he goes on to list several such personifications, notably Hans Christian Andersen's Snow Queen, whose characteristics of frigidity and intellect 'take their force from being reversals of conventional female qualities' and make her an 'anti-mother and anti-wife'.[13] (Lopez's interpretation of this story, in contrast, sees ice as symbolic of sexuality rather than a negation of it. This seems to me to run counter to a well-established cultural metaphor, of which the word 'frigid' provides an obvious example.)[14]

Refraining from defining his poem as allegory, Crane locates this personification of negativity in 'North Labrador'. Graham is not so shy. By calling his poem after a fictive place which is in turn named after a fictive person, he equates the Arctic with fiction itself. Crane's address to the Darkly Bright is stranded inside inverted commas and unattributed, as if to say that he, too, is a non-person, a homeless voice. Similarly, Mooney (who is, of course, writing a diary, not speaking at all) doubts both his voice and the location from which it speaks (*NCP*, p. 153). Crane asks only two questions, to neither of which he receives a reply, but Mooney asks them constantly, with the same result: '[. . .] how should he know?', 'What is to read there [. . .]?', 'why is it there has to be / Some place to find [. . .]?', 'Have I not been trying to use the obstacle / Of language well?', 'Why did you choose this place / For us to meet?', '[. . .] is / It right to stay here [. . .]?', 'And what's the news?' (*NCP*, pp. 154–6). These answerless questions are combined with equally rhetorical imperatives like 'lead / Me where the unblubbered monster goes' and 'Come and sit' (*NCP*, p. 153, p. 156).

Crane's interlocutor is a woman, whose femininity is negated by coldness and infertility (her breasts glitter and do not blush). Mooney also thinks of a woman, his wife Elizabeth, the 'furry / Pelted queen of Malcolm / Mooney's Land', but she is only a hallucination: 'I made / You here beside me / For a moment out / Of the correct fatigue' (*NCP*, p. 157). Fridtjof Nansen, the explorer mentioned in the poem, has a similar hallucinatory passage in his account of his Arctic expedition:

> You have the power to recall all that is beautiful [. . .] By the light of the lamp she sits sewing in the winter evening. Beside her stands a little maiden with blue eyes and golden hair, playing with a doll. She looks tenderly at the child, and strokes her hair; but her eyes fill, and the big tears fall upon her work.[15]

Lopez's idea that there are two Elizabeths, one of them a muse present with Mooney on his expedition and the other the woman he has left behind, is thus unnecessary. The fact that Mooney refers to Elizabeth as 'queen / Of Malcolm Mooney's / Land' is not evidence that she is someone other than his wife. Since Mooney's land is named after him and is an extension of his fictive being, it is not surprising that he refers to her as its queen.[16]

As in earlier poems we have looked at, then, Graham creates an uncanny textual community which acts as a substitute for the human world of kinship and love. In 'The White Threshold' and 'The Nightfishing', images of death and haunting provided the uncanny element. In 'Malcolm Mooney's Land', it is the theme of hallucination which ensures that Mooney's companions have no substance and makes them appear like ghosts. There is a psychological rightness to the device – as well as Nansen's dream, one thinks of Eliot's note to 'The Waste Land' in which he mentions the delusion experienced by an Antarctic expedition 'that there was *one more member* than could actually be counted'.[17] Mooney's hallucinations provide him with temporary and insubstantial versions of everything he has lost by being part of the textual wasteland: 'Yet not mistake this / For the real thing' (*NCP*, p. 155). Sexuality, fertility and home – even warmth, since she is clad in furs – are represented by Elizabeth. Friendship and creativity appear in the form of the mysterious 'friend who loves owls'.[18] This friend reminds Mooney of fertile summers when creativity had the character of orality rather than text: 'When to speak was easy' (*NCP*, p. 154). He is so much a creature of the oral world that he does not see, but only hears. He even walks at Mooney's ear. This passage reminds one not only of Eliot's Shackleton note, but also of the 'familiar compound ghost' in 'Little Gidding' who instructs the poet on the sufferings he will have to endure in age.[19] Like that ghost, he disappears at the end, 'Becoming shapeless' (*NCP*, p. 155). Shape, or individuality, cannot be sustained for long in the 'blizzard' of text.

Where Crane addressed the Arctic as a woman and complained that she did not reply, Graham surrounds himself with bodiless voices: 'Enough / Voices are with me here and more / The further I go', 'The blizzard grew and proved / Too filled with other voices / High and desperate / For me to hear him more', 'Out at the far-off edge I hear / Colliding voices', 'the foolish / Voices are lighting lamps' (*NCP*, pp. 154–6). Because they are bodiless, these voices do not bring with them the comfort of human presence. Just as a frozen woman is an image of the unfeminine and the sterile, so a bodiless voice, by negating the physicality that normally goes with speech, comes to represent writing, or language without the presence of a human interlocutor. The voices collide as words 'clash' in the impersonal space of text according to Barthes, or as the reader collides with the poem according to Graham himself.[20] The 'foolish voices' 'lighting lamps' are a somewhat bizarre reference to the foolish virgins in the New Testament, no doubt inspired by the lamps fuelled by blubber or 'train-oil' which Nansen used on his expedition.[21] The voices are virgin, like Crane's personified Arctic, and lack the animal fuel to sustain a light, just as the monster in Section 2 was 'unblubbered' (*NCP*, p. 153). Text supplements Mooney's loneliness with unnatural, insubstantial, unlocated company in the same way that Rousseau's masturbatory fantasies famously analysed by Derrida surrounded him with imaginary women.[22] The voices are not incompatible with 'silence', and Mooney, despite his hallucinations of presence ends the poem alone. 'I have made myself alone now', he says, in a phrase that ambiguously defines fiction as both solitude and solipsism (*NCP*, p. 157). Earlier, in the most startling of his hallucinations, the telephone had rung, but it, like the two-way communication it represents, was out of reach (*NCP*, p. 154).

In her analysis of the concept of impersonality in the writings of Pound and Eliot, Maud Ellman points out that these two writers, in spite of their distaste for many of Bergson's ideas, inherited from him an opposition between time and space: 'Like Bergson, they honour time with metaphors of speech, denouncing space with metaphors of writing.'[23] Or, of course, tenor and vehicle may be transposed, so that time is a metaphor for speech, space a metaphor for writing. I have already demonstrated how Graham (who cited Pound and Eliot among his chief influences) broke time into innumerable static moments in 'The

Nightfishing' by switching beween present and past tenses.[24] In 'Malcolm Mooney's Land', the verb forms are naturalistically determined by the story, but the whole structure of the poem is created by the transformation of time into space, a process whose most obvious metaphor is freezing. The diary form turns days into areas of text, so that Mooney can refer to 'This diary of a place / Writing us both in' (*NCP*, p. 156). In section 4, the place is a tent, and the stanzas themselves take on the appropriate shape (the only instance I can think of in which Graham used a form of concrete verse). The tent is not a real home, and Mooney will soon have to find another place 'to speak from' (*NCP*, p. 155). When he meets the 'furry queen' in section 5, his first question to her is 'Why did you choose this place / For us to meet?' (*NCP*, p. 155).

This, then, is the timeless space of the poem which Mooney explores as Nansen explored the Arctic. Nansen's expedition had two stages. His original idea was to test his theory that currents in the Arctic Ocean would enable a ship to drift east to west through the ice by setting out from Siberia in an exceptionally strongly built and well-provisioned ship and deliberately getting it locked into the ice. When this expedition was well under way, however, he decided to take advantage of his comparative proximity to the North Pole to leave the ship and travel by dog-sled in an attempt to get as far north as possible. The *Fram* continued its drift towards Spitzbergen, while Nansen and his one companion, Johansen, reached the most northerly point yet attained by any explorers, and then returned over the ice to Frantz Josef Land. The two parts of the expedition arrived safely in Norway within a few days of each other.

Malcolm Mooney's Land is indeed a land rather than a stretch of frozen sea, as the name, a parody of Frantz Josef Land, implies, and Mooney is not part of the jolly shipboard life described in the first volume of Nansen's book *Farthest North*.[25] The voyage of the *Fram* itself, though full of interesting details, would be an unlikely model for a portrait of the artist as hero. Locked in the pack ice, the crew had little to do except to take scientific measurements and entertain themselves. Their provisions were ample and their lives comfortable. On special occasions, such as the birthdays of crew-members, they celebrated with impressive menus and music. On Boxing Day, 1893, Nansen commented, 'I am almost ashamed of the life we lead, with none of those darkly painted sufferings of the long winter night which are indispensable to a properly exciting Arctic expedition. We shall have nothing to write about when we get home.'[26] During his two-man dog-sled expedition, however, he had to endure considerable hardship and danger. Like

Mooney, he slept in a tent, and would wake to find that his sleeping-bag had frozen.[27] Other episodes from this trip appear to have suggested incidents in 'Malcolm Mooney's Land'. The mysterious lines addressed to the 'benign creature with the small ear-hole', are reminiscent of Nansen's and Johansen's encounters with walruses, which frequently appeared around their kayaks and then submerged again. Describing one of these encounters, Nansen explains that he tried to shoot 'at a spot behind the ear, where it is more easily wounded' (*NCP*, p. 153).[28] Mooney's meeting with this Arctic animal is juxtaposed with an encounter with another creature:

> A fox was here last night (Maybe Nansen's,
> Reading my instruments.) The prints
> All round the tent and not a sound.

(NCP, p. 154)

Nansen, too, was visited by foxes, and though the idea of a fox reading instruments is surreal, they did at any rate steal instruments:

> Meanwhile the foxes continued to annoy us [. . .] one morning [we] found that the foxes [. . .] had gone off with the thermometer again. The only thing we found this time was the case, which they had thrown away a little way off. The thermometer itself we were never to see again; the snow had unfortunately drifted in the night, so that the tracks had disappeared. Goodness only knows what fox-hole it now adorns.[29]

Other details correspond less exactly with those related in *Farthest North*. Nansen and his men had many meetings with bears, though none that corresponds to Mooney's discovery of the sleeping 'sulphur bear' (*NCP*, p. 156). A yellow bear is described early in the expedition, but it is not asleep.[30] Similarly, Nansen had problems with bugs only when he was on the *Fram*, not in his tent (*NCP*, p. 154). (Insects were, however, discovered by the Scott expedition in Antarctica, a fact of some significance for my later argument.)[31]

Graham is highly selective, then, in his use of details from Nansen. He takes only those aspects of the expedition which fit his metapoetic theme. Although Mooney is on land in the spring, he does not find the flowers that Nansen discovers with such joy, or the equally welcome sight of bare rock.[32] The landscape of Malcolm Mooney's Land consists only of snow and ice, and, though Mooney camps for the night at the end of each section, the scenery usually has the starkness of daylight. Night scenes including the stars and moon would disturb the pure white background appropriate to his metaphor. Mooney's Arctic is a bleaker place than Nansen's. The tone of Mooney's meditations is sombre and melancholy, while Nansen is often enthusiastic. 'This is as good a night, a place as any,' Mooney says, while a typical comment by Nansen is:

> We found a camping-ground not far off. The tent was soon pitched, our catch cut up and placed in safety, and, I may say, seldom has the drift-ice housed beings so well satisfied as the two who sat that morning in the bag and feasted on seal's flesh, blubber and soup as long as they could find any room to stow it.[33]

Passages like this bring to mind Barthes's essay about Verne and Rimbaud which I have already had occasion to quote in my discussion of 'The Nightfishing'. Just as a ship is essentially homely in Barthes's view, so the whole ethos of Verne's adventure stories stems from a 'delight in the finite, which one finds also in children's passion for huts and tents'. The hero of *L'Île mystérieuse*:

> re-invents the world, fills it, closes it, shuts himself up in it, and crowns this encyclopaedic effort with the bourgeois posture of appropriation: slippers, pipe and fireside, while outside the storm, that is, the infinite, rages in vain.[34]

Barthes's insight into the fiction of Verne is also an insight into the nature of real-life adventure (which is, after all, a lived narrative with a beginning, an end and a sustaining tension, and which is often the raw material for a book). *Farthest North* is structured by the opposition between hardship and comfort, desolate exteriors and cosy interiors. All three forms of domicile mentioned in Barthes's account of Verne, ship, hut and tent, are present in Nansen's story.[35] If one sometimes feels that Nansen exaggerates his comfort, this may be partly due to his explorer's stiff upper lip, but is no doubt also influenced by an unconscious conformity with the conventions of adventure narrative:

> It is no trial now to turn out in the mornings with a good day's march before one, and cook, and lie snug and warm in the bag and dream of the happy future when we get home. Home...?
> Have been engaged on an extensive sartorial undertaking to-day; my trousers were getting the worse for wear. It seems quite mild now to sit and sew in -18° Fahr. in comparison with -40°. Then certainly it was not enjoyable to ply one's needle.[36]

I stress this domestic element of Nansen's narrative because it is a significant feature that is absent from 'Malcolm Mooney's Land'. Nansen describes nearly every meal, while Mooney does not mention food at all. The practicalities of life are Nansen's overriding concern; when he comes across a bear or walrus, his immediate reaction is to kill and eat it, while in Mooney's version these creatures become scenery and mate-rial for a 'story' (*NCP*, p. 156). Nansen's voyage, like those of other real-life explorers, is one of appropriation, a process of making oneself at home in the wilderness by exploiting its resources and proving that human beings and their culture can survive there. Mooney, on the other hand, is not at home there, and that is the point of the poem. Furthermore, while Nansen is immensely purposive, planning his expedition in detail, and setting himself the North Pole as an ultimate target, Mooney is the opposite. Instead of having set out with the determination to attain the Pole, Mooney appears to have just found himself in the Arctic territory named after him. He moves on reluctantly, with no hope of ever arriving anywhere different. 'This is as good [. . .] a place as any,' he says, and 'I [. . .] could / Hardly bear to pass' and 'why is it there has to be / Some place to find [. . .]?' (*NCP*, pp. 153–5). He is not so much an explorer as an anti-explorer, and his 'land' is not an objective but a condition.

'Malcolm Mooney's Land', then, is a parody of Nansen, in which the comforts, objectives and successes of exploration have been removed. Mooney is an explorer without hope, and in this he resembles Robert Falcon Scott in the last stages of his Antarctic expedition more than Nansen. Indeed, so strong is this resemblance that Graham's insistence on Nansen as an influence on his work seems almost suspicious. Graham told Lopez that 'Nansen helped [him] to steer' 'The Nightfishing'; he mentioned him in his comments on *Malcolm Mooney's Land* in the *Poetry Book Society Bulletin*; and, of course, Nansen is named in the poems, too – in 'Malcolm Mooney's Land' itself and in 'Implements' (*NCP*, p. 154, p. 246).[37] Graham's apparent lack of interest in Scott is surprising in view of the latter's mythic significance in twen-tieth-century Britain.[38] Michael and Margaret Snow tell us:

> He was critical of Captain Scott because he believed that he had not taken sufficient care of his men but Nansen he much admired as a humane leader, responsible for his companions.
>
> (*NFM*, p. 187)

And yet Scott is there in the work as a repressed presence, the latent content of a polar dream whose manifest content is Nansen.

The two explorers are, literally, poles apart, Nansen at the North and Scott at the South. Nansen, as we have seen, is a very positive figure; his carefully planned trip to the Arctic reached the most northerly point yet attained and he and his shipmates arrived back safe and well. Scott, on the other hand, was a failure. He reached the Pole too late, defeated by Nansen's countryman and protégé, Roald Amundsen, and died, together with the rest of his advance party, on the way back. It is this failure, and, in particular, the grim and noble deaths of the explorers, which account for the Scott myth. He was an unsuccessful explorer, but he was a martyr to the sublime.[39] He was also an apt symbol of the Romantic artist-hero, a man who wrote his suffering as he lived it. His last journey is glimpsed in 'the English imagination' through a blizzard of words: 'Great God! this is an awful place' (with its subtle pun on 'awful' which simultaneously invokes the sublime and tackles it with heroic vernacular bathos), the masterly understatement of Oates's exit line 'I am just going outside and may be some time', and Scott's final cry, 'For God's sake look after our people.'[40] Nansen was a successful explorer who ultimately demonstrated his attunement with social values by becoming a delegate to the League of Nations; Scott was an explorer-poet doomed to die in the polar opposite of home, writing on alone after the deaths of Wilson and Bowers, agonizingly aware at the last of the distance separating him from his 'people' (and preventing him from fulfilling his responsibility to them). Surely it is obvious which figure would have the greater appeal for a writer of Graham's tempera- ment. And Scott is certainly a presence in Graham's poetry, even if he is one that cannot be named. The title of the early poem 'His Companions Buried Him', he notes on one manuscript 'was a phrase which seemed to me to occur again and again in accounts of exploration and man's endurance against the elements' (*NCP*, pp. 37–8)[41] 'Again and again' perhaps, but not in the benign pages of *Farthest North*; the phrase, to most readers, is irresistibly reminiscent of the fate of Evans in the Scott expedition. The substitution of Nansen for Scott is also evident in a 1950s manuscript poem in which Graham describes 'the death of Nansen' by freezing.[42] As for 'Malcolm Mooney's Land' itself, Lopez has noted its echoes of Scott's story. He cites Dr Wilson's poem 'The Barrier Silence' with its Grahamesque title, and mentions 'the figure [of Oates] walking off into the snow' like Mooney's friend at the end of Section 3. Like Scott, Mooney has a son to worry about. (Nansen had a daughter.) Lopez points out, too, that the reference to Nansen (whose fox, we remember, is reading Mooney's instruments) explicitly distinguishes between Mooney and his supposed prototype.[43] It does more. The passage makes it clear that Nansen is the narrator's rival, just as Amundsen was Scott's. The foxlike cunning of the two Norwegians makes them a threat. Amundsen's foresight and efficiency has traditionally been seen in the Scott myth as somehow unsporting. Since Mooney's business is with the sublime self-sacrifice of text rather than winning races and raising flags, the presence of Nansen in his wilderness is even more of an affront than Amundsen's was to Scott.

Why, though, should Scott be repressed? I have suggested that Nansen and Scott can be seen as an opposed pair, one representing success and social integration, the other failure and ultimate isolation – though these latter qualities are touched with glamour. As we have seen many times in this study, Graham wanted to reconcile two conditions which were equally opposed in his imagination: textuality and community. Text was a wilderness one could only reach by leaving home. Graham insisted that it was (or ought to be) possible to go through that wilderness and come out into a transcendent community on the other side. If we take the League of Nations to be a transcendent community of a sort, Nansen had actually achieved something close to Graham's goal. By proclaiming his identification with Nansen, he declares his faith in community. As in the drowning poems, he insists that his exploration of textuality is not an abandonment of home and family but a self-sacrifice undertaken for communal ideals. Scott's (textual) cry 'For God's sake, look after our people' is a moving statement of human love and longing uttered from a place of total isolation, but it is also a confession of delinquency. If Scott had behaved otherwise, he could have looked after his people himself. By plunging after that heroic figure into the heart of the wilderness, Graham allows himself to echo his cry, to feel the love, intensified and glamorized by distance, that Scott proclaimed. But he dare not admit the hopelessness of his cause or his responsibility for his ultimate separation from his people. He is forced to conceal his suspicion that he is not Nansen but Scott.

We have seen, then, that 'Malcolm Mooney's Land' repeats themes that were present in Graham's poetry from the start. Mooney is stranded in a wilderness of text which isolates him from human contact. However, it offers him a substitute for such contact in the form of uncanny companions – disembodied voices and hallucinations, a wife and son who are both there and not there. Such company is always insufficient and he does not mistake it 'for the real thing'. The main difference between this and earlier poems on the same theme is that Graham's uneasy balance between the joy and despair of writing seems finally to be tilting towards despair. Mooney ends the poem alone, like Scott in his tent, and, like Scott, he has only himself to blame.

One-Way Telephone Calls

For Malcolm Mooney, the ringing telephone at the bottom of a crevasse was a particularly poignant hallucination. The image is repeated in a negative form in 'What Is the Language Using Us For?', where Mooney complains that he is 'in a telephoneless blue / Green crevasse' (*NCP*, p. 199). The two complaints amount to the same thing. Mooney's Arctic is a place without telephones, even if he sometimes dreams of them. The telephone was important enough for Graham to mention it in his explanatory note on *Malcolm Mooney's Land*, in a passage I have already quoted in Chapter 1:

> I am always very aware that my poem is not a telephone call. The poet only speaks one way. He hears nothing back. His words as he utters them are not conditioned by a real ear replying from the other side.[44]

This belief that text does not permit reciprocity is, I have suggested, the consequence of Western cultural convention. In our survey of his career so far, we have seen Graham first celebrate its autonomy in the early poems, then try to turn it into the membership of a transcendent community in the poems of the middle period. This attempt persists, as my reading of 'Malcolm Mooney's Land' shows, into the late poems, but the emphasis now falls on stasis rather than flux, and on the inadequacy of the linguistic community rather than its transcendence. He attempts to counter the resultant dissatisfaction with a more direct attempt to communicate, to make up for language's shortcomings as a community by testing to the full its claim to provide a conduit. Despite his contrary claim, he writes as if his words really were 'conditioned by a real ear replying from the other side', pretending to believe a poem can be a direct personal address.

This strategy has led one of Graham's critics, Ruth Grogan, to claim that he has 'a dialogical imagination'. 'More than three-quarters of these last poems,' she writes, 'explore the relationship between a speaker, "I", and an unanswering listener, "you"'. The title of her essay suggests that Grogan intends to apply the theories of Mikhail Bakhtin, but in fact she is dubious about the relevance of Bakhtin's 'heteroglossia' to Graham's work.[45] Bakhtin himself thought that heteroglossia could not figure in poetry except 'in the "low" poetic genres' which would be able to use it for 'the speeches of characters'. Certainly Graham has a very recognizable poetic 'voice'; there is little evidence in his work of the 'social diversity of speech types' which Bakhtin finds characteristic of the novel (and which undoubtedly does characterize 'The Waste Land' and *The Cantos*). On the other hand, it would be quite wrong to say of Graham, as Bakhtin does of poetry, that 'in the finished work language is an obedient organ, fully adequate to the author's intention.'[46] For all his fantasies of controlling it, language is constantly escaping from him, as we shall see shortly when we look at his treatment of greetings. And for Graham's poetry, as for Bakhtinian dialogue, 'every word is directed towards an *answer*', even to the extent that, like Sterne's Tristram Shandy, he leaves a space in one of his poems for the reader to write one (*NCP*, p. 249).[47]

The second person is, of course, a familiar poetic convention, which might seem ridiculous if readers were not so used to it. There are odes which address not only people but also skylarks and clouds, nightingales and urns; there are love-poems which address a beloved person; there are even elegies addressed to the dead. Graham's use of the second-person goes beyond these conventional addresses, but they are nevertheless important to him. He is not a writer of odes, but his love-poems and elegies are adapted to his metapoetic obsession.

In the poems 'I Leave This At Your Ear' and 'To My Wife At Midnight', he addresses his wife as she sleeps. Clearly, these poems constituted a genuine act of communication, since Nessie Dunsmuir undoubtedly read them soon after they were written. The communication is nevertheless deferred, and this changes its nature. Such deferral is a feature of all writing, which introduces both a time-lag and a mediating object between addresser and addressee, but by setting this in the context of sleep, Graham introduces a powerful image of isolation. Dunsmuir cannot answer his questions; she is not even aware that he is writing them. Furthermore, the acts of personal communication between husband and wife are only one aspect of these utterances. Like all pieces of writing, they remain available for the duration of their physical existence to be read by anyone who encounters them. In this case, as with many other 'private' love-poems, the message has been made available to the public by the sender himself, and was probably written with such publication in mind. The poems' status as love-notes is thus fictive; the attempted communication they depict is a synecdoche for the communication between any writer and reader, obstructed not by a few hours' sleep but by the nature of text itself. These two poems beat at this barrier – they portray a love which is not unrequited but unresponsive. In 'To My Wife', the poet asks a string of questions – six in the first fifteen-line section alone – to which he knows he cannot expect an answer. Nevertheless, he goes on asking them, repeating compulsively such enquiries as 'Is the cat's window open?' The questions he asks are mostly, in Jakobson's categorization of utterances, phatic: 'messages primarily serving to establish, to prolong, or to discontinue communication, to check whether the channel works [. . .], to attract the attention of the interlocutor or to confirm his continued attention'.[48] He asks Dunsmuir if she is asleep, if she can hear him, if she intends to say good-night and then turn her back. Even the question about the cat's window seems to be a metaphor for the other kinds of access problematized in the poem (*NCP*, pp. 263–5). Paul De Man's analysis of the doubleness of rhetorical questions is relevant here: Graham's use of this trope is caught between a non-rhetorical attempt to exact a reply and a rhetorical desire to demonstrate that no reply is possible in text.[49] Similarly the title 'I Leave This At Your Ear' both explains itself as a written message and gestures towards an impossible oral one: the poem is left at Dunsmuir's ear as if she could hear it. The house the poet returns to is silent, and his hope that she is listening is unfulfilled (*NCP*, p. 166).

The conventional 'you' of the love poem, then, becomes a way of exploring the nature of text in Graham's treatment. More significant in his work, though, is the elegy. We have already considered in the previous chapter Graham's elegy for his mother. His poems for the drowned are also in a sense elegies, as are the poems which mention his dead father. In 'To Alexander Graham' the poet dreams that he meets his father by the quay, but the dream, like writing, is soundless. The son asks his father three questions but the latter tries and fails to reply. Graham insists 'I think he wanted to speak'. Death is the ultimate barrier to communication; the father's inability to address his son in a dream would not matter if his death had not made that dream the only possible occasion for such an address (*NCP*, p. 222–3). The last two books also contain three important elegies for painters in which this one-way communication is further explored.

'The Thermal Stair', in effect, sets up a meeting with the dead Peter Lanyon. 'I called today, Peter, and you were away' the poet tells him. It is a natural enough phrase, despite being an iambic pentameter, the sort of note one might easily put through a letter box. In this case, though, Lanyon is away permanently; nevertheless, the poem tries to become a space where they can meet and converse. This space is the 'thermal stair' of the title, the current of air on which a glider pilot rises to the required altitude. In using the idea of a thermal as an image for the virtual space of art, Graham is following Lanyon himself, whose painting 'Thermal' is a image of that which cannot be realistically painted because it is invisible.[50] The poet therefore asks this painter who has perfected the art of painting what eludes the senses to find this space for him: 'Find me a thermal to speak and soar to you from' (*NCP*, p. 164). The place of their meeting is the space of an abstract painting, but because it is abstract it is an encapsulation of other places. The poem is full of Cornish place names, reminding us that Lanyon – unusually for a member of the art colony – was a native Cornishman.[51] Abstraction, whether that of an abstract painting or of a poem (since text, for Graham, is always abstract, as I mentioned in Chapter 1), provides a vantage point from which many real places can be seen, just as a glider pilot overlooks a number of towns, villages and fields, all of them equally distant. Their conversation takes place over Botallack, Ding Dong , Levant, Lanyon Quoit, Gurnard's Head and Little Parc Owles, all equally visible from the perspective of their thermal (*NCP*, pp. 163–4).

This theme of art as a thermal is a positive one; it affirms a faith that seems to underlie the paintings of the St Ives school, that the essence of the concrete can be captured in abstraction, a point made by the painter John Wells when he wrote:

> How can one paint the warmth of the sun, the sound of the sea, the jour-ney of a beetle across a rock, or thoughts of one's own whence and whither? That's one argument for abstraction. One absorbs all these feel-ings and ideas: if one is lucky they undergo a transformation into gold and that is creative work.[52]

But Graham is not content with the metaphor of the thermal, precisely because it contains no element of loss. The opening six stanzas of the poem are a statement of faith which might be taken as religious as well as artistic; the allusion to Methodism seems to bring them up short, as if the poet realizes that his thermal stair might equally be a vision of heaven, and that this unproblematic view of a continuing communion does not really represent his own feelings about the death of his friend (*NCP*, p. 164). The consolation traditional to the elegy has perhaps come too quickly. The poem resumes, then, in a different rhythm. The shorter lines suggest a communication of a more difficult kind, since the end of the sentence is deferred by a series of line-breaks – the first sentence in the new manner takes six lines, the second five. Even more significantly, the perspective has now altered. Where the view in the first part of the poem was from above, here it is from below. Poet and painter stand 'in the Engine / House below Morvah', and Lanyon asks:

'Shall we go down [. . .]

Before the light goes
And stand under the old
Tinworkings around
Morvah and St Just?'

(*NCP*, p. 164–5)

Lanyon and the poet are standing 'below Morvah' and 'under the old /
Tinworkings' not because they are underground but because of the hilly
nature of the west Cornish landscape. But the locations they have
chosen for their visits are designed to remind us of the subterranean
nature of mining, and to provide an underworld to counter the celestial
vision of the first part of the poem. In those six stanzas, it was the poet
who spoke, inviting Lanyon to take him gliding into the heaven of
abstraction. Now it is Lanyon who replies, implicitly pointing out that
he is dead and under the ground. Furthermore, his speech is not in fact
a reply at all but a reminiscence of a conversation they had when he was
alive and could speak. Throughout the poem, Lanyon is addressed, not
in the interrogative mode Graham used for his one-sided conversation
with Dunsmuir (though there is one question: 'Lanyon, why is it you're
earlier away?'), but in the imperative (*NCP*, p. 166). Instead of asking a
sleeping woman to speak, he asks a dead man to do things: to find him
a thermal, to sit on a sparstone, to give him his hand, to remember him
(*NCP*, pp. 164–6). Closely allied to these imperatives are the future tenses
used to set up their final drinking session: 'We'll take the quickest way',
'Climb here where the hand / Will not grasp on air', 'we'll sit and drink'.
Lanyon's side of the conversation belongs to the pastness of his real life,
while the poet's is future and hypothetical.

   The poet and painter, then, have nowhere to meet. They have neither
time nor place in common. At the end of the poem, they are going home
by different roads, and although the poet asks for the painter's hand, he
knows, too, that his friend is both 'earlier' and 'away'. The multiple
places possible in a poem or an abstract painting are all ultimately
unsatisfactory, which accounts for the restless movement of the protag-
onists. They soar, go down, climb, go and rise; the poet asks twice to be
steadied and at the end of the poem is turning aimlessly (*NCP*,
pp. 164–6).

   'Lines on Roger Hilton's Watch' is an address, not to the dead man,
but to the watch, making it a sort of ode after all. Graham even uses the
traditional vocative 'O' (*NCP*, p. 235). The watch replies to him, but this
somewhat ludicrous conversation, like that between Graham and

Lanyon, is subject to the dislocation of both time and space. In its narra-
tive 'It is Botallack o'clock' – that is, the place is Hilton's home and the
time is his lifetime (*NCP*, p. 236).

The elegy that has the strongest links to Graham's other poems in the
second person is 'Dear Bryan Wynter'. This is a poem that explicitly
accepts its textuality, unlike 'The Thermal Stair' and 'Lines on Roger
Hilton's Watch', both of which purport to be conversations, however
problematic. If the poet cannot make his poem into a telephone call, he
can, perhaps, make it into a letter. Letters, as we have seen in Chapter 1,
are writing at its most personal, and Graham's determination to prove
the genuineness of his desire to communicate led to a lifelong preoccu-
pation with the form. His letter poems present themselves as maimed,
lacking an addressee. 'Dear Bryan Wynter' is a dead letter, a letter to a
man who cannot receive it:

> Speaking to you and not
> Knowing if you are there
> Is not too difficult.
> My words are used to that.

> (*NCP*, p. 258)

The metaphor round which the poem is structured has broken down
already. Speaking is the standard for all communication so far as
Graham is concerned – even though he has granted textuality for the
sake of argument, he cannot help taking it back again. As in 'To My Wife
At Midnight', and 'Malcolm Mooney's Land', he asks a string of ques-
tions to which he cannot receive answers:

> Anyhow how are things?
> Are you still somewhere
> With your long legs
> And twitching smile under
> Your blue hat walking
> Across a place? Or am
> I greedy to make you up
> Again out of memory?
> Are you there at all?

> (*NCP*, p. 258)

The problem here, as in 'The Thermal Stair', is one of place. Now Wynter
is dead, they can only meet in a poem, which is not a true meeting-place
because only one person speaks there. To write a poem is like writing to
the dead, who never reply. As Derrida puts it, 'Writing in the common
sense is the dead letter, it is the carrier of death.' [53]

Graham's poems in the second person attempt to put back into text what is missing from it. We have seen that questions (which demand answers) and imperatives (which demand a practical response) are two linguistic functions which he uses to emphasize the isolation of text from personal contact. Another linguistic function which he uses compulsively to represent this missing element is greeting.

Greetings are ritual speech acts. In Jakobson's classification, they, too, are no doubt phatic, since they are used to open and close communications. Indeed, one of his examples of a phatic communication is the phrase 'Hello, can you hear me?' He goes on to say that they 'may be displayed by a profuse exchange of ritualized formulas'.⁵⁴ Nevertheless, one feels that the truly Grahamesque utterance 'Hello, can you hear me?' conflates two slightly different functions, a technical enquiry and a ritual acknowledgement of another's presence.

Like many of the strategies of the late poems, greeting appears in earlier work too. 'Letter I' from *The Nightfishing* is largely a meditation on the theme. The phrases 'welcome', 'farewell', 'good morning' and the epistolary salutation 'dear' are played with throughout the poem:

> Welcome then anytime. Fare
> Well as your skill's worth
> You able-handed sea-blade
> Aglint with the inlaid
> Scales of the herring host
> And hosting light. Good morning
> Said that.

> (*NCP*, p. 121)

The basic idea of the poem is that greetings, divorced from the social contexts which normally govern them, take on a life of their own. 'Good morning' speaks because there is no extralinguistic person to speak it and no extralinguistic place for it to be spoken in. The words lose some of their ritual character and regain some of their original meaning: 'good morning' becomes a statement about morning, 'fare well' an injunction to the reader to voyage successfully through 'this difficult element'. At this stage of his career, Graham eagerly accepts the performative power of his words, newly liberated from their dependence on him:

> These words said welcome. Fare
> Them well from what they are.

> (*NCP*, p. 122)

In later poems, the greetings seem to have regained their ritual charac-
ter without regaining the social contexts which make them meaningful.
In 'Approaches To How They Behave', language is a show-off which the
poet greets in the silence of the text:

> Language is expensive if
> We want to strut, busked out
> Showing our best on silence.
> Good morning.

(NCP, p. 179)

Silence is menacing later in the poem when the poet is unable to make
it respond to his greeting:

> [. . .] Hello
> Hello I shout but that silence
> Floats steady, will not be marked
> By an off-hand shout.

(NCP, p. 182)

In 'Private Poem to Norman Macleod', the ostensible addressee is asked
to send one greeting before both he and Graham are lost in the deper-
sonalizing vortex of text:

> Macleod. Macleod, say
> Hello before we both
> Go down the manhole.

(NCP, p. 228)

The manhole is a conduit leading nowhere, and the greeting uttered
before entering it takes on something of the doomed glamour of a pris-
oner's last words before execution. Greetings can still be used in text
even though the physical presence they exist to acknowledge has no
place there; stranded on the page in this way, they are both a faintly
comforting reminder of that presence and a final irony.

The Wrong Wood

Greeting can be a function of writing as well as speech. The salutation
that begins a letter, the valediction and signature that close it, are ritual
acts. They mark the beginning and end of the message, but, more impor-
tantly, they act as some kind of guarantee of the relationship between
writer and reader. In letters, the name of the addressee and of the

author are an essential part of the formula, guaranteeing that the communication is indeed personal. But in Graham's poem-letters these names are usually missing. 'Dear Who I Mean' begins with a salutation that clarifies nothing, as the reader cannot know who is referred to (*NCP*, p. 160). Similarly, 'Yours Truly' takes its title from a valediction, but the phrase is itself misleading. He cannot be the reader's 'truly', since he does not even know who his reader, the 'Dear Pen / Pal in the distance', is (*NCP*, pp. 159–60). Furthermore, the signature which ought to guarantee the personal and unique nature of the communication is missing. According to Derrida, the signature's guarantee of authorship is compromised by the iterability of the linguistic sign. Even in a letter, a signature proves nothing. In a printed document, like Derrida's essay 'Signature Event Context' it can only be an ironic joke.[55] Graham does not go so far with this joke as Derrida. Instead, he is seized with a kind of anxiety at the very thought of putting his name in a poem:

> Where is your pride I said
> To myself calling myself
> By my name even pronouncing
> It freshly I thought but blushed
> At the lonely idea.

> (*NCP*, p. 159–60)

Graham's fascination with names and naming, as with letters, goes back to the beginning of his career. One manifestation of this is his obsession with the children's rhyme 'Water Water Wallflower', which he quotes in full in 'Letter II':

> Water water wallflower
> Growing up so high
> We are all children
> We all must die.
> Except Willie Graham
> The fairest of them all.
> He can dance and he can sing
> And he can turn his face to the wall.

> (*NCP*, p. 124)

Even earlier, however, he had referred to it in 'Except Nessie Dunsmuir', published in *2ND Poems*, in which it is his future wife who is named, rather than himself (*NCP*, pp. 50–1). Derek Stanford tells how Graham persuaded some children to sing the rhyme to Nessie Dunsmuir in the street, and Robert Frame remembers him singing it, naming himself as

Sydney rather than Willie.[56]

As Lopez has pointed out, rhymes of this kind are used by children for the ritual definition of an individual's identity in the context of the community.[57] A name, as distinct from the first person singular, is a fixed identifier and is conferred on an individual by others, not by him- or herself. People do not customarily refer to themselves by name, but by the same deictic used by other people to describe themselves. A name is the marker of a fixed, communal identity, while 'I' on its own can only represent a shifting, personal one. The uncanny community of text does not provide him with such a name. In fact, of course, the words of authors are named as their property, though generally only outside the boundaries of the text proper, on covers and title pages, or at the foot of poems published in magazines. For Graham, apparently, this naming is not enough. His poems are racked with nostalgia for the communities of his childhood, and for the kind of naming he associates with them.

Naming was important to Graham in his life as well as his poetry. Julian Maclaren-Ross states that it was 'a terrible offence' to greet him without calling him Sydney, 'thus publicly proclaiming that you'd no wish to be considered a friend of his'.[58] He appears to have been a compulsive user of other people's names; a letter to Norman Macleod on the subject of 'The Nightfishing' repeats 'Norman' like an invocation: 'Now, Norman, think of the wonderful [. . .] beginning again [. . .] Norman, this first section, this time, I took easy [. . .] And of course, Norman [. . .] Norman, this section, which I used to think of as a song I have spoken out fairly [. . .] Norman Norman Norman what shall I say.'[59] This letter of seven typed pages uses the name 'Norman' 24 times, not counting the initial salutation. Frequently the name is repeated. The naming of the addressee seems at times to be more important than the message. (Interestingly, this message is concerned with such questions as the correct delivery of the lines 'I hear my name called' and 'Named me to the bone'.) Similarly his poems are often addressed to a named individual. 'The Don Brown Route', 'How Are the Children Robin' and the poems to Bryan Wynter, Roger Hilton and Macleod himself are examples:

> I walked up Fouste Canyon
> With a pack of beans and malt
> Whisky and climbed and shouted
> Norman Norman Norman
> Till all the echoes had gone.

>   (*NCP*, p. 227)

Such ironically 'personal' poems exist side by side with those addressed to an unknown reader. Even in 'personal' poems, the unknown reader gets in and diverts the message, which by that very fact loses some of its content. It is naming that anchors meaning to an individual and prevents its escape into the impersonal – hence Graham's insistence on it. Nevertheless, this strategy is doomed to fail in a printed poem. As I remarked in Chapter 1, he cannot be sure that the reader will distinguish between the real people named in his poems, such as Bryan Wynter, and fictive characters like Malcolm Mooney. A name is no guarantee of reality.

The multiplicity of Graham's own names is itself a reminder of 'the fluidity of identity'. His friends in the Cornish artistic community sometimes called him Sydney and sometimes Jock. To Sven Berlin, he was Joke Grim, a variant of Jock Graham. Stanford states that in London he was called 'Willie or Sydney without distinction'.[60] He seems to have been known as Willie in his childhood, as witness 'Letter II' and the name used by his relation Sam in 'What Is the Language Using Us For?': 'He shouted Willie and I crossed the street' (*NCP*, p. 201). On his book jackets, he was W.S. Graham, a form, perhaps chosen in imitation of T.S. Eliot, that erects an additional barrier between poet and reader by hiding his forenames. It seems likely that Graham himself connived in this shifting identity, that he wanted the protection afforded by multiple names. Just as his poems yearn for a community that he had voluntarily deserted, so his pretended longing for the communal validation conferred by a name is belied by his deliberate adoption of replacements for it.

In his note in *Contemporary Poets of the English Language*, Graham listed the prose of Samuel Beckett as an influence on his work. He must have been intrigued by the way Beckett's trilogy, *Molloy*, *Malone Dies* and *The Unnamable*, gradually moved from the confident characterization of traditional fiction to a refusal to fix identity in words – a refusal epitomized by the shifting names of the hero of the last volume.[61] The dim metafictional space of that novel has its equivalent in the wood of the late poems, as we shall see shortly. Like Graham, the Unnamable tries and fails to find a name that can be used in such a space. The heroes of the previous volumes, Molloy and Malone, together those of other Beckett novels, pass in procession before the nameless narrator:

> I see him in profile. Sometimes I wonder if it is not Molloy. Perhaps it is Molloy, wearing Malone's hat. But it is more reasonable to suppose it is Malone, wearing his own hat. Oh look, there is the first thing, Malone's

hat. I see no other clothes. Perhaps Molloy is not here at all. Could he be, without my knowledge? The place is no doubt vast. Dim intermittent lights suggest a kind of distance. To tell the truth I believe they are all here, at least from Murphy on.[62]

In 'The Lying Dear', as we have seen, the lover's lie, that is, her calling of the wrong name during intercourse, precipitates a Fall (*NCP*, pp. 158–9). In 'Five Visitors to Madron', the possession of a name is tied up with an image of childhood. Now that this is lost, the speaker is left nameless:

> The hint was as though a child running
> Late for school cried and seemed
> To have called my name in the morning
> Hurrying and my name's wisp
> Elongated. Leaves me here
> Nameless at least very without
> That name mine ever to be called
> In that way different again.

(*NCP*, p. 190)

In 'The Secret Name', both writer and reader are nameless, confronting each other in the wood which is a major symbol in *Implements in Their Places*, and which, like the Arctic waste of 'Malcolm Mooney's Land', represents text. Lopez's claim that this wood is derived from Kipling's poem 'The Way Through the Woods' is surely too categorical, since he had earlier pointed out connections with the woods of Scots ballads and with Birnam Wood in Macbeth.[63] There is, however, another literary reference which may be present in 'The Secret Name', the wood where things have no names in Lewis Carroll's *Through the Looking-Glass*:

> 'This must be the wood,' she said thoughtfully to herself, 'where things have no names. I wonder what'll become of *my* name when I go in? I shouldn't like to lose it at all – because they'd have to give me another, and it would be almost certain to be an ugly one.'[64]

The reader's name escaping into the trees in the third line of the poem is perhaps a reminiscence of the fawn in the novel, which runs back into the safety of the wood as soon as it realizes its own identity and that of the child accompanying it. In the same way, the writer and reader might have been named to each other if they had met in the open:

> If I had met you earlier walking
> And with the poetry light better

We might we could have spoken and said
Our names to each other.

(NCP, p. 237)

The confrontation resembles the one between writer and reader at the beginning of 'The Dark Dialogues'. Once again, it takes place in the dark and the identity of the two people who meet is unknown. But at the end of the poem, Graham tells the reader he or she has another name, the 'secret name' of the title: 'You maybe did not know you had another / Sound and sign signifying you'. This name, like so many of those referred to in the poems, is not revealed. Nevertheless, the possibility of finding a new name in the text is a partial compensation. People lose by going into the wood, as Alice lost her name and her memory to the extent that she even forgot what a tree was, but they also gain. Alice and the fawn could be friends in the wood, but not outside. That curious provisional intimacy is echoed in the line 'even the words are shy', and the fact that it does duty for the sense of real community between people is shown a few lines later: 'They move / As a darkness of my family'.

The conjunction of naming and the wood occurs again in 'Implements in Their Places', where a sequence of 'wood' pieces is apparently set off by a naming of the poet at the end of number 58: 'Grampus homes on the Graham tongue' (*NCP*, p. 253). Numbers 59 and 61 deal directly with the question of whether the wood can contain a name. The two twigs in number 59 have numbers, not names, and they are bothered by the fact that they cannot separate their identity from that of the trunk, in the same way that a poet's words belong to the language as a whole. The speaker says confidently: 'I think they were wrong.' The confidence seems to have been generated by his naming in the previous section: 'I carved my name / On the bark' (*NCP*, pp. 254). In number 61, however, the name has disappeared:

> You will observe that not one
> Of those tree-trunks has our initials
> Carved on it or heart or arrow
> We could call ours. My dear, I think
> We have come in to the wrong wood.

(NCP, p. 254)

He is back to the 'wrong place' of 'The Secret Name'. Graham would be happy, he claims, if he could go into the poems and take his name with him. Instead, he has to accept another name conferred by textuality. The wrong place is the poem itself.

In 'The Nightfishing', as we saw, Graham's suggestion that it was his parents who first 'named [him] to the bone' introduced a Derridean note, implying that community was always already invaded by the absences of writing (*NCP*, p. 105). Derrida's argument is based on a passage from Lévi-Strauss's *Tristes Tropiques* dealing with the prohibition against uttering a name among a South American tribe. In this community, the use of names was prohibited, but the names themselves already existed, as Derrida points out. He sees naming as a form of violence or violation, and this view is apparently shared by the tribespeople themselves.[65] Robert Graves, in a passage that must have given 'The Secret Name' its title, remarks that 'in ancient times, once a god's name had been discovered, the enemies of his people could do destructive magic against them with it.'[66] The same awe of naming is noted by Iona and Peter Opie among British schoolchildren:

> Children attach an almost primitive significance to people's names, always wanting to find out a stranger's name, yet being correspondingly reluctant to reveal their own.[67]

For Graham, too, as we have seen, the name has a mystical significance and is associated with childhood. But his earlier tentative attempt to bring the lifeworld and the text closer by arguing that community is always already textual is not continued in the late poems. He now seems convinced that the name is not the beginning of the erosion of presence which culminates in the text, but the marker of the uncorrupted identity of childhood, the place where language and the self meet and merge perfectly, leaving no remainder. In the adult world, this naming has become plural and therefore contaminated with impersonality. The 'fluidity of identity' is produced by the loss of innocence.

This yearning for a name is an aspect of Graham's nostalgia, and participates in its ambivalence. Every state to which he reverts in fantasy is already fallen. From the viewpoint of the adult, the street of childhood seems a safe place, while from the dangers of that street, the unviolated walls of home doubtless seemed more desirable. Similarly, within the home a relationship with his mother unshared with other males (his father and brother) was the object of nostalgia – and even that primary relationship involves the acknowledgement of the separation of birth. When he fantasizes about playing in the street, it is full, as we saw in Chapter 2, of his family, with none of the strangers one might expect to find there. In claiming to wish to return to the security of the street, Graham conceals the alienation that must have characterized it in his own experience. His nostalgia for the name as the only pure and unfallen text seems as disingenuous as every other aspect of his myth of community. His idyllic community of game-playing children was not, one suspects, as innocent as it appears in hindsight. The street, after all, is where bad children may call one names.[68]

CHAPTER 6

Dreams and Clusters:
Some Unpublished Writings

Dreams of Greenock, Dreams of Crete

In 1973, Graham published an extract 'From a Poem in Progress' called 'A Dream of Crete' in the magazine *Aquarius* (*NCP*, pp. 343–4). It seems an intriguing opening to a poem, but no more. (Indeed, it has a section numbered '1', but no succeeding sections.) Yet this is the only version of 'A Dream of Crete' he published. After his death, Robin Skelton and Margaret Blackwood published another version in *Aimed at Nobody*, which, like the other texts in that volume, is taken from a manuscript sent to Robin and Sylvia Skelton (*NCP*, pp. 307–8). In their notes, Skelton and Blackwood quote from the letter Graham sent to accompany the poem:

> 'Maybe you will remember that I pin things up on my wooden wall and as well as drawings I sometimes put up words not saying HOME SWEET HOME or BLESS THIS HOUSE. But phrases which might be usable or otherwise mean something to me. It so happens at the moment, my dears I have up – A DREAM OF CRETE (I feel it would be truer to spell it with a K.) which, as a title, more than charms me.'
>
> (*AAN*, p. 65)

Skelton and Blackwood seem not to know of the version of the poem published in *Aquarius*, but their note does refer to 'other later passages from a projected and never completed poem with the same title' published by Ruth Grogan in her article 'Dear Pen Pal in the Distance'. This article is based on Ronnie Duncan's archive of the letters and manuscripts sent to him by Graham. It does not, however, give a sense of the importance of the poem in the archive.[1] There is also a manuscript which Graham sent to Michael Schmidt in the Graham archive at the John Rylands University Library of Manchester. Some of the imagery of these manuscripts appears in other writings, both published and unpublished. Skelton and Blackwood include a poem called 'In Crete' and another called 'In the Street of Knives' which also has a Cretan setting, as does one of the sections of 'Surrealgraphs' (*NCP*, pp. 308–10, p. 299). As they point out in their notes, a later poem entitled 'The Street of Knives' was published in Graham's *Uncollected Poems* (*NCP*, pp. 283–4). In 'Implements in Their Places', Cretan material appears in numbers 11, 65, 70 and 71 (*NCP*, p. 243, p. 255, pp. 256–7). Number 11 includes the Scops owl, with its call 'POLEEP', which is mentioned in the drafts so frequently as to seem an obsession. Lopez discusses the symbolism of the owl, and its connection to ancient Greece, but does not mention Graham's experience of modern Greece, or the Cretan poems.[2] (The significance of the call is explained below.)

'A Dream of Crete', (the title by which I shall refer to the overall project represented by this assortment of fragments), has an important place in Graham's late work despite being unfinished – indeed, it seems likely, as I shall go on to explain, that it was its importance to him that prevented him finishing it. It was his most ambitious treatment of an analogy that he was exploring in several other poems of this period, that between text and dreams.

Images of sleeping and waking occur sporadically in the poems of the middle period. There are passing references in 'The Lost Other' in the phrases 'And New York turns Dechmont in sleep' and 'night-speaking pillow', but these are hard to differentiate from the generally dreamlike tone (*NCP*, p. 72, p. 74). In 'Listen. Put on Morning', the poem, or 'song' is implicitly compared to King Arthur and other great sleepers of myth; it 'sleeps to be wakened' at some time in the future when the past will be perfectly reconstituted. Dreams are an inadequate substitute for the daylight plenitude which will be attained by 'the handclapping centuries' of posterity. Even as morning is proclaimed again in the final lines of the poem, however, the condition of being awake is equated by the pun on 'mourning' with bereavement, suggesting that that plenitude is itself the product of a dream (*NCP*, pp. 59–61). In 'The Nightfishing' Graham writes:

> To work at waking. Yet who wakes?
> Dream gives awake its look.

> (*NCP*, p. 107)

This suggests the possibility that the entire experience of the fishing trip, with its nocturnal setting and uncanny quality, is a dream. The last word of the poem, after all, is 'awoke' (*NCP*, p. 120). This possibility remains largely implicit but can provide a useful aid to the reader's attempt to understand the experience described. In the same way, although there is no reference to dreaming in 'The Dark Dialogues', we almost feel when we read it that 'language' has been substituted for 'dream'. Like 'The Nightfishing' it takes place at night; the scenes shift in a magical way, as those of a dream do; the speaker revisits the scenes of his childhood; and above all, he finds himself becoming different characters – his mother in section 2 and his father in section 3 (*NCP*, pp. 169–70). This common dream phenomenon, mentioned by Freud, allows readers with a taste for realism to infer that the poem is, on one level, a mimetic account of a familiar experience.[3]

But it is in the poetry of the last two volumes that dreams come into their own both as theme and as narrative device. In 'Greenock At Night I Find You', the speaker lies half-asleep imagining himself back in Greenock. Then in the second section imagination becomes dream: 'See, I am back' he says, but the meeting in the Cartsburn Vaults is an uncanny one; the family shine like apparitions, and Graham himself is not encountered personally by them but 'only remembered' as one absent or even dead. This is the hide-and-seek referred to in the first section, a childhood game which turns out to have prefigured the impossibility of reciprocal contact (*NCP*, pp. 219–20).

Similarly in 'To Alexander Graham', as we have seen, the dream encounter with the poet's father is incomplete. The poem is structured around the father's desire to speak, which is continually frustrated and continually renewed. The repetition itself is uncanny and 'recalls the sense of helplessness experienced in some dream states'.[4] Graham displaces his own desire for his father to acknowledge him on to the father himself, and at the same time frustrates it (*NCP*, pp. 222–3). 'The feeling of being inhibited' according to Freud, 'serves admirably to represent in dreams *a conflict of will* or a *negative*.[5] This dream fits Freud's model, enacting both the son's desire to be recognized by his father and, more subtly, his desire to be ignored. It is not only a place where the father can apparently be reclaimed, but also one where he can be controlled. The price of such control, however, is the failure to achieve true reciprocity.

Graham evokes a different phase of his past in 'The Night City' where it is the literary London of the 1940s that appears in the dream, though here it is peopled also by the figures from the poet's earlier fantasies of it, Whistler, Holmes and John Donne as well as Eliot and Paul Potts (the Canadian poet best known for his autobiographical prose work *Dante Called You Beatrice* – *NCP*, p. 215). Suddenly, however, 'the City is empty':

> The fire had burnt out.
> The plague pits had closed
> And gone into literature.
>
> Between the big buildings
> I sat like a flea crouched
> In the stopped works of a watch.

This emptiness, like his father's silence, signifies the unavailability of the past. The stopped watch has a dual meaning: London, that intricate machine which had so fascinated the young Graham, is no longer functional, and it is only accessible to him through the breakdown of time occasioned by the dream. I have referred to dreams as a device, and both here and in 'To Alexander Graham' they are indeed seen as mechanical, but as machines that are in some sense defective. The watch has stopped; the film has no soundtrack. One is reminded of the imagery of artifice in the first three books and in 'The Nightfishing'. Text itself is mechanical in Graham's imagination; here, however, the emphasis is on the failure of the mechanism rather than its ingenuity.

Dreams, then, bring the past to the present and the dead back to life, but only in a provisional and defective way. They also act as a separator between living people. In 'I Leave This At Your Ear', Nessie Dunsmuir is cut off from the poet by the solipsism of dreams: 'Your dreams blindfold you by the light they make.' (*NCP*, p. 166.) In 'To My Wife at Midnight', the dream is a suit of 'drowsy armour' which shuts out all human contact, protecting the poet even from his wife (*NCP*, p. 265). In one dream he plays 'the games of Greenock / Beside the sugar-house quays', while in another, presumably dreamt by Dunsmuir, whose dream situates her 'among [her] Dunsmuir clan', he is a wounded soldier 'on the field at Culloden'. He is punished, not only for his bad behaviour at Culloden but for all 'the terrible acts of [his] time', but by entering his dream he escapes. As he drifts off, his 'responsibility' drifts off, too. Whereas one dream can only provide a simulacrum of community, two, when taken together, offer a magical reciprocity in which he can experience love and independence at the same time, unharmed by the wounds of the one and the loneliness of the other. Dreams are an unsatisfying substitute for community, but by imagining a community *of* dreamers, Graham hopes to make the substitution more satisfying. Ultimately, though, this community is only another level of fantasy superimposed on the original one. Dream is, by its nature, a 'lonely place'. 'To My Wife At Midnight' is his last important poem (it was written too late for inclusion in *Implements in Their Places*, and the later poems published in *Uncollected Poems* are trivial) and this fact suggests that there was much at stake for him in its ingenious but doomed attempt to break down the barrier between dream and reality, solipsism and community. If a dream is a fulfilment of a wish, it is only a fulfilment in its own fantastic terms.

Of all his metaphors for text, dream is the most deeply felt because it epitomizes the solipsism which is what really keeps him from human contact. The theme goes deeper than its ostensible meaning; it conceals the message that he is not lonely because he has chosen to be a poet – rather, he is a poet because he has chosen to be lonely. Dreams are a more basic means even than writing of creating a personal world. As long as they remain dreams, there is no possibility of reconciling that world with reality. Dreams, therefore, were the fundamental problem Graham had to solve if he really wanted to heal his breach with community. 'To My Wife at Midnight' was his final failure to heal that breach. It was not an artistic failure, but he wanted to do more than merely write a good poem. This is shown by his deferral of the conclusion of 'A Dream of Crete', his refusal to settle for any textual resolution that would condemn it to be a finished poem with all the limitations that implies. In this respect, it resembles those dreamers described by Freud who repeatedly dream of a traumatic event in a vain attempt to resolve the trauma.[6] The continual shifting and displacement of this process actually gives the poem some of the dynamism and fluidity which a real dream shares with the lifeworld, features which a published poem must sacrifice.

Graham and his wife made two visits to Crete, the first in 1964 in the company of Nancy Wynne-Jones, and the second in 1977 with Ronnie and Henriette Duncan.[7] The main attempts to write a Cretan poem occur between these two visits, and the fantasy that generated the poems led eventually to the second visit. This no doubt explains why most of the manuscripts were sent to the Duncans, whose own previous trip helped to stimulate Graham's imagination.[8] However, the bulk of the manuscripts are dated considerably earlier than the second journey to Crete, around 1970-2, which rules out one explanation for their incompleteness: that the real experience drove away the desire to write.

The opening paragraph of the version published in *Aquarius* announces a dream, but does so through a reverse metaphor, that of waking (*NCP*, pp. 343–4). The speaker is described as falling, and this falling is revealed first to be slow and eventually, in the second paragraph, to be a metaphor for sinking. His great weight is referred to, and is associated with his profession of poet ('my making tons'). A similar reversal to the one in the first line shows us the sea-bed rising to meet him and discovering him rather than the other way about. Inversions, as we shall see in our discussion of the automatic writing, are characteristic of Graham's looking-glass world of text. At the bottom of the sea is a Crete populated by 'heroic ghosts'. The invocation to his mother introduces another metaphor for this fall / sinking / dream, that of birth. The opposite metaphor, death by drowning, is implied by the trail of bubbles which he leaves behind. In this metaphor Crete is an afterlife, as implied by its ghosts. His arrival is analogous to a soldier going into battle, perhaps as part of an invading army. In this case his writing equipment is the equivalent of a weapon. Writing is also implied by the words / worlds that he trails behind him. (The Cretan poems have many symbolic allusions to writing, such as the black and white contrast between the garments of the women and the place-name 'The White Mountains', and the octopus, with its blinding sprays of ink, which is referred to in one of the Duncan manuscripts and figures later in section 71 of 'Implements' – *NCP*, p. 276).

This extraordinary complex of metaphors can be summarized as a series of statements about the speaker's experience:

— I dreamed I was in Crete

— I awoke in Crete

— I tripped and fell into Crete

— I sank (drowned) and found myself in Crete

— I was 'born' into Crete

— I invaded Crete

— I was met by Crete

— I was discovered by Crete

— I wrote about Crete.

It is possible to subordinate all these metaphors into a hierarchy. One may say that the speaker dreamed he was sinking through the sea into

Crete, that waking, falling, drowning, being born, invading, being met and being discovered are all metaphorical ways of describing this experience, and that the entire dream is a metaphor for the process of writing the poem. This structure can be represented thus:

Writing

    Dreaming

        Sinking

            {Waking

            {Falling

            {Drowning

            {Being born

            {Invading

            {Being met

            {Being discovered.

But while this structure is no doubt the way most readers would rationalize the poem, the overwhelming impression is of confusion, a drifting from metaphor to metaphor without being able to fix on one. Such drifting is characteristic both of a dream and of the early stages of writing. Indeed, in publishing his 'fragment', Graham was emulating the *Work in Progress* of his literary hero, Joyce, which also deals with a dream. Having satisfied himself that text is a frozen space rather than a dynamic one, he can only achieve a dreamlike fluidity, a state of creative flux, by refusing to complete the text. As long as the Art object is not finished, the distance separating it from community is not measurable. To finish the poem would be to awaken from the dream and realize that the wish it represents remains unfulfilled.

The lack of closure of the *Aquarius* text is typified by the nonsensical question 'why did you let / Me out of you both [. . .]?' which, as I mentioned in Chapter 2, fuses two of the avatars of Graham's mythical Fall, birth and the leaving of the family home. To finish the poem would have necessitated deciding between the two possible causes of his unhappiness. And yet, for Graham, life is best depicted as a series of falls, like going over a set of rapids, and any reversal of the process, any imaginary undoing of one of the falls, would still leave him already fallen. To go back to the time before birth, even in fantasy, would be to go back to a state before he existed as an individual capable of appreciating his unfallen state. An unfinished poem allows the expression of incoherent and even nonsensical desires.

In one of Duncan's manuscripts, the association of drowning and growing up is made more explicit.

> Now I am diving in one slow fall
> Out of my mother's arms into
> Myself at fifty-two going down
> Brightly beyond myself into
> Myself. Do you see how I go?

Another consequence of the incompleteness of the poem is apparent here. The manuscript depends on our knowledge of other versions in order to be fully understood, and this, as I noted in Chapter 1, is incompatible with the commodification of literature in contemporary Western culture; the mythic text is supposed to be an autonomous object. The image of the middle-aged poet falling out of his mother's arms is ludicrous in itself, but without the knowledge of the drowning theme (which is not mentioned in this draft), the phrase 'diving in one slow fall' makes no sense. This dependence of one text on another seems highly relevant to the themes of unity and separation stated in the lines themselves. The poem itself is reluctant to be born. It remains attached to the maternal body of the language.

It is easy enough to see why Graham was interested in dreams, but his desire to write about Crete requires some explanation. He wrote to Ronnie and Henriette Duncan on 31 October 1972:

> My time in Crete went in so deep. I can recall every wisp of it and I certainly must put down a poem about it.[9]

What was it about Crete that 'went in so deep'? One clue is provided by that other letter to the Duncans which I quoted earlier. The poem was to provide an equivalent of those capitalized mottoes Graham did not pin on his wall, 'HOME SWEET HOME' and 'BLESS THIS HOUSE'. Crete had reminded him of home.

We can see this in one of the Duncan manuscripts which suddenly breaks into prose, as if the undersea world he encountered was too big and detailed, too non-literary, to be contained in Graham's verse framework:

> When Demetrios enters with a pockmarked man from Athens, the taverna darkens. Introduced, I shake hands with the brother of a girl who used to sit in front of me at school in Greenock. He does not recognize me, but turns to talk of ballcocks and cisterns in ancient crows' nest

monasteries. He speaks in early Greek I know, but which I cannot under-
stand. His name is Elias. He wags his peppered jaw and spills his drach-
mas on the table for ouzo.

The five black-dressed women have left their preparations and now
they sit at another table. They know me but they will not look. They are
eating fish although I can't smell it. I am frightened one of them, the
nearest, might turn round and it would be my mother's face sitting talk-
ing to my aunt Julia. I slide down under the table and nobody sees me go.
It is even darker here. Their Greek feet are so delicate. Clawhammer toes,
shaggy ankles, goat-pads like sponges to leap and land on. I crouch here
but know I can stand up. Table-roof is soaring up over my head in the
dark. Nobody will believe. I can see it is funny. I know well I am not a
dwarf standing trying to listen in the octopus jar. I must speak to my
mother but she can't be here. If I could take off this mask.

The dream world he finds at the bottom of the sea is in some respects
foreign, but in others it is the Clydeside of his childhood. No doubt the
taverna in which he sees himself drinking ouzo is the equivalent of the
Cartsburn Vaults he mentions in 'What Is the Language Using Us For?'
among other poems (*NCP*, p. 201). He finds there the brother of a school-
friend and fears to find his mother and his aunt Julia. The talk is comi-
cally proletarian. He is both of this society and not of it, recognizing
Elias's Greek and not understanding it at the same time, ignored when
he speaks. The goats' feet and legs of the women serve a multiple func-
tion: goats are appropriate to a Greek landscape; the concept of satyrs
and fauns is part of Greek myth and emphasizes the doubleness of
everything that goes on in the dream (the landscape partakes equally of
Crete and the seabed, Greenock and abroad); finally, the image implies
that the women have not shaved their legs. They are not interested in
Western ideas of glamour, and are content to remain, in a phrase
deleted from the manuscript 'old black hags'. Perhaps in this respect
they remind Graham of the middle-aged or elderly women of his child-
hood.

In another of the Duncan manuscripts, he tells us:

[. . .] I have come
To meet my Greenock dead father
Who acts as quick as life wearing
His Sunday suit and no moustache.

Having left his parents in the Fall of the opening lines, he rejoins them
in Crete. He has come home. His time in Crete went in deep because the
working-class, maritime community he discovered there reminded him
of Greenock. Its rejection of some aspects of modernity (leg-shaving, for

example) must have contributed to the impression that he had stepped back in time. Similarly, the sense of kinship among the inhabitants had an intensity he associated with his past.

Once again, then, Graham has fallen asleep and dreamed of the community of his childhood. It has returned in garbled form, as real people and events turn up disguised in a dream: the men have moustaches which mark them as different from his clean-shaven father, ouzo is drunk instead of whisky or beer, goatherding and olive-growing rather than shipbuilding are the main industries. (In the later version, 'The Street of Knives', he uses the more industrial imagery of metal-working – *NCP*, p. 283, p. 309.) The dominant image of Crete, however, is the Scops owl. The Duncan manuscripts include such passages as:

POLEEP. POLEEP. It is the voice
Of Scop's owl in the banana grove.

POLEEP, POLEEP, the Crete owl says

POLEEP. POLEEP. Not our home sound.
It is Scop's owl, not knowing
I am a Scotsman overhearing.

And, as I have noted, it makes its appearance in the published poetry, too:

. . . POLEEP. POLEEP.
The owl calls through the olive grove.

(*NCP*, p. 243)

The call welcomes Graham to a dream version of his native community. 'POLEEP' is an anagram of 'PEOPLE'. This dream dissolved in language is 'where the people are'.

Syntax Gram and the Magic Typewriter

The late Robin Skelton's archive of Graham manuscripts, now in the library of the University of Victoria, Canada, contains one item in particular of exceptional interest. It is a copy of the book *Toward the Well-Being of Mankind* by Robert Shaplen which Graham has defaced with graffiti-like annotations and by pasting in prose manuscripts (I use the word to include typescripts, which the vast majority of them are) of his own.[10] It is these pasted-in pieces, the 'clusters' as I shall call them, that I want to consider in this section. Most of them are dated; Graham had the fortunate habit of dating manuscripts, often incorporating the date into the text or using it as part of a heading as one does with a letter. The manuscripts were written between 1967 and 1973. The book was used as a convenient medium for transmitting them to Skelton, who was paying Graham a small regular income in exchange for them. (Some of the material was also sent in the form of letters to his friend Ruth Hilton.)[11] These prose manuscripts are Graham's most intensive experiments with automatic writing, and represent an exceptionally frenzied spell of creative activity; many phrases and images which eventually appeared in his last two collections were generated in this way. Automatic writing was a significant factor in the production of Graham's late poetry.

'Clusters' was Graham's own word for his automatic prose, and one of the results of his commitment to this technique is the poem 'Clusters Travelling Out', which is also related to his interest in the Madron slaughterhouse and his much more structured efforts to write a poem about that. (There are so many drafts of 'Clusters Travelling Out' that Skelton devoted an entire folder to them.) But 'Implements in Their Places' owes still more to the clusters, both in its use of automatically generated phrases and images and in its fragmented structure. Clusters, then, have become 'implements', implying that Graham has fashioned useful objects out of naturally occurring formations. (I shall consider later the full significance of the peculiar vocabulary he applied to the products of his writing.)

Automatic writing presupposes an agency which will take power away from the conscious mind and thus make possible meanings which are unknown to it. This agency is usually identified with the Freudian unconscious, but for Graham, as we shall see, the agency was language itself, regarded as an entity possessing superhuman powers. André Breton's method of making contact with the agency was to write as quickly as possible:

> I resolved to obtain from myself [. . .] a monologue spoken as rapidly as possible without any intervention on the part of my critical faculties, a monologue consequently unencumbered by the slightest inhibition and which was, as closely as possible, akin to *spoken thought*. It had seemed to me, and still does [. . .] that the speed of thought is no greater than the speed of language, and that thought does not necessarily defy even the fastest moving pen. It was in this frame of mind that Philippe Soupault [. . .] and I decided to blacken some paper, with a praiseworthy disdain for what might result from a literary point of view.[12]

To write rapidly like this is the best way of obtaining unmediated access to what Breton calls neither 'the unconscious' nor 'language' but simply 'thought'. He regards speech as having privileged access to thought because it is faster than writing, so the speed of writing is an attempt to negate this distinction and so 'express [. . .] the actual functioning of thought'.[13] His formula for doing this is: 'Write quickly, without any preconceived subject, fast enough so that you will not remember what you're writing and be tempted to reread what you have written.'[14]

Whether it is necessary to refuse to correct what has been written in this way is a point on which Breton is not entirely clear. He praises Soupault because 'he constantly and vigorously opposed any effort to retouch or correct, however slightly, any passage which seemed to me unfortunate'. On the other hand, in a footnote, he observes that 'one is at the mercy of [. . .] outside distractions' and suggests that the automatic text may contain 'obvious weaknesses' which must be blamed on such distractions.[15] This is a possibility he takes into account in his instructions for novices in the technique:

> If you should happen to make a mistake – a mistake, perhaps due to care-lessness – break off without hesitation with an overly clear line. Following a word the origin of which seems suspicious to you, place any letter whatsoever, the letter 'l' for example, always the letter 'l', and bring the arbitrary back by making this letter the first of the following word.[16]

Breton accepts, then, the possibility that automatism will not always be successful. Something – conventional patterns of thought, or the conscious mind – will intervene in the transaction between writer and writing agency. How is the writer to know that the work produced is indeed the authentic product of this agency, unaffected by such interventions? For Breton, the test of authenticity is the quality that most readers would acknowledge as the distinguishing feature of Surrealist texts, 'their *extreme degree of immediate absurdity*'.[17] In the spontaneously-generated sentence which instigated his own experiments, this absurdity took the form of an incongruous image: 'There is a man cut in two by the window.'[18] Graham's automatic writing, too, as we shall see, is characterized by absurdity.

It seems clear that Graham composed the clusters swiftly, for they show signs of a feature which has been identified by J. Gratton in the writings of Breton as 'runaway', described as 'a creative *élan* [. . .], an impulse which thrives on critical moments of deflection, or even dislocation, yet releases an urge towards flux and sheer uninterruptedness', and as 'an agent of *radical continuity*.'[19] We have seen many times in the course of this study that flux is an important theme in Graham's poetry, and that it is represented both by the narrative shifts of a poem such as 'The Nightfishing' and by the use of liquid imagery. In the clusters, flux is a feature of the syntax – not for the first time, for he used unorthodox syntax sporadically throughout his career, in poems like 'The Dual Privilege' and 'Enter a Cloud', but more consistently and daringly than anywhere else in his work (*NCP*, p. 44, p. 216). He is taking runaway further than the Surrealists themselves took it, for their writing, as I remarked in Chapter 3, is well-formed; Graham's dreamlike distortions of words and syntax derive from *Finnegans Wake*.

Joyce, listed by Graham as one of the major influences on his poetry, was arguably the greatest and most durable of them all.[20] Although the Surrealists were the pioneers of automatic writing, Graham seems always to have associated it in his own practice with an attempt to imitate his literary hero. Explaining one of his manuscripts from the 1950s, he wrote (with a grammatical and orthographic carelessness itself reminiscent of the clusters):

> Automatic prose, part of which seem to me a little comic when it is not being to self-consciously punny. Rejoyce.[21]

Throughout his life he wrote letters in a playful, punning style imitated from *Finnegans Wake*, whose linguistic exuberance forms a link between the early poems and the clusters:

> Thus Tom Mick a Muse-meant for yews elf use Jams Joss – BUST IN HELL WARLID. Thus double in boy mucks goo. Ruskin wee day illso. O mush as end glims nigh so snorely noire arain the chummies' gabbles sloopin bemoth an a'sternlauft. Lay mint. Sick cloth to Waly Greymoo.[22]

He was also, as we have seen, obsessed with the theme of dreaming, which is Joyce's justification for his use of language in the novel. While the late dream poems are written in a lucid, almost oversimplified style, the clusters can be seen as the dark side, the unconscious, of that style.

Their syntactic flux often allows us to picture the process by which the clusters came into being. The following sentence, for example, is very characteristic of their dynamics: 'I can hear anything while father's ego sleeps bear his bones in my bones' ('Clusters', 21 March 1967). This suggests that he intended to write 'I can bear anything', but struck the wrong key on the typewriter ('B' and 'H' are adjacent on the keyboard); on noticing his mistake, he added the word at the point he had already reached, producing a change of direction by using the word in a different sense.

The appearance of so much of this material in greatly changed form in later poems shows that Graham regarded automatism as a starting-point for further work rather than an end in itself. This attitude is typical of the Surrealists, as Anna Balakian points out:

> These 'Surrealist texts', as they are called, must not be taken for poems. They are just a means of developing or enriching poetic consciousness.[23]

Indeed, Graham actually applied the method to poems he was already working on. In one manuscript, following an attempt to write a passage of verse which eventually became Implement number 51, he writes 'try it in clusters', and immediately switches to unpunctuated prose (*NCP*, p. 252, 'Clusters', 21 March 1967).

Most pages of the clusters begin with a title which is typed in capitals, and which is, given the nature of the exercise, more of a starting-point than a summary. André Breton and Paul Éluard had made use of titles to stimulate writing in their joint text *L'Immaculée Conception*.[24] If, as I suspect, this is a coincidence, it nevertheless demonstrates the extent of Graham's imaginative attunement with the movement Breton and others had founded some forty years earlier. It is mainly from these titles that I have been able to deduce the meaning of the word 'clusters'. One sheet has the title 'CLUSTERS TRAVELLING TOGETHER' ('Clusters', 21 March 1967). Others are simply headed 'CLUSTERS', 'C L U S T E R S' or 'c l u s t e r s' ('Clusters', 28 May 1967, 27 May 1967). Some headings are much more cryptic. One reads 'SYNTAXVOC THE CORN'S PEER OER GRAMMERSOW GANGBLIN' ('Clusters', 21 March 1967). While much apparent nonsense in the clusters is decipherable given a knowledge of Graham's themes, images and idiosyncratic vocabulary, this phrase continues to elude me, though it has clear references to syntax and grammar (his favourite joke on the Cornish word 'grammersow'). The effect in the titles of the unnatural syntax, which sometimes seems compressed, and the capital letters in a prominent position is reminiscent of a newspaper headline, and this impression was not lost on Graham, who parodied such a headline in the heading of one page:

CHINKS OF HOPE IN THE PALL OF GLOOM CHINKS OF GLOOM
IN THE PALL OF HOPE   SELFSHRINKING HEADS   SHARES
OF MARG ACHIEVE NEW CEILING   New low for low me.

('CLUSTERS', 15 March 1967)

The gist of this is an analogy between financial and personal depression. The headline style re-emerges several paragraphs later in the line:

ARTICULATED TRAILER LIFTS IMPEDIMENTED MAN OF 48

The 'impedimented man of 48' is, of course, Graham himself, whose 48th birthday was in November 1966, and who saw the condition of art as an 'impediment' to human relations and himself as maimed or 'Grahamstrung' (*NCP*, p. 154, p. 164, 'Clusters', 22 March 67). (There is also a connection with a knee injury he suffered falling off a roof.)[25] The 'articulated trailer' is his automatic writing, with its changes of direction (articulation) and continuity (trailing), which has made him feel better. 'Articulated' also means 'verbalized', and this punning account of text as articulated flux occurs also in 'The Nightfishing', in the phrase 'my ghostly constant is articulated' (*NCP*, p. 111).

Headings like this provide further clues to Graham's working methods. The parody headline 'CHINKS OF HOPE . . .' suggests that he took real or stereotypical texts and rearranged them in various ways, using the resulting combinations to generate ideas. Such modifications are a key component of poetry according to Riffaterre's theory; he would describe the original phrase as a 'hypogram', and uses the term 'scrambling' for this particular form of modification, in which elements of the hypogram are rearranged.[26] There are many clues in the clusters to this scrambling technique. The heading of one page reads 'SOMEWHERE BEGIN MUST WE BEGIN HEADTAIL TO TELL SOMEWHERE' ('Clusters', 22 March 1967)). Clearly, he has started with the phrase 'WE MUST BEGIN SOMEWHERE', an admission that he is so far devoid of ideas. He has reversed this to produce 'SOMEWHERE BEGIN MUST WE'. Then he has added another 'BEGIN' to produce a question ('MUST WE BEGIN') which fights against the initial (reversed) assertion while coexisting with it in the same sentence. Following this he has added a word descriptive of his method: 'HEADTAIL'. Then he has taken the second part of this compound word as a pun and used it to generate a familiar phrase 'TAIL [TALE] TO TELL'. Finally, by adding another 'SOMEWHERE' to the end, he produces a vague impression of a palindrome. These peculiar wordgames act as a kind of prompt to him, suggesting a possible direction for the rest of the piece. In this case, the phrase that counts is 'TAIL TO TELL', since it suggests to him the idea of writing a story, which he goes on to do.

An elaborate example of scrambling including reversal occurs in a piece without a heading. It begins with the following sentence:

'ITeenthirt March Four Two Seven away put started across which lumi-
nous sand know never shall.' ('Clusters', 13 March 1967.) 'Teenthirt' is an
obvious inversion of 'thirteen', at the level of syllables rather than
letters or words. Inverting the rest of the date, however, does not help,
since it has three numbers in it. The month 'March' itself has suggested
a pun, to which it is possible that two of the three numbers refer. The
four and the two may belong to a march rhythm of 1–2–3–4, while the
seven is what remains from the date 1967.[27] The sentence is a condensed
and scrambled form of the date 13 March 1967, and the statement 'I
march away across which luminous sand I shall never know.' The phrase
'put started' fits rather more awkwardly. Graham has 'started' his clus-
ter and his hope may be to put it 'across', though equally, since it is
private, he may be merely putting it 'away', as the sentence suggests
when read the other way round.

A phrase which confirms once and for all Graham's reliance on the
technique of inversion occurs on an undated page: 'Poet young A was
Maharg'. It is significant, I think, that this inverted form of the poet's
surname resembles the M- names of Beckett's novels, Murphy, Molloy,
Moran, Malone, Mahood – it is another in the series of shifting identities
which culminates in the fictive non-identity of the Unnamable (see
Chapter 5). This inversion, together with the fact that Graham used a
distorted form of the name 'SYDNEY GRAHAM' in the heading 'SYNTAX
GRAM AND THE MAGIC TYPEWRITER', suggests that the parody-head-
line discussed earlier, 'SHARES OF MARG ACHIEVE NEW CEILING', is
more complex than it appears ('Clusters', 21 March 1967). 'MARG' is the
inverted form of 'GRAM', or Graham. A new ceiling for Graham's
inverted self, the one that exists in the clusters, is, we are told, a 'new
low for low me'. The world of the clusters is a looking-glass world, for
Lewis Carroll, as well as Beckett, is a presence in them. The 'Maharg'
piece ends with an evocation of the inverted spirit of Madron:

> Nordam's a backword place. Her towers are deep. Her ups are furred with
> the softest down. Her beasts are bosom-slaps. Gnirps si gnimoc. LLEW-
> ERAF. Oireehc.

> ('CLUSTERS', NO DATE)

This inversion is associated with text in Graham's published work, too,
as in 'Approaches to How they Behave', when he states: 'Backwards the
poem's just as good', or in 'Untidy Dreadful Table' when he tells the
reader, 'Of course I see you backwards covered / With words backwards
from the other side' (*NCP*, p. 181, p. 206). The conceit underlying this is

that the writer is behind or underneath the words on the page and therefore 'on the other side / Of language' (*NCP*, p. 188, p. 310). To write is to submit to a reversal or scrambling of identity in order to permit oneself to become readable. This reversibility has been noted by Ong as a product of the objectification of language brought about by writing.[28] By turning his name backwards, Graham attempts to make himself a suitable inhabitant of the textual world. This is no doubt one reason why he insistently claims that his name does not belong in his work: the only appropriate form would be Maharg.

The clusters are full of puns, which are, in effect, another form of scrambling. The punning technique Graham favoured is paronomasia, the distortion of an original phrase which can be deduced by the reader. One might describe the trope as a process by which words are made to differ from themselves, retaining the context and memory of their original shape while acquiring a new one. In the space of this difference, new meanings are created. These devices are classified by Freud in his study of jokes as 'modification jokes'. An Italian example he gives 'is the well-known cry "*Traduttore – Traditore!*"' [Translator – traitor]. They have an obvious similarity to Freudian slips of the tongue or pen, and to mishearings or misreadings.[29]

A typical Graham paronomasia is the phrase:

> Sign me a right in the pillow of cloudy night. By day a fire-distinguisher.
>
> ('CLUSTERS', 13 March 1967)

The idea of a sign has suggested a passage from Exodus 13.xvii:

> And the Lord went before them by day in a pillar of cloud, to lead them the way; and by night in a pillar of fire, to give them light.

Graham distorts and condenses the passage even as he transcribes it, writing 'pillow of cloudy night' for 'pillar of cloud by night' and then apparently remembering that the pillar of cloud appeared by day and adding the phrase as an afterthought. Since he cannot go back and change anything, he must assign the fire to day instead of night. The pillars of cloud and fire are examples of signs, and the phrase 'sign me a right' (or 'aright') is the poet's request for such a sign. By transforming 'pillar' to 'pillow', Graham changes the signs seen by the Israelites in the desert into another kind of sign, a dream. The reassignment of cloud to night is appropriate both for the vagueness of a dream and the white fluffiness of a pillow. But this reversal has left him with the rather undramatic image of a pillar of fire by day which would be difficult to distinguish against its sunlit background, and this unsatisfactory image suggests another paronomasia, 'extinguisher' / 'distinguisher'. When the passage finds its way into 'Implements', however, all traces of the process which generated it have been removed. The two pillars have been separated, leaving the 'pillow of cloudy night' on its own in Implement 17 and the 'extinguisher' / 'distinguisher' contrast, reapplied to stars and birds, in Implement 46:

Sign me my right on the pillow of cloudy night

(*NCP*, p. 244)

By night a star distinguisher
Looking up through the signed air.
By day an extinguisher of birds
Of silence caught in my impatient
Too-small-meshed poet's net.

(*NCP*, p. 251)

The shared origin of these two verses remains detectable in the theme of signs and in the contrast between day and night which still structures number 46.

Another punning technique is the portmanteau, which Graham owes, like paronomasia, partly to Carroll and partly to Joyce.[30] The portmanteau fuses two source-words into an object-word, which, in most cases, did not previously exist. 'Childhood', for example, is not a portmanteau word, although it looks like a fusion of the words 'child' and 'hood' (and Graham experimented with splitting it into these components by the use of line-breaks – *NCP*, p. 171). In one passage, he lists the denizens of a verbal circus, many of which are portmanteau animals. 'Paragriphons', for example, are a cross between griffins and paragraphs, 'elephantinies' are tiny elephants, 'donkrses' are formed from 'donkeys' and 'arses' (overdetermined by a hidden pun on 'ass'), and 'zebracorns' from zebras and unicorns ('Clusters', 21 March 1967). The attraction of these animals is that they exist only as words, so that to invent them is to inhabit a Wonderland or looking-glass world of language.[31] Indeed, some of their constituent animals are themselves mythical beasts such as the unicorn and the griffin, the latter already a cross between an eagle and a lion.

Graham's automatic writing technique in the clusters appears to be related to Breton's advice to 'bring the arbitrary back'. Whereas Breton recommended doing this by putting down a letter at random, Graham did it by rearranging the letters, syllables or words of whatever he was planning to write, using the resultant absurdity to generate a writing temporarily liberated from conscious planning. A phrase from one of the clusters, when unscrambled, gives us a rather touching portrait of the writer at this quixotic task: 'my hear can back to back killing echo' ('Clusters', 13 March 1967). 'Back to back', like the 'HEADTAIL' we have already considered, must be a metapoetic description of his inversion technique, for the three words which precede it, when reversed, read 'can hear my'. The only possible object to be found for this sentence-frag-ment is 'killing echo'. He was, after all, using a typewriter. The echo of his keys must have been a reminder that he was alone, engaged, not in a dialogue with another human being, but in an attempt to converse with the language itself.

Indeed, the clusters reveal, perhaps more clearly than any of his other writings, his devotion to a superhuman language which he equates with community and femininity. In a passage of lucid expository prose buried among them he wrote:

> The thing is to find or create (in this case the same thing) a language, a timbre of thought or voice, which I will live in. It will never be adequate except for its moment but it will be the nearest to my soul speaking and as I change so it shall.
>
> ('CLUSTERS', 19 March 1967. See also *NFM*, p. 210)

Language cannot be personal because it transcends the personal, because individuals participate in it rather than creating it. As Blanchot has pointed out, if automatic writing puts us in touch with language, it does so only at the expense of our individuality and hence of the power to speak.[32] But for Graham this transcendence is analogous to the way a community transcends the personal. The nearest he can come to person-alizing language, therefore, is to create a home for himself in it, some-where he can live, just as an individual's relationship to the community is defined geographically, as a home. It is only by colonizing writing in this way that he can come close to abolishing the difference between writing and speech, to create a written 'voice'.

Language, then, is a form of community which Graham strives to turn into a home. The focus of a home for him, as I argued in Chapter 2, is the mother, and therefore to create a home in language is to discover a mother. Graham found precedents for this maternal presence within language, as Lopez has shown, in the traditional concept of the Muse, in particular as expounded by Robert Graves in *The White Goddess*.[33] In one of the clusters, this figure is invoked as follows:

Cuntess Muse, her stays enlocked stitched wornout to the gloves of Astra Khan. As little cistern closets mingle to big sea sewers so rushed thundering negativwards his last fake frantic experients in keeping mum. Is the word?

('CLUSTERS', 15 March 1967)

The Countess with her aristocratic yet carnal title and astrakhan gloves is also a celestial tyrant ('Astra Khan' as in Genghis Khan). Language is both a formidable restraint ('stays enlocked') and a frayed and tattered material ('stitched wornout'). In the next sentence, language is represented by the sea, as it is in 'The Nightfishing' and related poems. The relationship of the individual utterance to the system, of *parole* to *langue* in Saussure's terms, is that of a river to the sea it flows into, but this fairly conventional analogy is given a scatological turn so that the sea is also a sewer filled by the product of individual 'little cistern closets'.[34] (There is a pun here, characteristically involving kinship: the 'little cistern closets' and the 'big sea sewers' are sisters.) It is true, of course, that utterances modify the language, but the reverse flow was more important to Graham, since he was deliberately trying to open himself to the promptings of the personified language, to become the voice of the Muse. In his case, therefore, the river flows 'negativwards' (one reason for his cult of inversion). 'Mum', the maternal muse, may be a kept woman, but does he have the 'experients' to keep her? These 'frantic experi[m]ents' are his attempts to do so, but in the silence of writing ('mum is the word') he is forced to rely on the dubious meanings of words isolated from the personal context of speech, leaving him with an unfinished question: 'Is the word?'

A sentence in an earlier piece also equates maternity and language: 'Fluxy mother me utters to abridge us time again' ('Clusters', 13 March 1967). Language is fluid, feminine, generative and dominating – a fluxy mother. (The adjective suggests the themes which we have traced in Graham's work above all of the middle period, but it alludes also to menstruation.) Her offspring, the poetic utterance is, as so many of Graham's poems complain static, unlike the mother who has given birth to it. If *langue*, the entity with which he is trying to communicate in automatic writing, is feminine and equated with the mother, Graham identifies the other term of this binary opposition, *parole*, with the masculine and the son. In a passage probably written on the same day as the 'Cuntess Muse' cluster, we read:

What are you frightened for it's all language. We're in it somewhere.

Lines and spaces. Good boys all deserving doubtful favours.

('CLUSTERS', no date)

'We're in it somewhere' is another way of saying that 'the shape of all of
us in [the] language', except that that 'somewhere' demonstrates the
perplexity of the poet as he tries to find his home in this daunting
community. Graham's ultimate model of a community is always the
family, or rather his own family. Hence the 'good boys', for his family
was one with two boys. The phrase 'good boys all deserving doubtful
favours' is of course an adaptation of the mnemonic for the lines of a
musical stave. He is comparing language, a system of differences, with
music, a system of intervals or 'lines and spaces'. We may surmise that
it is the spaces he is frightened of. Language's favours to 'good boys' are
doubtful because it has, in Saussure's formulation, 'no positive terms'.[35]
Indeed, if the lines of the stave are equated with boys, we can go further
and suggest that the spaces represent not just difference but femininity.
The combination of sex, music and language continues:

> Suffle your molecules all guys between Madhoven fucks Cecilia's daugh-
> ters who lose their keys in the shoe-string band. It's gramar as wolf kills
> us better. Melt predicate unparsable with which us cares for laughs.

The guys (lines) are between the girls (spaces). The shuffling of the mole-
cules is the process of rearranging words which Graham is currently
engaged in. Madhoven, the Madron equivalent of Beethoven (who is
perhaps mad) has sex with the daughters of Cecilia, the patron saint of
music, who have lost their phallic keys. Grammar is also 'grandma', the
wolf in 'Little Red Riding Hood', who kills 'us', no doubt the same 'us'
who are 'in it somewhere'. Language is the matriarch which kills and
swallows the individual. The last sentence really is 'unparsable' and a
predicate missing a subject. Presumably it is grandma who has eaten
the subject and melted the predicate, leaving the sentence unparsable.

In these examples, we see that the feminine language where Graham
is trying to find a home is associated with anxiety as well as longing.
Language is a Big Bad Wolf, a Cuntess Muse. This anxiety about the femi-
nine is a familiar theme of psychoanalysis, and an investigation of the
clusters reveals a thinly disguised castration symbolism. I have
suggested that the uttered 'me', the *parole*, is masculine and identified
with Graham himself. It is also identified with the male genitals, seen as
isolated from the body to which they belong. Words, in Graham's shift-
ing terminology, are 'molecules', 'clusters', 'implements', 'particles', all
terms that could be taken as euphemisms for the male genitals. This last

word occurs shortly after the passage we have just looked at: 'some-
where our belonging particals believe'. This phrase was later used in the
couplet which opens and closes 'Implements in Their Places':

> Somewhere our belonging particles
> Believe in us. If we could only find them.

(NCP, p. 240, p. 257)

The word 'particles' refers to linguistic fragments, and is also a diminu-
tive suggesting a possibly rather pathetic smallness. However, remem-
bering the prevalence of portmanteau words in the clusters and that
this passage has its origins there, I would suggest that the word in this
instance is overdetermined by a similar wordplay: Graham treats it as if
it were constructed from a combination of 'parts' and 'testicles'. (Indeed,
the phrase 'private particles' appears in a cluster of 22 March 1967.)
Suddenly this rather cryptic complaint makes sense. The poem is cut off
from the poet like genitals cut off from the male body. To be in language
offers the fantasy of being reunited with the mother, but the price paid
for such pleasurable union is absorption into a feminine system of
differences, one's lines swallowed by female spaces, a good boy receiving
extremely doubtful favours. Once again, the union takes place in that
mysterious 'somewhere', a home the poet can never find because he has
been cast out from it. Graham's claim that he is 'maimed' or 'impedi-
mented' can now be seen to be something more than a romantic asser-
tion of the stigma of genius. It is easy to see that there is a genuine
neurotic guilt behind this imagery, and that his quest for a union with
the language is also a quest for a reunion with his home and mother,
and between the separated parts of his own self.

The themes of exile and castration are linked in the clusters. The
condition of separation is both Graham's crime (he has rejected his
upbringing by leaving home and becoming a writer), his punishment
(he feels deprived of human contact) and his hope of redemption
(language may provide him with an alternative home, though one that
will never be truly satisfactory). In terms of the castration metaphor, the
text is isolated from its author like castrated genitals, but it may still be
able to achieve a kind of remote sexual contact with the reader.
Graham's descriptions of words often imply that they have a subhuman
life of their own, and is reminiscent of the mischievous independence
sometimes ascribed to the penis in popular culture. Words are beasts, as
in the following passage:

> These words (Who they were? The beasts!) recorded it past me, the blem-
> ish thus now this is so them now each paticle agog for changing into light
> not fast enough for finishing events of their own. Language or silence
> illmannered leave me for saying my own piece alone to share another.
> Whose fragments afloat in memory's distorting distortions of space still
> carry kindly an echo of their original? Speaking's for putting down nerve-
> end highjinks somersaulted arestoelbow in a destined oner.
>
> ('CLUSTERS', 21 March 1967)

This passage anticipates the exclamation 'the beasts!' in Implement 52 (*NCP*, p. 252). Words are animated, made into independent agents, by writing. The problem ('blemish') here is that the words are not being put down fast enough to take over entirely. They change into light, that is, become visual rather than aural, but do not succeed in 'finishing events of their own'. Separated from the body of language, the particles are 'fragments'. Exiled to space, they suffer 'distorting distortions' like those to which conventional syntax is subjected by Graham's own automatic prose. There is another buried sexual metaphor here, one familiar enough from Derrida's deconstruction of Rousseau: writing ('saying my own piece alone') is analogous to masturbation, speech to sex ('to share another'). Graham's description of speech 'nervend highjinks somer-saulted arestoelbow') has a clear sexual charge.[36]

So far I have written as if the Oedipal theme of the clusters were entirely represented by Graham's frustrated longing for his mother. But the Freudian family romance is, at the least, a triangle, and castration anxiety is directed at the father rather than the mother. One manifesta-tion of the father in the clusters, as elsewhere in Graham's work, is God, who turns up in an inverted disguise in the sentence: 'To say what to who for reason such as why in the name of Dog.' ('Clusters', 15 March 1967). The same Dog / God, inverted by writing and possessing the phal-lic, animal qualities of Graham's verbal beasts, appears in the published poem 'Dear Who I Mean' as a 'quick brown pouncing god' (*NCP*, p. 161).[37]

As Freud remarked, the fear of the outraged and castrating father is complicated by the son's love for him.[38] In 'Notes on a Poetry of Release', Graham showed a certain pride in the fact that 'my history has my eyes and mouth and a little likeness of my father' (*NFM*, p. 379). His guilt separates him from his father as well as his mother, and it is his father who punishes him, at least in his fantasies; however, since the guilt is of heterosexual origin, it is also something father and son have in common, a bond between them. The automatic prose of 21 March 1967 (a particularly productive day) contains the seed of some of this later writing:

I can hear anything while father's ego sleeps bear his bones in my bones
for ever beside the horde unlimited stretching back to the branivin
lizards bottled in the ouzo marches.

I have already discussed the correction Graham made here. Perhaps he
found the idea of a son bearing his father too feminine, however, for he
removed it from the version which eventually appeared in Implement 7:

My father's ego sleeps in my bones
And wakens suddenly to find the son
With words dressed up to kill or at
The least maim for life another
Punter met in the betting yard.

(*NCP*, p. 241)

This Oedipal theme of conflict and equivalence between father and
son is also present in Graham's ballad 'The Broad Close' (*NCP*, pp. 141–5).
Words are the son's weapon against the father, but the permanence of
writing means that the latter is never really dead, while the inter-
changeability of person it makes possible means that the son and the
father become identical. Words are both castrated 'particles' and pene-
trating 'implements'. Whatever violence the son may carry out against
the father, the latter is always preserved in the 'magic medium' of
language, as if by bottling. The only way back to the family is through
language with its permanent traces of 'the horde unlimited'. The
'branivin lizards' whatever they may be, are bottled in ouzo, which is
associated with Crete and the possibility of rediscovering his family
through a community which reminded Graham of the Greenock of his
childhood.

Paradoxically, then, writing, because of its permanence, is a link to
the father, offering a substitute for heredity. But what precisely is
preserved? The father's recognition of his son is symbolized by the pass-
ing on of his name. For Graham, as we saw in Chapter 5, naming is prob-
lematized in the realm of writing, a shadowy place haunted by shifting
pronouns where numbers are more appropriate. This theme continues
a little later in the passage:

Only let me begin a new life ignorant of an old other. Make me twig No.
999955 on the greatest oak in a forest of terrible thousands. But save me
from life as a dressing-table leg. Make me a puffball, healthy and true, but
save me from the chopsticks of the Red Guard. Make me forget to stir the
lentil pot of my moral broth. Make me make. Make me make me.

In this passage, which anticipates Implement 59 with its discussion between numbered twigs, he is, once again, trying to find his name in the linguistic wood (*NCP*, p. 254). In the automatic writing, it should be remembered, he is communing with his Muse, the personified spirit of language, and it is not surprising, therefore, that the words should have the form of a prayer. He asks to forget his 'old other' life, the world of Greenock, and begin a new one. He will be satisfied, he says, with being a number. What he asks is not to be cut off, a fate that combines alienation and castration: 'Save me from life as a dressing-table leg'. It is perhaps the castration theme that generates the otherwise incongruous image of the puffball. (The way puffballs reproduce by puffing out their spores also gives them an appropriateness as a phallic symbol. In addition to this, some woodland varieties, as Graham may well have known, have phallic-looking stalks.) His ambivalence about communities in general and his own place in them is shown by the phrase 'save me from the chopsticks of the Red Guard'. This clearly started out as 'save me from the chop', and the fact that the line ends at this point perhaps gave Graham the idea of one of his trick enjambments. The 'chop' he is frightened of needs no further explanation, but the 'chopsticks of the Red Guard' are somewhat more difficult. He is afraid both of being turned into chopsticks (as he was of becoming a dressing-table leg) and of being eaten. The transformation of the word allows him to make a connection to another image of a depersonalizing community, Communist China, famous for its enormous population and with a reputation for treating that population in a mechanically systematic way – associated, that is, with numbers of people, and with giving people numbers.

From the Red Guard, Graham makes a huge jump to 'the lentil pot of my moral broth'. The connection, of course, is food, but where he was afraid of being eaten before, here he seems to be doing the cooking. And why lentils, which hardly seem the right diet for the Chinese? The answer is to be found in the story of Jacob and Esau in the Bible. Graham, who was himself an elder brother, is identifying with Esau, the elder brother of Jacob, who 'came out red' from the womb.[39] (This is another connection to the Red Guard.) Esau was tricked out of his birthright by his younger brother Jacob in exchange for a 'red pottage [. . .] of lentiles' (another occurrence of the colour red). The story ends: 'thus Esau despised his birthright'.[40] In Graham's version, it is he, the elder brother, who is the cook, for he cannot blame his brother for tricking him out of his birthright. The mess of pottage of the biblical story has become a 'moral broth', soup and brother at the same time. He worries that his own cooking (or writing) activities constitute the despising of his birthright, the anxiety that we have traced throughout his career. His prescription for this anxiety is, as always, to carry on as before, constructing poetic objects ('make me make') and, at the same time, a new identity ('make me make me'). This identity will be defined not by any living community but by the community of language; it will be a thing of words rather than flesh and blood, not Sydney Graham but Syntax Gram.

Graham Through the Looking Glass

Graham's unpublished writing is his attempt to escape from the fixity and impersonality he associates with printed text, to bathe in the sea of language without freezing to death in the Arctic of the completed poem. That is why there is so much of it. The late unpublished writing constitutes almost an alternative oeuvre to the poems of *Malcolm Mooney's Land* and *Implements in Their Places*, one whose creative energy and radical technique represents a remarkable avant-garde challenge to the institution of literature.[41] Perhaps in his dreams and clusters Graham has come as close as it is possible to come to what Barthes called the 'writerly' text, since it is necessary in effect to make a text of it for oneself, to finish its writing, before one can begin to read it.[42] In challenging readers to this task, Graham is also challenging the commodification of literature to which he so uneasily acquiesced in the late published poems.

At the same time, there is something tragic about these projects, as there is about his career as a whole. Like all his work, they are an attempt to achieve the impossible, to combine absolute control with absolute love. On the one hand, the shifting metaphors of 'A Dream of Crete' and the runaway syntax of the clusters approximates to the flux of the lifeworld to which he had sought to find a written equivalent from the middle period on, but on the other this flux is achieved at the cost of a greater isolation than that of any published text. Automatic writing is apparently a means of submitting oneself to a force beyond one's own will, and Graham, as we have seen, regarded this force not as an unconscious part of his psyche but as a transcendent community; he believed that he was giving up control to his 'fluxy mother', language. Nevertheless, he kept the products of these experiments private.

Although he shared some of them with selected individuals, he refrained from introducing them into the public arena where control would be shared by the community of readers. He wanted to keep his mother to himself.

The clusters, like some of the late poems, are reminiscent of Lewis Carroll. 'A Dream of Crete', too, with its slow descent into a magical world of hallucinatory transformations, has much in common with the adventures of Alice. In Chapter 1, I suggested that Graham valued the autonomy of the text because he saw it as a playground where he could amuse himself without interference from others – and Wonderland and the looking-glass world are the ultimate children's playgrounds, playgrounds where reality itself is kept out. For Elizabeth Sewell, nonsense is primarily a game, and as such requires control of that which is to be played with; in nonsense literature like the Alice books, words (and indeed numbers) are 'safe, distinct and manageable' playthings affording such entertainment.[43] Far from submitting himself to the control of language, then, it may be that Graham in his wordplay is exercising a control of his own. Jean-Jacques Lecercle has argued that 'non-sense is also meta-sense' and that 'nonsense texts are reflexive texts'.[44] My own theory of Graham's reflexivity, advanced in Chapter 1, is that it is an attempt to defeat the indeterminacy of language, to exert an individual control over its social nature. It seems possible, then, to put these three assertions together and conclude that these writings seek control by means of the self-referentiality of nonsense.

Before we settle for this formula, however, there are some objections to be dealt with. The first of these is that Lecercle sees the orthodox syntax of classic nonsense literature as a crucial part of its attempt to impose order on chaos, and points out that Carroll actually advocated the reform of spelling to make this second aspect of language more precise; this punctiliousness is in striking contrast to Graham's wild syntax and erratic spelling.[45] But this only shows that Graham was not a classic nonsense-writer. He did not have the education of Victorian gentlemen like Carroll and Lear and his grasp of formal orthographic and grammatical rules was never very confident. It would have been beyond him to create a Wonderland on Carroll's mathematical lines, but he was still capable of seeing its attraction. Nonsense was only one of the constituents of his fantasy world, together with such influences as Surrealism and *Finnegans Wake*.

The second possible objection to seeing the unpublished writing as a variety of nonsense is Sewell's interesting opposition between game and dream: 'in dreams [...] things are not separate and controllable and the mind cannot play with them'.[46] Dream, for her, is the opposite of control since the dreamer is entirely at the mercy of his or her hallucinated reality, and this would suggest that 'A Dream of Crete', at any rate, cannot be a fantasy of control. But she has to admit that the transformations of dream run through the Alice books, as games do: the opposition, that is, is internal to nonsense.[47] The point, surely, is that to write a dream is not to lose control, but to play at doing so and thus to exercise a kind of control over the most uncontrollable area of one's life. There is also, as we have seen, another aspect of dreams which makes them most desirable as playthings – they are entirely private and thus not liable to any interference from other people. A voluntary dream, if such existed, would be the best toy of all.

This brings us to the third objection, which is that Graham's intention is ostensibly to relinquish control, not to exert it. In leaving his poem unfinished or submitting his prose writings to the chance intervention of typographical errors and the promptings of an unknown part of his psyche, he liberates his work from the tidiness and rationality of the conscious mind, and thus puts himself at the service of a power greater than himself, language. And yet his treatment of this language, particularly in the clusters, is hardly that of a servant: he coins new words, distorts and parodies established phrases and rearranges conventional syntax. In effect, he is trying to make language his own, a plaything and a private domain, taking its creative use beyond the limits which a conventionally minded reading public would normally insist on. The great nonsense philosopher of language is, of course, Humpty Dumpty, who insisted on being its master.[48] Graham's attitude is more complex – he insists on being mastered, but on his own carefully stipulated terms.

'A Dream of Crete' and the clusters, then, mark both the culmination of Graham's quest for a community of language and a sort of *reductio ad absurdum* of it, and with them we reach the end of this study. We have seen how in the early poems he celebrated text as a closed-off space where he could demonstrate his prowess and energy. The flux of the life-world was only admitted to this playground to be transformed into textual stasis. The themes of love and community that were to become all-important to him are present here, but they do not disturb his concentration as he plays his verbal games. In the poems of the middle period, however, there is evidence of a deep anxiety about the theme of community, a theme which he dramatized in his poems of drowning.

He still believed in the autonomy of language, but it now became neces-
sary for him to prove through his rhetoric that language was an alter-
native community, more powerful and demanding than the one he felt
he had deserted, but at the same time lacking its human substance and
satisfactions. In 'The Nightfishing' – in my opinion, his greatest achieve-
ment – he attempts to chart the process by which the flux of the life-
world is transformed into static moments not only by writing but also
by memory. He thus comes close to abolishing the distinction between
life and text which was still so valuable to him. In the late poems, his
emphasis is on the inadequacy of his chosen substitute for community,
the frozen fixity of text rather than the living flux of the sea of
language. He demonstrates both his public-spiritedness and the limita-
tions of text by his attempts to use it as a conduit to communicate with
the reader, while community continues to be the object of his nostalgic
and guilty dreams. Finally, the unpublished writings bring us almost
back to where we started. They are verbal games whose privacy allows
him greater freedom than was possible in his published work.
Nevertheless, he still feels the necessity of justifying them in communal
terms by insisting that it is language, his fluxy mother, who masters
him rather than the other way about.

Ironically, this is true. Language is communal property and individu-
als, *pace* Humpty Dumpty, cannot control it. Even in his private games,
Graham had to take the language as a given which he then attempted to
manipulate within the limits of his own socially acquired linguistic
capacity, and once he made the decision to send the manuscripts to
friends the words became hostages to indeterminacy. His error as I see it
was to believe that language's overpowering community was closed and
therefore only analogous to the communities of the lifeworld instead of
being part of them. Its communal power was thus magical, the power of
the dead rather than the living, and Graham invoked it both to excuse
his adventures in the playground of the text and to explain why they
never offered him the control he sought. Now his words and his reputa-
tion are entirely in the hands of others. For my part, I think he is an
extraordinary poet. His wit and imagination are dazzling and the inge-
nuity of his rhetoric deeply impressive. He is a brilliant expositor of
language's indeterminacy, its failure to act as a conduit and the impos-
sibility of using it for the mimesis of flux; his view of it as closed is
deeply engrained in twentieth-century Western culture, and for that
reason alone his attempts to reconcile this condition with the demands
of community would repay study. His notions of text as the locus of

absolute control and community as that of absolute love are indeed myths, but myths, as we all know, are the raw material of literature. Besides, poets have embraced worse myths in the last hundred years, and few more interesting.

Notes

Introduction

1 Tony Lopez, *The Poetry of W.S. Graham* (Edinburgh, Edinburgh University Press, 1989), p. 1. (Subsequent references to this study will use the abbreviation *PWSG*).

2 *PWSG*, pp. 1–2.

3 Robert Frame, 'W.S. Graham at Sandyford Place' *Edinburgh Review* (February 1987) , no. 75, 60–65 (pp. 60–61). (This issue commemorating Graham will hereafter be referred to as ER.) W.S. Graham, *Cage Without Grievance* (Glasgow: Parton Press, 1942).

4 *PWSG*, pp. 3–5.

5 *PWSG*, pp. 6–7; Nancy Wynne-Jones, 'W.S. Graham in Cornwall', ER, 66-9.

6 W.S. Graham, *The Seven Journeys* (Glasgow: William Maclellan, 1944), *2ND Poems* (London: Nicholson and Watson, 1945), *The White Threshold* (London: Faber and Faber, 1949), *The Nightfishing* (London: Faber and Faber, 1955), *Malcolm Mooney's Land* (London: Faber and Faber, 1970), *Implements in Their Places* (London: Faber and Faber, 1977), *Collected Poems: 1942–1977* (London: Faber and Faber, 1979), *Selected Poems* (New York: Ecco Press, 1980).

7 *PWSG*, p. 3.; Frank Ruhrmund, 'Literary World Mourns W.S. Graham', *The Cornishman*, 16 January 1986, p. 1.

8 Letter to Edwin Morgan, 23/11/49, quoted in Edwin Morgan, 'W.S. Graham: A Poet's Letters', *ER*, 39–48 (p. 44).

9 Penelope Mortimer, A Poet's Interview With Himself', *Observer Magazine*, 19 November 1978, pp. 61–2.

10 *PWSG*, p. 6.

¹¹ W.S. Graham, *New Collected Poems*, ed. by Matthew Francis (London: Faber and Faber, 2004).

Chapter One

¹ F. de Saussure, *Course in General Linguistics*, ed by Charles Bally and Albert Sechehaye, with the collaboration of Albert Riedlinger, trans. by Roy Harris (London: Duckworth, 1983); Noam Chomsky, 'On Cognitive Capacity' in *Reflections on Language* (London: Temple Smith, 1976), pp. 3–35; Friedrich Nietzsche, 'On Truth and Lies in a Nonmoral Sense' in *Philosophy and Truth: Selections from Nietzsche's Notebooks of the Early 1870's*, trans. and ed. by Daniel Breazeale (New Jersey: Humanities Press, 1979), pp. 79–97 (p. 84); Jacques Derrida, *Of Grammatology*, trans. by Gayatri Chakravorty Spivak (Baltimore: Johns Hopkins University Press, 1976), pp. 3–5; Edward Sapir, 'The Status of Linguistics as a Science' in *Selected Writings of Edward Sapir: In Language, Culture and Personality*, ed. by David G. Mandelbaum (Berkeley: University of California Press, 1949), pp. 160–8 (p. 162); Benjamin Lee Whorf, 'The Relation of Habitual Thought and Behaviour to Language' in *Language, Thought and Reality: Selected Writings of Benjamin Lee Whorf*, ed. by John B. Carroll (New York: John Wiley & Sons, 1962), pp. 134–59; Jacques Lacan, 'The Direction of the Treatment and the Principles of Its Power' in *Écrits: A Selection*, trans. by Alan Sheridan (London: Routledge, 1980), pp. 226–80 (p. 234).

² *PWSG*, p. 2.

³ From a 1949 notebook in the National Library of Canada, Ottawa (Elizabeth Smart Papers, Series J). I am assuming that 'read' here is an imperative rather than a past tense. The notebook is not a diary, and there would be little point in keeping lists of books one had already read.

⁴ Michael J. Reddy, 'The Conduit Metaphor: A Case of Frame Conflict in Our Language About Language' in *Metaphor and Thought*, ed. by Andrew Ortony, 2nd ed. (Cambridge, Cambridge University Press, 1993), pp.164–201.

⁵ George Lakoff and Mark Johnson, *Metaphors We Live By* (Chicago: University of Chicago Press, 1980), p. 10.

⁶ Reddy, 'The Conduit Metaphor', pp. 189–201.

⁷ Reddy, 'The Conduit Metaphor', p. 168, p. 166.

⁸ Reddy, 'The Conduit Metaphor', pp. 171–4.

⁹ Catherine Belsey, *Critical Practice* (London: Routledge, 1980), p. 4; Colin MacCabe, *James Joyce and the Revolution of the Word* (London: Macmillan, 1978), p. 14.

¹⁰ Antony Easthope, *Poetry as Discourse* (London: Methuen, 1983), pp. 11–12; Roman Jakobson, 'Linguistics and Poetics' in *Selected Writings*, ed. by Stephen Rudy, 6 vols (The Hague: Mouton, 1981), III, pp. 18–51 (p. 21).

¹¹ Reddy, 'The Conduit Metaphor', p. 188.

12 Reddy, 'The Conduit Metaphor', pp. 176–7.

13 Lakoff and Johnson, *Metaphors We Live By*, p. 6; George Lakoff and Mark Turner, *More Than Cool Reason: A Field Guide to Poetic Metaphor* (Chicago: University of Chicago Press, 1989), p. 2.

14 Lakoff and Johnson, *Metaphors We Live By*, pp. 7–9.

15 Lakoff and Turner, *More Than Cool Reason*, p. 66.

16 Lakoff and Johnson, *Metaphors We Live By*, p. 8.

17 Lakoff and Johnson, *Metaphors We Live By*, p. 13, pp. 10–13.

18 Lakoff and Johnson, *Metaphors We Live By*, pp. 236–7.

19 Lakoff and Johnson, *Metaphors We Live By*, pp. 65–8.

20 Lakoff and Turner, *More Than Cool Reason*, pp. 8–9. See also their analysis of a Shakespeare sonnet on pp. 26–34.

21 Lakoff and Turner, *More Than Cool Reason*, pp. 1–8.

22 Sigmund Freud, 'Negation' in *On Metapsychology: The Theory of Psychoanalysis*, trans. by James Strachey, ed. by Angela Richards (Harmondsworth: Penguin, 1984), pp. 437–42. See also Michael Riffaterre, *Semiotics of Poetry* (Bloomington: Indiana University Press, 1978), p. 54.

23 Lakoff and Johnson, *Metaphors We Live By*, pp. 14–21.

24 Reddy, 'The Conduit Metaphor', p. 189.

25 For Lopez, however, the voyage is one of self-discovery, *PWSG*, p. 24, pp. 126–7.

26 Reddy, 'The Conduit Metaphor', p. 191.

27 Reddy, 'The Conduit Metaphor', p. 192.

28 Lakoff and Johnson, *Metaphors We Live By*, p. 12.

29 Stanley Fish, 'Is There a Text in This Class?' in *Is There a Text in This Class: The Authority of Interpretive Communities* (Cambridge, MA: Harvard University Press, 1980), pp. 303–21.

30 J.L. Austin, *How to Do Things With Words* (Oxford: Clarendon Press, 1962), pp. 142–3.

31 Walter J. Ong, *Orality and Literacy: The Technologizing of the Word* (London: Methuen, 1982), p. 31.

32 Ong, *Orality and Literacy*, p. 91; 'The written form of a word strikes us as a permanent, solid object', Saussure, *Course in General Linguistics*, p. 26.

33 Ong, *Orality and Literacy*, p. 32.

34 Ong, *Orality and Literacy*, p. 136.

35 Ong, *Orality and Literacy*, pp. 78–9.

36 Ong, *Orality and Literacy*, p. 126.

37 Ong, *Orality and Literacy*, p. 78, pp. 102–3.

38 Ong, *Orality and Literacy*, p. 130.

39 Derrida, *Of Grammatology*, p. 7.

40 Ong, *Orality and Literacy*, p. 169.

41 Derrida, *Of Grammatology*, p. 12.

42 Derrida, 'Signature Event Context' in *Margins of Philosophy*, trans. by Alan Bass (Brighton: Harvester Press, 1982), pp. 309–30 (p. 311).

43 Graham, letter to Ronnie and Henriette Duncan, 15/4/73 in Ronnie Duncan's collection of Graham manuscripts, quoted in Ruth Grogan, '"Dear Pen Pal in the Distance": A Selection of W.S. Graham's Letters', *PN Review*, 16, no. 5 (1989), 14–21. (p. 16).

44 Ong, *Orality and Literacy*, p. 102; Derrida, 'Signature Event Context', p. 316.

45 Graham, letter to Ronnie and Henriette Duncan, 24/1/76, Duncan Collection, quoted in Grogan, 'Dear Pen Pal', p. 18, letter to Ronnie and Henriette Duncan, 24/3/80, Duncan Collection.

46 Graham, letter to Ronnie and Henriette Duncan, 12/2/72, Duncan Collection.

47 Ong, *Orality and Literacy*, p. 74.

48 *PWSG*, p. 82.

49 David Wright, 'W.S. Graham in the Forties: Memories and Conversations', *ER*, 49–56 (p. 55).

50 'For isn't the writer dead as soon as the work exists? He sometimes has such a presentiment himself: an impression of being ever so strangely out of the work.' Maurice Blanchot, *The Space of Literature*, trans. by Ann Smock (Lincoln: University of Nebraska Press, 1982), p. 23.

51 Roland Barthes, 'The Death of the Author' in *Image, Music, Text* trans. by Stephen Heath (London: Fontana, 1977), pp. 142–148.

52 Gayatri Chakravorty Spivak, 'Translator's Preface' in Derrida, *Of Grammatology*, pp. ix-xc (p. xvii).

53 Ludwig Wittgenstein, *Philosophical Investigations*, trans. by G.E.M. Anscombe (Oxford: Basil Blackwell, 1963), pp. 12–13.

54 The significance of deictics in poetry is noted by Jonathan Culler, *Structuralist Poetics: Structuralism, Linguistics and the Study of Poetry* (London: Routledge & Kegan Paul, 1975), pp. 164–70, and by David Trotter, *The Making of the Reader: Language and Subjectivity in Modern American, English and Irish Poetry* (London: Macmillan, 1984), pp. 14–15.

55 *PWSG*, p. 84.

56 For a discussion of the use of this concept in literary theory, see Timothy Bahti, 'Ambiguity and Indeterminacy: the Juncture', *Comparative Literature*, 38, no. 3 (Summer 1986), 209–23. The classic critique of indeterminacy is E.D. Hirsch, Jr, *Validity in Interpretation* (New Haven: Yale University Press, 1967), pp. 224–35.

57 Reddy, 'The Conduit Metaphor', pp. 171–6.

58 A good explanation of the difference between meaning and reference is given in Raymond Tallis, *Not Saussure: A Critique of Post-Saussurean Literary Theory* (London: Macmillan, 1998), pp. 82–3.

59 Wallace Stevens, 'Notes Toward a Supreme Fiction' in *The Palm at the End of the Mind: Selected Poems and a Play*, ed. by Holly Stevens (New York: Vintage Books, 1972), pp.207–34 (p. 207); W.S. Graham, 'From a 1949 Notebook: Given to the Late Elizabeth Smart in the 1950s', *ER*, 24– 36 (p. 32); Notebook 3 in Robin Skelton's Collection of Graham manuscripts, c/o, University of Victoria, Canada

60 The most famous New Critical statement of this theme is W.K. Wimsatt and Monroe Beardsley, 'The Intentional Fallacy' in W.K. Wimsatt, *The Verbal Icon: Studies in the Meaning of Poetry* (Lexington: University of Kentucky Press, 1967), pp. 3–18.

61 Italo Calvino, *If On a Winter's Night a Traveller*, trans. by William Weaver (London: Minerva, 1992), p. 3.

62 'Meta-poetry' is suggested as a useful term by Réné Wellek, 'The Poet as Critic, the Critic as Poet, the Poet-Critic' in *Discriminations: Further Concepts of Criticism* (New Haven: Yale University Press, 1970), pp. 253–74 (p. 261).

63 Robert Alter, *Partial Magic: The Novel as a Self-Conscious Genre* (Berkeley: University of California Press, 1975), p.x; Patricia Waugh, *Metafiction: The Theory and Practice of Self-Conscious Fiction* (London: Methuen, 1984), p.6; Linda Hutcheon, *Narcissistic Narrative: The Metafictional Paradox* (New York: Methuen 1985), p. 20.

64 Ong, *Orality and Literacy*, p. 79.

65 Ong, *Orality and Literacy*, p. 32.

66 Reddy, 'The Conduit Metaphor', p. 172.

67 Graham, 'W.S. Graham Writes . . . ', *Poetry Book Society Bulletin* no. 64 (Spring 1970), no page number, quoted in *ER*, p. 37.

68 W.S. Graham, letter to John Knight, 15/10/74, quoted in Michael and Margaret Snow, 'Dear Who I Mean . . . ', *CS*, pp. 91–7 (p. 94).

69 Fish, 'Normal Circumstances, Literal Language, Direct Speech Acts, the Ordinary, the Everyday, the Obvious, What Goes Without Saying, and Other Special Cases' in *Is There a Text in This Class?*, pp. 268–92 (p. 284).

70 Reddy, 'The Conduit Metaphor', p. 174.

Chapter Two

1 On communion and the kiss as a model of community, see Jean-Luc Nancy, 'The Inoperative Community', trans. by Peter Connor, in *The Inoperative Community* (Minneapolis: University of Minnesota Press, 1991), pp. 1–42 (pp. 36–7).

2 Exodus 3.ii.

3 Letter to Bill Featherston, 19/7/73, quoted in *PWSG*, p. 7.

4 Richard Hoggart, *The Uses of Literacy: Aspects of Working-Class Life, with Special Reference to Publications and Entertainments* (London: Chatto & Windus, 1957), pp. 32–8; p. 37.

5 Hoggart, *The Uses of Literacy*, p. 33.

6 Hoggart, *The Uses of Literacy*, p. 241.

7 Hoggart, *The Uses of Literacy*, p. 34.

8 Hoggart, *The Uses of Literacy*, p. 51.

9 Hoggart, *The Uses of Literacy*, p. 57.

10 Hoggart, *The Uses of Literacy*, p. 58.

11 Hoggart, *The Uses of Literacy*, p. 58.

12 Hoggart, *The Uses of Literacy*, p. 268.

13 Roland Barthes, 'Operation Margarine' in *Mythologies*, trans. by Annette Lavers (London: Paladin, 1973), pp. 41–2.

14 Freud argues that dreams of stressful events, such as exams, which the dreamer survived serve to reassure him or her of similar success in the future. Sigmund Freud, *The Interpretation of Dreams*, trans. by James Strachey, ed. by James Strachey assisted by Alan Tyson, revised by Angela Richards (London: Penguin, 1976), p. 378.

15 Michael Young and Peter Willmott, *Family and Kinship in East London* (London: Routledge & Kegan Paul, 1957), p. 92.

16 Graham Crow and Graham Allan, *Community Life: An Introduction to Local Social Relations* (Hemel Hempstead: Harvester Wheatsheaf, 1994), p. 24, p. 26.

17 Raymond Williams, *Keywords: A Vocabulary of Culture and Society* (London: Fontana, 1976), pp. 75–6.

18 Williams, *Keywords*, pp. 227–8.

19 F.R. Leavis and Denys Thompson, *Culture and Environment: The Training of Critical Awareness* (London: Chatto & Windus, 1948), p. 3.

20 Raymond Williams, 'Culture is Ordinary' in *Resources of Hope: Culture, Democracy, Socialism*, ed. by Robin Gable (London: Verso, 1989), pp. 3–18 (p. 9).

21 Williams, 'Culture is Ordinary', p. 10.

22 Williams, *The Country and the City* (London: Chatto & Windus, 1973), pp. 9–12. See also Williams, *Culture and Society: Coleridge to Orwell* (London: Hogarth Press, 1993), pp. 259–60.

23 Williams, *Keywords*, p. 228; *Culture and Society*, p. 264.

24 Quoted in Williams, *Keywords*, pp. 228. Coleridge's distinction will be discussed in Chapter 3. In 'A Note on "Organic"' in *Culture and Society*, Williams gives five implications of the term, of which one is 'an idea of "wholeness" in society'. Williams, *Culture and Society*, p. 264.

25 For example in 'Culture is Ordinary', pp. 3–5, pp. 9–10, and *The Country and the City*, pp. 2–8.

26 Williams, *Culture and Society*, p. 328.

27 Williams, 'Culture is Ordinary', p. 8. A critique of organicism which draws on that of Williams while drawing attention to its deficiencies is provided by Terry Eagleton, *Criticism and Ideology: A Study in Marxist Literary Theory* (London: Verso, 1976), particularly pp. 102–61 for the literary tradition of organicism and pp. 21–42 for the critique of Williams.

28 Anthony P. Cohen, *The Symbolic Construction of Community* (London: Tavistock Publications, 1985), p. 21.

29 Cohen, *The Symbolic Construction of Community*, pp. 45–6, pp. 40–41, p. 11.

30 Jean-Luc Nancy, 'The Inoperative Community', p. 9.

31 Nancy, 'The Inoperative Community', p. 10.

32 Nancy, 'Myth Interrupted', trans. by Peter Connor, in *The Inoperative Community*, pp. 43–70 (p. 50).

33 Ian Sansom suggests that Graham's fondness for this image derives from a wish 'to be picked up and petted'. '"Listen": W.S. Graham' in *W.S. Graham: Speaking Towards You*, ed. by Ralph Pite and Hester Jones (Liverpool: Liverpool University Press, 2004), pp. 11–23 (p. 19).

34 Hoggart, *The Uses of Literacy*, p. 241.

35 *PWSG*, p. 1.

36 *PWSG*, pp. 1–3; Hoggart, *The Uses of Literacy*, pp. 244–5.

37 *PWSG*, p. 7

38 Grogan, 'Dear Pen Pal', p.20.

39 Wynne-Jones, 'W.S. Graham in Cornwall', p. 66.

40 Hoggart, *The Uses of Literacy*, p. 27.

41 Hoggart, *The Uses of Literacy*, p. 27; Graham, 'Notes on a Poetry of Release', *Poetry Scotland*, no. 3 (July 1946), 56–8, reprinted in *NFM*, pp. 379–83 (p. 381).

42 Nancy, 'The Inoperative Community', p. 9.

43 Lacan, 'The Function and Field of Speech and Language in Psychoanalysis' in *Écrits: A Selection*, pp. 30–113 (p. 55); Plato, *The Timaeus of Plato*, ed. by R.D. Archer-Hind (London: Macmillan, 1888), p. 107.

44 For example, the front cover of *Promenade*, no. 65 (1955), the magazine that he edited, and his letter to Roger Hilton, 8 November 1968, in *NFM* p. 223.

45 Lakoff and Turner, *More Than Cool Reason*, p. 50.

46 Saussure, *Course in General Linguistics*, p. 77.

47 Saussure, *Course in General Linguistics*, p. 73, p. 74; p. 78.

48 John Haffenden, 'I Would Say I Was a Happy Man: W.S. Graham Interviewed by John Haffenden', *Poetry Review*, 76, no. 1–2, 67–74 (p. 73). See 'O Why Am I So Bright', *NCP*, pp. 271–2.

49 Lakoff and Turner, *More Than Cool Reason*, p. 103.

51 *NFM*, p. 380, p. 383.

51 *NFM*, p. 380; manuscript dated 13 March 1967, in a copy of Robert Shaplen, *Toward the Well-Being of Mankind: Fifty Years of the Rockefeller Foundation* (New York: 1964), Skelton Collection, Notebook 4. Hereafter this notebook will be referred to as 'Clusters').

Chapter Three

1 Dennis O'Driscoll, 'W.S. Graham: Professor of Silence' in *CS*, pp. 51–65 (p. 51, p. 53).

2 Letter to Michael Schmidt, 11 July 1979, Achives of Carcanet Press, John Rylands University Library of Manchester.

3 *PWSG*, pp. 26–40.

4 Paul C. Ray, *The Surrealist Movement in England* (Ithaca: Cornell University Press, 1971), pp. 277–8.

5 William Montgomerie, 'Introduction' in *SJ*, no page number.

6 Lakoff and Turner, *More Than Cool Reason*, pp. 49–56.

7 Clement Greenberg, 'Avant-Garde and Kitsch' in *The Collected Essays and Criticism*, ed. by John O'Brian, 2 vols (Chicago: University of Chicago Press, 1986), I, pp. 5–22 (p. 9).

8 Noam Chomsky, *Syntactic Structures* (The Hague: Mouton & Co, 1964), p. 15. Most of the early poems are grammatically well-formed, but there are a few exceptions, such as these lines from 'The Dual Privilege': '(Looked off Heaven and saw / Creelsmashed headlong in sacred poles and cages / Different not lawless retraced to warfare / On furious maps farfetched below the sky / Perpendicular to bugleing towns that fare / In turns in the blue eye of a Sunday.' (*NCP*, p. 44.)

9 Montgomerie, 'Introduction' in *SJ*; *PWSG*, p. 32.

10 I.A. Richards, *Practical Criticism: A Study of Literary Judgment* (London: Routledge & Kegan Paul, 1929), p. 136.

11 This is also a characteristic of surrealist poetry. Anna Balakian, *Surrealism: The Road to the Absolute* (Chicago: University of Chicago Press, 1986), p. 164.

12 Quoted in *The New Princeton Encyclopedia of Poetry and Poetics*, ed. by Alex Preminger and T.V.F. Brogan (Princeton: Princeton University Press, 1993), p. 873.

13 *The New Princeton Encyclopedia of Poetry and Poetics*, p. 172.

14 Ibid.

15 The source domain corresponds to I.A. Richards's 'vehicle' and the target domain to his 'tenor'. See Lakoff and Turner, *More Than Cool Reason*, pp. 49–56, and I.A. Richards, *The Philosophy of Rhetoric* (New York: Oxford University Press, 1965), pp. 96–9.

16 Riffaterre, *Semiotics of Poetry*, pp. 1–22, p. 21.

17 Jonathan Culler, 'Riffaterre and the Semiotics of Poetry' in *The Pursuit of Signs: Semiotics, Literature, Deconstruction* (London: Routledge & Kegan Paul, 1981), pp. 80–99 (p. 93).

18 Thomas, 'Altarwise By Owl-Light' in *Collected Poems*, pp. 65–9 (p. 68).

19 Hart Crane, 'Voyages' in *The Complete Poems and Selected Letters and Prose of Hart Crane*, ed. by Brom Weber (New York: Doubleday, 1966), pp. 35–41 (p. 36); *PWSG*, p. 31.

20 Gerard Manley Hopkins, 'The Wreck of the Deutschland' in *Poems and Prose*, ed. by W.H. Gardner (Harmondsworth: Penguin Books, 1953), pp. 13–24 (p. 16). Graham quotes these lines in a letter to William Montgomerie, 20/8/44 in the National Library of Scotland (Acc. 9154).

21 Hopkins, 'God's Grandeur' in *Poems and Prose*, p. 27

22 Crane, 'Voyages', p. 37.

23 'The year 1935,' according to Paul C. Ray, 'may be said to mark the turning-point in the career of English Surrealism.' Ray, *The Surrealist Movement in Britain*, p. 86. A controversial exhibition of Surrealist work was held in London in 1936. (Ray, pp. 134–166). Graham's studies at Newbattle Abbey, arguably the turning-point in his own career, began in October 1938. (*PWSG*, p. 1). The influence of Surrealism on Graham is briefly discussed by Lopez, *PWSG*, p. 35.

24 Balakian, *Surrealism*, p. 149. She also notes the Surrealist cult of 'juxtaposition and apposition, producing [. . .] stupefying parallels of concurrent realities' (p. 165).

25 J.H. Matthews, *An Introduction to Surrealism* (University Park: Pennsylvania University Press, 1965), pp. 111–13.

26 Lakoff and Turner, *More Than Cool Reason*, p. 9.

27 On overdetermination in poetry, see Riffaterre, *Semiotics of Poetry*, p. 21. The penultimate line of 'The Seventh Journey' brings the poet back to his watery and celestial starting point: 'The eye is a lake. The sky is Neptune hovering.'

28 Samuel Taylor Coleridge, 'Kubla Khan' in *Complete Poems*, ed. by Morchard Bishop (London: Macdonald, 1954), pp. 212–13 (p. 212).

29 Thomas, 'I, In My Intricate Image' in *Collected Poems*, pp. 30–33 (p. 30).

30 T.S. Eliot, 'The Waste Land' in *Collected Poems: 1909–1962* (London: Faber and Faber, 1963), pp. 61–86 (p. 63); Ezra Pound, 'Hugh Selwyn Mauberley' in *Selected Poems* (London: Faber and Faber, 1977), pp. 98–112 (p. 101).

31 *PWSG*, p. 48, p. 63, p. 51.

32 Nessie Dunsmuir, 'I Would Have Chosen Children' in *Nessie Dunsmuir's Ten Poems* (Warwick: Greville Press, 1988), p. 1.

33 A similar phrase, 'anarchy within a cage' occurs in the poem 'The Narrator', originally published in *The Seven Journeys*. (*NCP*, p. 38.)

34 Balakian, *Surrealism*, p. 154 (emphasis removed).

35 Valentine Cunningham, *British Writers of the Thirties* (Oxford: Oxford University Press, 1988), p. 226, and discussion pp. 226–8. See also Samuel Hynes's discussion of Graham Greene's *Journey Without Maps* in *The Auden Generation: Literature and Politics in England in the 1930s* (New York: Viking Press, 1977), pp. 229–31.

36 See the discussion by Lopez, *PWSG*, p. 37.

37 Rainer Maria Rilke, 'letter, 17 Mar 1926 to an unnamed young girl', quoted in Eudo C. Mason, *Rilke* (Edinburgh: Oliver and Boyd, 1963), p. 50.

38 Rainer Maria Rilke, 'The Panther' in *The Selected Poetry of Rainer Maria Rilke*, ed. and trans. by Stephen Mitchell (London: Picador, 1987), p. 25.

39 André Breton, 'Manifesto of Surrealism' in *Manifestoes of Surrealism*, trans. by
    Richard Seaver and Helen R. Lane (Ann Arbor: University of Michigan Press,
    1972), pp.3–47 (pp. 9–10).

40 David Gascoyne begins his *Short History of Surrealism* with a portrait of man
    imprisoned in the world of everyday reality. David Gascoyne, *A Short History of
    Surrealism* (London: Frank Cass, 1935), p. ix.

41 Ian Higgins, 'Postscript: *Pas De Patrie?* Language, Freedom and Society in
    Surrealist Poetic Theory' in *Surrealism and Language: Seven Essays*, ed. by Ian
    Higgins (Edinburgh: Scottish Academic Press, 1986), pp. 87–94 (p. 88). Ray
    remarks, 'The Surrealist plea for freedom from conventional reality, from
    logic, taste and morality, extends to language also.' *The Surrealist Movement in
    Britain*, p. 45.

42 Cunningham, *British Writers of the Thirties*, p. 78. Cunningham gives many
    examples of the use of cage imagery (pp. 78–105), and suggests that the self-
    referential texts of Beckett, Woolf and Joyce can be seen as verbal cages (pp.
    103–5).

43 Derrida, *Of Grammatology*, p. 44.

44 It was Mallarmé who remarked to Valéry that 'one does not make poetry with
    ideas but with *words*'. (Emphasis original.) Paul Valéry, 'Poetry and Abstract
    Thought' in *The Art of Poetry*, trans. by Denise Folliott (London: Routledge &
    Kegan Paul, 1958), pp. 52–81 (p. 63).

45 T.S. Eliot, 'Tradition and the Individual Talent' in *Selected Essays* (London: Faber
    and Faber, 1941), pp. 13–22 (p. 18).

46 Ray, *The Surrealist Movement in Britain*, pp. 28–9.

47 Briony Fer, 'Surrealism, Myth and Psychoanalysis' in Briony Fer, David
    Batchelor and Paul Wood, *Realism, Rationalism, Surrealism: Art Between the Wars*
    (New Haven: Yale University Press, 1993), pp. 171–249 (pp. 221–4).

48 *NFM*, p. 379; 'One cannot step twice into the same river, nor can one grasp any
    mortal substance in a stable condition [. . .]', Heraclitus, 'Fragment LI',
    quoted in Charles H. Kahn, *The Art and Thought of Heraclitus: An Edition of the
    Fragments With Translation and Commentary* (Cambridge: Cambridge University
    Press, 1979), p. 53. The original fragment has not survived, and the idea is
    attributed to Heraclitus by Plutarch. The importance of the Heraclitean flux
    in Graham's work is stressed by Lopez, *PWSG*, p. 62.

49 Randall Stevenson, *Modernist Fiction: An Introduction* (Hemel Hempstead:
    Harvester Wheatsheaf, 1992), p. 136 (see also Ray, *The Surrealist Movement in
    Britain*, p. 263; Sanford Schwartz, *The Matrix of Modernism: Pound, Eliot and
    Twentieth-Century Thought* (Princeton: Princeton University Press, 1985), p. 20.

50 Christopher Buckingham Stephens, *'St Ives' Artists and Landscape* (Unpub. Ph. D.
    dissertation, University of Sussex, 1996), p. 198, p. 200.

51 T.E. Hulme, 'The New Philosophy' in *The Collected Writings of T.E. Hulme*, ed. by Karen Csengeri (Oxford: Clarendon Press, 1994), pp. 85–8 (p. 86).

52 Schwartz, ibid.

52 *PWSG*, p. 29.

54 Samuel Taylor Coleridge, *Shakespearean Criticism*, ed. by Thomas Middleton Raysor, 2 vols (London: Dent, 1960), II p. 198.

55 *The New Princeton Encyclopedia of Poetry and Poetics*, p. 868.

56 Peter Bürger, *Theory of the Avant-Garde,* trans. by Michael Shaw (Manchester: Manchester University Press, 1984), p. 47.

57 The phrase comes from Henry Treece, *Dylan Thomas: Dog Among the Fairies* (London: Lyndsay Drummond, 1949), p. 15.

58 G.S. Fraser, 'Apocalypse in Poetry' in *The White Horseman: Prose and Verse of the New Apocalypse*, ed. by J.F. Hendry and Henry Treece (London: Routledge, 1941), pp. 3–31 (p. 9).

59 Treece, *Dylan Thomas*, p. 16.

60 Treece, *Dylan Thomas*, p. 18.

61 T.E. Hulme, 'Romanticism and Classicism' in *Collected Writings,* pp. 59–73 (pp. 71–2).

62 Henri Bergson, *Creative Evolution*, trans. by Arthur Mitchell (London: Macmillan, 1912), pp. 186–7.

63 Nessie Dunsmuir, 'Stanis Pit', 'Raith Pit'.'The Night-Walking Men Taken Into the Dark', in *Nessie Dunsmuir's Ten Poems*, p. 6, p. 8, p. 10.

64 Treece, *Dylan Thomas*, p. 27.

65 Naum Gabo, one of the founders of Constructivism, was living in Cornwall during the war years, at the same time as Graham. Gabo had trained as an engineer. Tom Cross, *Painting the Warmth of the Sun: St Ives Artists 1939–1975* (Cambridge: Lutterworth Press, 1995), p. 51.

66 The OED (2nd edition) gives only one sense for the noun, 'an organic compound', and the earliest use of this given is dated 1953.

67 Graham, 'From a 1949 Notebook: Given to the Late Elizabeth Smart in the 1950s', *ER*, 24– 36 (p. 31). Letter to Sven Berlin, 12 March 1949, NFM, p85. (Emphasis original.)

Chapter Four

1 John Heath-Stubbs, 'Drowned Man', quoted from *Poetry of the Forties*, ed. by Robin Skelton (Harmondsworth: Penguin Books, 1968), p. 211; Vernon

Watkins, 'Griefs of the Sea', quoted from *Poetry of the Forties*, p. 212; Tom Scott, 'Sea-Dirge', quoted from *Poetry in Wartime*, ed. by M.J. Tambimuttu (London: Faber and Faber, 1942), p. 157.

2 Linda M. Shires, *British Poetry of the Second World War* (London: Macmillan, 1985), p. 85. The theme was familiar enough for Evelyn Waugh to allude to 'the Drowned Sailor motif' in a depiction of a wartime literary party. Evelyn Waugh, *Unconditional Surrender* (Harmondsworth: Penguin Books, 1964), p. 51.

3 *PWSG*, p. 2.

4 Graham uses the word 'keening' in the last stanza of the early drowning poem 'Many Without Elegy' (*NCP*, p. 40).

5 J.M. Synge, *Riders to the Sea* in *Plays, Poems and Prose* (London: Dent, 1975), pp. 19–30 (p. 25). Graham misquotes this line in a marginal note to a letter to Sven Berlin, dated '1st Saturday after the 9th March' (probably 1949), National Library of Scotland (Acc. 7389, Acc. 7581): 'And the black hags flying low over the sea'.

6 The sea possesses three of the attributes associated by Burke with the sublime: terror, power and vastness. Edmund Burke, *A Philosophical Enquiry into the Origin of our Ideas of the Sublime and Beautiful*, ed. by James T. Boulton (London: Basil Blackwell, 1987), pp. 57–8, pp. 64–70, pp. 72–3.

7 Synge, *Riders to the Sea*, pp. 26–7.

8 Synge, *Riders to the Sea*, pp. 27–8.

9 Eliot, 'The Waste Land', p. 75.

10 Psalms 107. 23–6.

11 William Shakespeare, *The Tempest* in *Complete Works*, ed. by W.J. Craig (London: Oxford University Press, 1943), I. 2. 394–401; Eliot, 'The Waste Land', p. 67.

12 A similar theme of a seagoing community penetrated by the ocean is explored by Robert Lowell in his poem 'The Quaker Graveyard in Nantucket': 'The empty winds are creaking and the oak / Splatters and splatters on the cenotaph.' Robert Lowell, 'The Quaker Graveyard in Nantucket' in *Poems: 1938–1949* (London: Faber and Faber, 1950), pp. 18–24 (p. 24). Lowell had also rejected his Protestant heritage.

13 For an exception, see 'The Wedding' by Roland Gant in *Poetry of the Forties*, p. 210. There is, of course, a significant body of literature dealing with drowned women, whose deaths, from Ophelia onwards, tend to be private and self-inflicted.

14 *PWSG*, p. 23; *NFM*, p. 5.

15 Max Weber, *The Protestant Ethic and the Spirit of Capitalism*, trans. by Talcott Parsons (London: George Allen & Unwin, 1930), p. 35.

16 Fiona Green, 'Achieve Further Through Elegy' in Pite and Jones (eds.), *W.S. Graham*, pp. 132–157 (p. 144).

17 Matthew 14.22–33; Mark 6.45–52; W. R. Rodgers, 'Christ Walking On the Water' in *Poetry of the Forties*, pp. 181–3 and in W.R. Rodgers, *Collected Poems* (London: Oxford University Press, 1971), pp. 82–3. Graham praises the poem in a letter to William Montgomerie, dated 21 August 1946. Another Rodgers poem, 'Europa and the Bull', is perhaps the source of Graham's use of this myth in 'The Dark Dialogues' , though Ralph Pite notes that Graham's friend Peter Lanyon 'produced a series of *Europa* paintings in 1953–4'. (Rodgers, *Collected Poems*, pp. 57–71, *NCP*, pp. 158–65, Ralph Pite, 'Abstract, Real and Particular: Graham and Painting' in Pite and Jones (eds.), *W.S. Graham*, pp. 65–83 (p. 80).)

18 Sigmund Freud, 'The "Uncanny"' in *Art and Literature*, trans. by James Strachey, ed. by Albert Dickinson (Harmondsworth: Penguin, 1985), pp. 339–381), p. 364. On repetition, see p. 359.

19 Freud, 'The "Uncanny"', p. 347.

20 Kahn, *The Art and Thought of Heraclitus*, p. 150

21 Bergson, *Creative Evolution*, pp. 263–4.

22 *Contemporary Poets of the English Language*, ed. by Rosalie Murphy (Chicago: St James Press, 1970), p. 436.

23 Letter to Sven Berlin dated 12th March 1949, *NFM*, p. 84.

24 Kahn, *The Art and Thought of Heraclitus*, p. 168, citing Aristotle's *Metaphysics*.

25 Memory is the subject of a cryptic note in his 1949 notebook. W.S. Graham, 'From a 1949 Notebook: Given to the Late Elizabeth Smart in the 1950s', *ER*, 24– 36 (p. 25); Notebook 3, Skelton Collection, c/o, University of Victoria, Canada.

26 G.S. Fraser, letter to the editor, *London Magazine*, 2, no. 9 (1955), 67–9 (p. 68): *PWSG*, pp. 61–74, especially p. 62.

27 *PWSG*, p. 67.

28 Hugh Kenner, in *The Pound Era* (London: Faber and Faber, 1972), explains (p. 144; pp. 458–9) how Pound derived the phrase 'tensile light' from a characteristic misreading of Chinese ideograms, and used it *The Unwobbling Pivot* (1945). 'Tensile' is also used of light in 'Canto LXXIV' – see Ezra Pound, *The Cantos of Ezra Pound* (London: Faber and Faber, 1975), p. 429. This is the first of *The Pisan Cantos*, first published in Britain in July 1949, at exactly the time Graham was writing 'The Nightfishing'.

29 *PWSG*, p. 97.

30 Numbers 20.10.

31 *PWSG*, p. 63.

32 'The Continual Sea', *TLS*, 8 July 1955, p. 379

33 Coleridge, *Complete Poems*, p. 228; the comparison is made by Lopez, *PWSG*, p. 63, p. 74.

34 Sven Berlin, *Alfred Wallis: Primitive* (London: Nicholson & Watson, 1949), pp.117–9; Graham wrote to Berlin: 'I like the death paintings best'. Letter to Sven Berlin dated 21 February 1949, National Library of Scotland (Acc. 7389, Acc. 7581).

35 Roland Barthes, 'The *Nautilus* and the Drunken Boat' in *Mythologies*, pp. 65–7 (p. 67).

36 W.S. Graham, 'From a 1949 Notebook: Given to the Late Elizabeth Smart in the 1950s', *ER*, 24– 36 (p. 25); Notebook 3, Skelton Collection, c/o, University of Victoria, Canada.

37 Derrida argues that names are a form of writing (*Of Grammatology*, pp. 110–11), while for Lacan, 'the subject [. . .] if he can appear to be the slave of language is all the more so of a discourse in the universal movement in which his place is inscribed at birth, if only by virtue of his proper name. 'The Agency of the Letter in the Unconscious or Reason Since Freud' in *Écrits*, pp. 146 – 178 (p. 148).

Chapter Five

1 Lopez, *PWSG*, pp. 86–7, points out the puns on 'rime' and 'print' but not that on 'cranes'.

2 In a 1950s manuscript entitled 'Notes On a Notebook' in the collection of the Harry Ransom Humanities Research Centre, University of Texas at Austin (Works 2 / Hanley II) Graham writes: 'gramersow' [*sic*] – the Cornish word for wood-louse. What a strange grotesque word it is, like a poem in itself.'

3 W.H. Auden, 'The Sportsmen: A Parable', reprinted in *The English Auden: Poems, Essays and Dramatic Writings 1927–1939*, ed. by Edward Mendelson (London: Faber and Faber, 1977), pp. 368–70.

4 The late Professor Robin Skelton possessed a tape of Graham reading 'Lament for the Makaris' by the medieval Scottish poet William Dunbar.

5 Cunningham, *British Writers of the Thirties*, p. 166.

6 Stephen Spender, 'Polar Exploration' in *The Still Centre* (London: Faber and Faber, 1939), p. 17.

7 Hugh MacDiarmid, 'The World of Words' in *Complete Poems: 1920–1976*, 2 vols, ed. by Michael Grieve and W.R. Aitken (London: Martin Brian & O'Keefe, 1978), II, pp. 805–840 (p. 823).

8 Francis Spufford, *I May Be Some Time: Ice and the English Imagination* (London, Faber and Faber, 1996), pp. 16–40.

9 Crane, 'North Labrador' in *Complete Poems*, p. 15.

10 Crane, 'The Bridge' in *Complete Poems*, pp. 43–117 (p. 82).

11 Spufford, *I May Be Some Time*, p. 20.

12 Spufford, *I May Be Some Time*, p. 24.

13 Spufford, *I May Be Some Time*, p. 137; p. 141.

14 *PWSG*, pp. 87–8.

15 Fridtjof Nansen, *Farthest North*, 2 vols (London: George Newnes, 1898), II, p. 216.

16 *PWSG*, pp. 87–9.

17 Eliot, 'The Waste Land', p. 85. (Emphasis original.) The connection is pointed out by Lopez, *PWSG*, p. 85.

18 Lopez identifies this friend as the blind poet John Heath-Stubbs. *PWSG*, p. 112, Graham, 'For John Heath-Stubbs' (*NCP*, pp. 274–5). However, there may also be a link to the painter Tony O'Malley, to whom Graham addressed a poem called 'Tony as the Owl', Marion Whybrow, *St Ives 1883–1993: Portrait of an Art Colony* (Woodbridge: Antique Collectors' Club, 1994), p. 121. Graham himself writes almost obsessively about owls in his Cretan poems (discussed in Chapter 6) and mentions them in 'The Nightfishing' and 'Implements' (*NCP*, p. 105, p. 243). In a letter of 1965 to Elizabeth Smart, he writes: 'I write this late at night with the owls calling and the sashes rattling.' (*NFM*, p. 192.) The 'friend' may therefore be the poet accompanying his character.

19 Eliot, 'Little Gidding' in *Collected Poems*, pp. 214–23 (p. 217).

20 'The text is [. . .] a multi-dimensional space in which a variety of writings [. . .] blend and clash.' Barthes, 'The Death of the Author', p. 146; 'He has to make the poem stand stationary as an Art object. He never knows who will collide with it.' *Poetry Book Society Bulletin*, no. 64 (Spring 1970), quoted in 'From Poetry Society Bulletins', *ER*, p. 37.

21 Matthew 25.1–13; Nansen, *Farthest North*, II, p. 205.

22 Derrida, *Of Grammatology*, p. 151.

23 Maud Ellman, *The Poetics of Impersonality: T.S. Eliot and Ezra Pound* (Brighton: The Harvester Press, 1987), p. 13.

24 *Contemporary Poets of the English Language*, p. 436.

25 Lopez, in his article 'On *Malcolm Mooney's Land* by W.S. Graham', *Ideas and Production*, no. 4 (December 1985), 44–70, explains that Graham had originally intended to use the ship in his poem but changed his mind.

26 Nansen, *Farthest North*, I, p. 164; p. 169; p. 232.

27 Nansen, *Farthest North*, II, p. 5.

28 Nansen, *Farthest North*, II, p. 157.

29 Nansen, *Farthest North*, II, p. 207.

30 Nansen, *Farthest North*, I, p. 172

31 Nansen, *Farthest North*, I, p. 154 and p. 175; R.F. Scott and others, *Scott's Last Expedition*, 2 vols. (London: Smith, Elder, 1913), II, p. 243.

32 Nansen, *Farthest North*, II, p. 159.

33 Nansen, *Farthest North*, II, p. 118.

34 Barthes, 'The Nautilus and the Drunken Boat', p. 67.

35 Barthes, 'The Nautilus and the Drunken Boat', pp. 65-7.

36 Nansen, *Farthest North*, II, p. 32.

37 Lopez, p. 63; Graham, 'W.S. Graham Writes . . .', *Poetry Book Society Bulletin* no. 64 (Spring 1970), no page number.

38 Spufford, *I May Be Some Time*, pp. 4-5.

39 Spufford, *I May Be Some Time*, p. 26.

40 Scott and others, *Scott's Last Expedition*, I, p. 544, p. 592, 595.

41 Annotated typescript of 'His Companions Buried Him' in the University Libraries, State University of New York at Buffalo, TMSS, 1943.

42 Poem beginning 'I surfaced and I saw the terrible sight' in [Poetical Notebook] Works 2 / Hanley II, University of Texas at Austin.

43 *PWSG*, pp. 84-5; p. 85; p. 86. Wilson's poem appears opposite page 1 in Scott and others, *Scott's Last Expedition*, II.

44 *Poetry Book Society Bulletin*, no. 64, quoted in *ER*, p. 37.

45 Ruth Grogan, 'W.S. Graham: A Dialogical Imagination', *English Studies in Canada*, 15 (June 1989), 196-213 (p. 197, p. 200).

46 Mikhail Bakhtin, 'Discourse in the Novel' in *The Dialogic Imagination: Four Essays*, ed. by Michael Holquist, trans. by Caryl Emerson and Michael Holquist (Austin: University of Texas Press, 1981), pp. 259-422 (p. 287; p. 263; p. 286.)

47 Bakhtin, 'Discourse in the Novel', p. 280 (emphasis original).

48 Jakobson, 'Linguistics and Poetics', p. 21.

49 Paul De Man, *Allegories of Reading: Figural Language in Rousseau, Nietzsche, Rilke and Proust* (New Haven: Yale University Press, 1979), pp. 9-11

50 Cross, *Painting the Warmth of the Sun*, p.131.

51 Cross, *Painting the Warmth of the Sun*, p.76.

52 Quoted in Cross, *Painting the Warmth of the Sun*, p. 200.

53 Derrida, *Of Grammatology*, p. 17.

54 Jakobson, 'Linguistics and Poetics', p. 21.

55 Derrida, 'Signature Event Context', p. 330.

56 Derek Stanford, *Inside the Forties* (London: Sidgwick & Jackson, 1977), pp. 139–40; Frame, 'W.S. Graham at Sandyford Place', p. 65.

57 *PWSG*, p. 76.

58 Julian Maclaren-Ross, *Memoirs of the Forties* (London: Alan Ross, 1965), p. 183.

59 Letter to Norman Macleod dated 'January 1960' in *NFM*, pp. 167–75.

60 Wynne-Jones, 'W.S. Graham in Cornwall', p. 66; Sven Berlin, *The Coat of Many Colours* (Bristol: Redcliffe Press, 1994), p. 137; Stanford, *Inside the Forties*, p. 138.

61 Damian Grant, 'Walls of Glass: The Poetry of W.S. Graham' in *British Poetry Since 1970: A Critical Survey*, ed. by Peter Jones and Michael Schmidt (Manchester: Carcanet Press, 1980), pp. 22–38 (p. 28).

62 Samuel Beckett, *The Unnamable* in *The Beckett Trilogy: Molloy, Malone Dies, The Unnamable* (London: Picador, 1979), p. 268.

63 *PWSG*, p. 123, p. 114.

64 Lewis Carroll, *Through the Looking-Glass and What Alice Found There* (London: Macmillan, 1971), p. 56 (emphasis original). Carroll was admired by the Surrealists, as Ray points out (*The Surrealist Movement in Britain*, p. 60). See Chapter 6 for a further discussion of his influence.

65 Derrida, *Of Grammatology*, pp. 110–11.

66 Robert Graves, *The White Goddess: A Historical Grammar of Poetic Myth* (London: Faber and Faber, 1952), p. 48.

67 Iona and Peter Opie, *The Lore and Language of Schoolchildren* (Oxford: Clarendon Press, 1959), p. 156.

68 In a manuscript of 1967, one of the 'clusters' of automatic writing to be discussed in the next chapter, Graham writes 'we all are that pelted in thin-skin a prey to our names miscalled in echo in shame-names over by sticks and stones that rough boy angels call'. ('Clusters', 21/3/67.)

Chapter Six

1 Grogan, 'Dear Pen Pal', p.16, p.17.

2 *PWSG*, pp. 111–12.

3 Freud, *The Interpretation of Dreams*, p. 164, p. 435.

4 Freud, 'The Uncanny', p. 359.

5 Freud, *The Interpretation of Dreams*, p. 345 (emphasis original).

6 Freud, 'Revision of the Theory of Dreams' in *New Introductory Lectures on Psychoanalysis*, trans. by James Strachey, ed. by James Strachey assisted by Angela Richards (Harmondsworth: Penguin Books, 1973), pp. 35–59 (pp. 57–9; p. 58).

7 Wynne-Jones, 'W.S. Graham in Cornwall', p. 69; Grogan, 'Dear Pen Pal', p.20; Ronnie Duncan, 'A Journal of Crete', *Aquarius*, no. 25/25 (2002), 146–155.

8 Grogan, 'Dear Pen Pal', p.20.

9 Quoted in Grogan, 'Dear Pen Pal', p.16.

10 Because of the eccentricity of these writings, I shall refrain from confirming unusual phrases with the word 'sic'.

11 Letters to Ruth Hilton, 21 March 1967 and 22 March 1967, *NFM*, pp. 209–11.

12 Breton, 'Manifesto of Surrealism', p. 22–3. (Emphasis original).

13 Breton, 'Manifesto of Surrealism', p. 26.

14 Breton, 'Manifesto of Surrealism', pp. 29–30.

15 Breton, 'Manifesto of Surrealism', p. 24, and note.

16 Breton, 'Manifesto of Surrealism', p. 30.

17 Breton, 'Manifesto of Surrealism', p. 24. (Emphasis original.)

18 Breton, 'Manifesto of Surrealism', p. 21.

19 J. Gratton, 'Runaway: Textual Dynamics in the Poetry of André Breton' in *Surrealism and Language*, pp. 30–45 (p. 31). (Emphasis original.)

20 *Contemporary Poets of the English Language*, p. 436.

21 'Notes on a Notebook', manuscript in the University of Texas at Austin (Works II / Hanley II)]

22 Letter to Edwin Morgan, undated, *NFM*, p. 123

23 Balakian, *Surrealism*, pp. 146–7.

24 Jacqueline Chénieux-Gendron, 'Toward a New Definition of Automatism: L'Immaculée Conception', *Dada Surrealism*, 17 (1988), 74–90 (pp. 76–80). Earlier, Breton had condemned Soupault's use of titles as an 'error'. ('Manifesto of Surrealism', p. 24).

25 *PWSG*, p. 6.

26 Riffaterre, *Semiotics of Poetry*, p. 12; p. 139.

27 Alternatively, since four and two make six (the missing number from the date), he may be trying a mathematical game as opposed to his more usual verbal ones.

28 Ong, *Orality and Literacy*, p. 91.

29 Freud, *Jokes and Their Relation to the Unconscious*, trans. by James Strachey, ed. by James Strachey and Angela Richards (Harmondsworth: Penguin, 1976), p. 67; Freud, *The Psychopathology of Everyday Life*, trans. by Alan Tyson, ed. by James Strachey, Angela Richards and Alan Tyson (Harmondsworth: Penguin, 1975), pp. 94–183.

30 On the portmanteau and paronomasia in Carroll, see Jean-Jacques Lecercle, *Philosophy of Nonsense: The Intuitions of Victorian Nonsense Literature* (London: Routledge, 1994), pp. 44–8, pp. 65–7. On the portmanteau in Joyce, see Derek Attridge, 'Unpacking the Portmanteau, or Who's Afraid of Finnegans Wake' in *On Puns: The Foundation of Letters*, ed. by Jonathan Culler (Oxford: Basil Blackwell, 1988), pp. 140–55.

31 Compare Carroll's composite insects, the 'Rocking-horse-fly', 'Snap-dragon-fly' and 'Bread-and-butter-fly'. *Through the Looking-Glass*, pp. 51–3.

32 Blanchot, *The Space of Literature*, p. 179.

33 *PWSG*, pp. 93–4; Graves, *The White Goddess*, p. 24. A similar view of language as feminine and communal occurs at the end of Hugh MacDiarmid's poem 'The World of Words'.

34 Saussure, *Course in General Linguistics*, pp. 13–14 (where '*langue*' is translated as 'language' and '*parole*' as 'speech').

35 Saussure, *Course in General Linguistics*, p. 118.

36 Derrida, *Of Grammatology*, p. 151.

37 See also *PWSG*, pp. 81–2.

38 Freud, *Analysis of a Phobia in a Five-Year-Old Boy* in *Case Histories 1: 'Dora' and 'Little Hans'*, pp. 167–305 (p. 291).

39 Genesis 25.xxv

40 Genesis 25.xxix–xxxiv.

41 Bürger, *Theory of the Avant-Garde*, p. 47.

42 Roland Barthes, *S/Z*, trans. by Richard Miller (London: Jonathan Cape, 1975), p. 4.

43 Elizabeth Sewell, *The Field of Nonsense* (London: Chatto and Windus, 1952), p. 36.

44 Lecercle, *Philosophy of Nonsense*, p. 2.

45 Lecercle, *Philosophy of Nonsense*, pp. 51–9.

46 Sewell, *The Field of Nonsense*, p. 36.

47 Sewell, *The Field of Nonsense*, p. 41.

48 Carroll, *Through the Looking-Glass*, p. 114.

Bibliography

1. Books by W.S. Graham (in Order of Publication)

Cage Without Grievance (Glasgow: Parton Press, 1942).
The Seven Journeys (Glasgow: William Maclellan, 1944).
2ND Poems (London: Nicholson and Watson, 1945).
The White Threshold (London: Faber and Faber, 1949).
The Nightfishing (London: Faber and Faber, 1955).
Malcolm Mooney's Land (London: Faber and Faber, 1970).
Implements in Their Places (London: Faber and Faber, 1977).
Collected Poems: 1942–1977 (London: Faber and Faber, 1979).
Selected Poems (New York: Ecco Press, 1980).
Uncollected Poems (Warwick: Greville Press, 1990)
Aimed at Nobody: Poems from Notebooks, ed. by Margaret Blackwood and
        Robin Skelton (London, Faber and Faber, 1993)
Selected Poems (London: Faber and Faber, 1996).
W.S. Graham Selected by Nessie Dunsmuir (Warwick: Greville Press, 1998).
The Nightfisherman: Selected Letters of W.S. Graham ed. by Michael and
        Margaret Snow (Manchester: Carcanet Press, 1999)
New Collected Poems, ed. by Matthew Francis (London: Faber and Faber,
        2004)

2. Other Published Works by W.S. Graham (in Order of Publication)

'A Letter to Norman', *Tempest*, no. 1 (October 1943), 14–16.

'It All Comes Back to Me Now', *Poetry* (Chicago), 72, no. 6 (September 1948) 302–307.

'Notes on a Poetry of Release', *Poetry Scotland*, no. 3 (July 1946), 56–8.

Promenade, no. 65 (1955).

'W.S. Graham Writes . . . ', *Poetry Book Society Bulletin* no. 64 (Spring 1970), no page number.

'W.S. Graham Writes . . . ', *Poetry Book Society Bulletin* no. 94 (Autumn 1977), no page number.

'From a 1949 Notebook: Given to the Late Elizabeth Smart in the 1950s', *Edinburgh Review*, no.75 (February 1987), 24– 36.

'From Poetry Society Bulletins', *Edinburgh Review*, no.75 (February 1987), p. 37.

3. Unpublished Works by W.S. Graham

Collection of the Harry Ransom Humanities Research Centre, University of Texas at Austin.

Manuscripts in the Poetry / Rare Books Collection, University Libraries, State University of New York at Buffalo.

Private collection of Ronnie Duncan.

Letters to Elizabeth Smart, Elizabeth Smart Papers, Series J, National Library of Canada, Ottawa.

Letters to Michael Schmidt, Archives of Carcanet Press, John Rylands University Library of Manchester.

Letters to William Montgomerie and Sven Berlin, National Library of Scotland.

Robin Skelton Archive, University of Victoria, Canada.

4. Works About W.S. Graham

Anonymous, 'The Continual Sea', *TLS*, 8 July 1955, p. 379.

Barker, Sebastian, 'Memoir of W.S. Graham', *Edinburgh Review*, no.75 (February 1987), 88–91.

Bedient, Calvin, 'W.S. Graham' in *Eight Contemporary Poets* (London: Oxford University Press, 1974), pp. 159–80;

—— 'Absentist Poetry: Kinsella, Hill, Graham, Hughes', *PN Review*, 4, no. 1 (1977), 18–24.

Calder, Robert, 'W.S. Graham's Poetry', *Edinburgh Review*, no.75 (February 1987), 75–82.

Duncan, Ronnie and Jonathan Davidson (eds.), *The Constructed Space: A Celebration of W.S. Graham* (Lincoln: Jackson's Arm, 1994).

Fraser, G.S. letter to the editor, *London Magazine*, 2, no. 9 (1955), 67–9.

Grant, Damian, 'Walls of Glass: The Poetry of W.S. Graham' in *British Poetry Since 1970: A Critical Survey*, ed. by Peter Jones and Michael Schmidt (Manchester: Carcanet Press, 1980), pp. 22–38.

Grogan, Ruth, '"Dear Pen Pal in the Distance": A Selection of W.S. Graham's Letters', *PN Review*, 16, no. 5 (1989), 14–21;

—— 'W.S. Graham: A Dialogical Imagination', *English Studies in Canada*, 15, (June 1989), 196–213.

Haffenden, John, 'I Would Say I Was a Happy Man: W.S. Graham Interviewed by John Haffenden', *Poetry Review*, 76, no. 1–2, 67–74.

Lopez, Tony, 'On Malcolm Mooney's Land by W.S. Graham', *Ideas and Production*, no. 4 (December 1985), 44–70;

—— 'An Introduction to W.S. Graham', *Edinburgh Review*, no.75 (February 1987), 7–23;

—— *The Poetry of W.S. Graham* (Edinburgh, Edinburgh University Press, 1989);

—— 'T.S. Eliot and W.S. Graham', *Scottish Literary Journal*, 19, no. 1 (May 1992), 35–46.

Morgan, Edwin, 'The Poetry of W.S. Graham', *Cencrastus*, no. 5 (Summer 1981), 8–10;

—— 'The Sea, the Desert, the City: Environment and Language in W.S. Graham, Hamish Henderson and Tom Leonard', *Yearbook of English Studies* (1987), 31–45.

Mortimer, Penelope, 'A Poet's Interview With Himself', *Observer Magazine*, 19 November 1978, pp. 61–2

Pite, Ralph and Hester Jones (eds.), *W.S. Graham: Speaking Towards You* (Liverpool: Liverpool University Press, 2004).

Punter, David, 'W.S. Graham: Constructing a White Space', *Malahat Review*, no. 63, (October, 1982), 220–44.

Ruhrmund Frank, 'Literary World Mourns W.S. Graham', *The Cornishman*, 16 January 1986, p. 1.

Schmidt, Michael, 'W.S. Graham' in *A Reader's Guide to Fifty Modern British Poets* (London: Heinemann, 1979), pp. 297–304.

Silverberg, Mark Andrew, 'A Readership of None: The Later Poetry of W.S. Graham', *English Studies in Canada*, 24, no. 2 (June 1998), 139–55.

Stephens, Chris, 'The Constructed Space', *PN Review* 21, 1 (September-October 1994), 7–8.

Various authors, *Aquarius*, no. 25/26 (George Barker / W.S. Graham issue, 2002);

—— *Edinburgh Review*, no. 75 (W.S. Graham issue, February 1987).

5. Other Works

Alter, Robert, *Partial Magic: The Novel as a Self-Conscious Genre* (Berkeley: University of California Press, 1975).

Attridge, Derek, 'Unpacking the Portmanteau, or Who's Afraid of Finnegans Wake' in *On Puns: The Foundation of Letters*, ed. by Jonathan Culler (Oxford: Basil Blackwell, 1988).

Auden, W.H. *The English Auden: Poems, Essays and Dramatic Writings 1927–1939*, ed. by Edward Mendelson (London: Faber and Faber, 1977).

Austin, J.L. *How to Do Things With Words* (Oxford: Clarendon Press, 1962).

Bahti, Timothy, 'Ambiguity and Indeterminacy: the Juncture', *Comparative Literature*, 38, no. 3 (Summer 1986).

Bakhtin, Mikhail, *The Dialogic Imagination: Four Essays*, ed. by Michael Holquist, trans. by Caryl Emerson and Michael Holquist (Austin: University of Texas Press, 1981).

Balakian, Anna, *Surrealism: The Road to the Absolute* (Chicago: University of Chicago Press, 1986).

Barthes, Roland, *Mythologies*, trans. by Annette Lavers (London: Paladin, 1973);

—— *Image, Music, Text*, trans. by Stephen Heath (London: Fontana, 1977);

—— *S/Z*, trans. by Richard Miller (London: Jonathan Cape, 1975).

Beckett, Samuel, *The Unnamable from The Beckett Trilogy: Molloy, Malone Dies, The Unnamable* (London: Picador, 1979).

Belsey, Catherine, *Critical Practice* (London: Routledge, 1980).

Bergson, Henri, *Creative Evolution*, trans. by F.L. Pogson (London: Macmillan, 1912).

Berlin, Sven, *Alfred Wallis: Primitive* (London: Nicholson & Watson, 1949);

—— *The Coat of Many Colours* (Bristol: Redcliffe Press, 1994).

Blanchot, Maurice, *The Space of Literature*, trans. by Ann Smock (Lincoln: University of Nebraska Press, 1982).

Breton, André, *Manifestoes of Surrealism*, trans. by Richard Seaver and Helen R. Lane (Ann Arbor: University of Michigan Press, 1972).

Burke, Edmund, *A Philosophical Enquiry into the Origin of our Ideas of the*

Sublime and Beautiful, ed. by James T. Boulton (London: Basil Blackwell, 1987).

Bürger, Peter, *Theory of the Avant-Garde*, trans. by Michael Shaw (Manchester: Manchester University Press, 1984).

Calvino, Italo, *If On a Winter's Night a Traveller*, trans. by William Weaver (London: Minerva, 1992).

Carroll, Lewis, *Through the Looking-Glass and What Alice Found There* (London: Macmillan, 1971).

Chénieux-Gendron, Jacqueline, 'Toward a New Definition of Automatism: L'Immaculée Conception', *Dada Surrealism*, 17 (1988).

Chomsky, Noam, *Syntactic Structures* (The Hague: Mouton & Co, 1964); —— *Reflections on Language* (London: Temple Smith, 1976).

Cohen, Anthony P. *The Symbolic Construction of Community* (London: Tavistock Publications, 1985).

Coleridge, Samuel Taylor, *Shakespearean Criticism*, ed. by Thomas Middleton Raysor, 2 vols (London: Dent, 1960); —— *Complete Poems*, ed. by Morchard Bishop (London: Macdonald, 1954).

Corcoran, Neil, *English Poetry Since 1940* (London: Longman, 1993).

Crane, Hart, *The Complete Poems* and *Selected Letters and Prose of Hart Crane*, ed. by Brom Weber (New York: Doubleday, 1966).

Cross, Tom, *Painting the Warmth of the Sun: St Ives Artists 1939–1975* (Cambridge: Lutterworth Press, 1995).

Crow, Graham and Graham Allan, *Community Life: An Introduction to Local Social Relations* (Hemel Hempstead: Harvester Wheatsheaf, 1994).

Culler, Jonathan, *Structuralist Poetics: Structuralism, Linguistics and the Study of Poetry* (London: Routledge & Kegan Paul, 1975); —— *The Pursuit of Signs: Semiotics, Literature, Deconstruction* (London: Routledge & Kegan Paul, 1981).

Cunningham, Valentine, *British Writers of the Thirties* (Oxford: Oxford University Press, 1988).

De Man, Paul, *Allegories of Reading: Figural Language in Rousseau, Nietzsche, Rilke and Proust* (New Haven: Yale University Press, 1979).

Derrida, Jacques, *Of Grammatology*, trans. by Gayatri Chakravorty Spivak (Baltimore: Johns Hopkins University Press, 1976); —— *Margins of Philosophy*, trans. by Alan Bass (Brighton: Harvester Press, 1982).

Dunsmuir, Nessie, *Nessie Dunsmuir's Ten Poems* (Warwick: Greville Press, 1988).

Eagleton, Terry, *Criticism and Ideology: A Study in Marxist Literary Theory* (London: Verso, 1976).

Easthope, Antony, *Poetry as Discourse* (London: Methuen, 1983).

Eliot, T.S. *Selected Essays* (London: Faber and Faber, 1941);

—— *Collected Poems: 1909–1962* (London: Faber and Faber, 1963).

Ellman, Maud, *The Poetics of Impersonality: T.S. Eliot and Ezra Pound* (Brighton: The Harvester Press, 1987).

Fer, Briony, 'Surrealism, Myth and Psychoanalysis' in Briony Fer, David Batchelor and Paul Wood, *Realism, Rationalism, Surrealism: Art Between the Wars* (New Haven: Yale University Press, 1993).

Fish, Stanley, *Is There a Text in This Class: The Authority of Interpretive Communities* (Cambridge, MA: Harvard University Press, 1980).

Fraser, G.S. 'Apocalypse in Poetry' in *The White Horseman: Prose and Verse of the New Apocalypse*, ed. by J.F. Hendry and Henry Treece (London: Routledge, 1941).

Freud, Sigmund, *New Introductory Lectures on Psychoanalysis*, trans. by James Strachey, ed. by James Strachey assisted by Angela Richards (Harmondsworth: Penguin Books, 1973);

—— *The Psychopathology of Everyday Life*, trans. by Alan Tyson, ed. by James Strachey, Angela Richards and Alan Tyson (Harmondsworth: Penguin, 1975);

—— *The Interpretation of Dreams*, trans. by James Strachey, ed. by James Strachey assisted by Alan Tyson, revised by Angela Richards (London: Penguin, 1976);

—— *Jokes and Their Relation to the Unconscious*, trans. by James Strachey, ed. by James Strachey and Angela Richards (Harmondsworth: Penguin, 1976);

—— *Case Histories I*: 'Dora' and 'Little Hans', trans. by Alix and James Strachey, ed. by Angela Richards (Harmondsworth: Penguin, 1977);

—— *On Metapsychology: The Theory of Psychoanalysis*, trans. by James Strachey, ed. by Angela Richards (Harmondsworth: Penguin, 1984);

—— *Art and Literature*, trans. by James Strachey, ed. by Albert Dickinson (Harmondsworth: Penguin, 1985).

Gascoyne, David, *A Short History of Surrealism* (London: Frank Cass, 1935).

Graves, Robert, *The White Goddess: A Historical Grammar of Poetic Myth* (London: Faber and Faber, 1952).

Gratton, J. 'Runaway: Textual Dynamics in the Poetry of André Breton' in *Surrealism and Language: Seven Essays*, ed. by Ian Higgins

(Edinburgh: Scottish Academic Press, 1986).

Greenberg, Clement, *The Collected Essays and Criticism*, ed. by John
    O'Brian, 2 vols (Chicago: University of Chicago Press, 1986).

Higgins, Ian, 'Postscript: Pas De Patrie? Language, Freedom and Society
    in Surrealist Poetic Theory' in *Surrealism and Language: Seven
    Essays*, ed. by Ian Higgins (Edinburgh: Scottish Academic Press,
    1986).

Hirsch, Jr, E.D. *Validity in Interpretation* (New Haven: Yale University
    Press, 1967).

Hoggart, Richard, *The Uses of Literacy: Aspects of Working-Class Life, with
    Special Reference to Publications and Entertainments* (London: Chatto
    & Windus, 1957).

Hopkins, Gerard Manley, *Poems and Prose*, ed. by W.H. Gardner
    (Harmondsworth: Penguin Books, 1953).

Hulme, T.E. *The Collected Writings of T.E. Hulme*, ed. by Karen Csengeri
    (Oxford: Clarendon Press, 1994).

Hutcheon, Linda, *Narcissistic Narrative: The Metafictional Paradox* (New
    York: Methuen 1985).

Hynes, Samuel, *The Auden Generation: Literature and Politics in England in
    the 1930s* (New York: Viking Press, 1977).

Jakobson, Roman, *Selected Writings*, ed. by Stephen Rudy, 6 vols (The
    Hague: Mouton, 1981).

Kahn, Charles H. *The Art and Thought of Heraclitus: An Edition of the
    Fragments With Translation and Commentary* (Cambridge:
    Cambridge University Press, 1979).

Kenner, Hugh, *The Pound Era* (London: Faber and Faber, 1972).

Lacan, Jacques, *Écrits: A Selection*, trans. by Alan Sheridan (London:
    Routledge, 1980).

Lakoff, George and Mark Johnson, *Metaphors We Live By* (Chicago:
    University of Chicago Press, 1980).

Lakoff, George and Mark Turner, *More Than Cool Reason: A Field Guide to
    Poetic Metaphor* (Chicago: University of Chicago Press, 1989).

Leavis F.R. and Denys Thompson, *Culture and Environment: The Training of
    Critical Awareness* (London: Chatto & Windus, 1948).

Lecercle, Jean-Jacques, *Philosophy of Nonsense: The Intuitions of Victorian
    Nonsense Literature* (London: Routledge, 1994).

Lowell, Robert, *Poems: 1938–1949* (London: Faber and Faber, 1950).

Lucie-Smith, Edward (ed.), *British Poetry Since 1945* (Harmondsworth:
    Penguin Books, 1970).

MacCabe, Colin, *James Joyce and the Revolution of the Word* (London:

Macmillan, 1978).

MacDiarmid, Hugh, *Complete Poems: 1920–1976*, 2 vols, ed. by Michael Grieve and W.R. Aitken (London: Martin Brian & O'Keefe, 1978).

Maclaren-Ross, Julian, *Memoirs of the Forties* (London: Alan Ross, 1965).

Mason, Eudo C. *Rilke* (Edinburgh: Oliver and Boyd, 1963).

Matthews, J.H. *An Introduction to Surrealism* (University Park: Pennsylvania University Press, 1965).

Murphy, Rosalie (ed.), *Contemporary Poets of the English Language* (Chicago: St James Press, 1970).

Nancy, Jean-Luc, *The Inoperative Community* ed. and trans. by Peter Connor (Minneapolis: University of Minnesota Press, 1991).

Nansen, Fridtjof, *Farthest North*, 2 vols (London: George Newnes, 1898).

Nicholls, Peter, *Modernisms: A Literary Guide* (Basingstoke: Macmillan, 1995).

Nietzsche, Friedrich, *Philosophy and Truth: Selections from Nietzsche's Notebooks of the Early 1870s*, ed. and trans. by Daniel Breazeale (New Jersey: Humanities Press, 1979).

Ong, Walter J. *Orality and Literacy: The Technologizing of the Word* (London: Methuen, 1982).

Opie, Iona and Peter, *The Lore and Language of Schoolchildren* (Oxford: Clarendon Press, 1959).

Plato, *The Timaeus of Plato*, ed. by R.D. Archer-Hind (London: Macmillan, 1888).

'Poets on the Vietnam War', *The Review*, no. 18 (April 1968), (28–44).

Pound, Ezra, *The Cantos of Ezra Pound* (London: Faber and Faber, 1975);
—— *Selected Poems* (London: Faber and Faber, 1977).

Preminger, Alex and T.V.F. Brogan (eds.), *The New Princeton Encyclopedia of Poetry and Poetics* (Princeton: Princeton University Press, 1993).

Ray, Paul C. *The Surrealist Movement in England* (Ithaca: Cornell University Press, 1971).

Reddy, Michael J. 'The Conduit Metaphor: A Case of Frame Conflict in Our Language About Language' in *Metaphor and Thought*, ed. by Andrew Ortony, 2nd ed. (Cambridge: Cambridge University Press, 1993).

Richards, I.A. *Practical Criticism: A Study of Literary Judgment* (London: Routledge & Kegan Paul, 1929);
—— *The Philosophy of Rhetoric* (New York: Oxford University Press, 1965).

Riffaterre, Michael, *Semiotics of Poetry* (Bloomington: Indiana University Press, 1978).

Rilke, Rainer Maria, *The Selected Poetry of Rainer Maria Rilke*, ed. and trans. by Stephen Mitchell (London: Picador, 1987).

Rodgers, W.R. *Collected Poems* (London: Oxford University Press, 1971).

Sapir, Edward, *Selected Writings of Edward Sapir: In Language, Culture and Personality*, ed. by David G. Mandelbaum (Berkeley: University of California Press, 1949).

de Saussure, F. *Course in General Linguistics*, ed by Charles Bally and Albert Sechehaye, with the collaboration of Albert Riedlinger, trans. by Roy Harris (London: Duckworth, 1983).

Schwartz, Sanford, *The Matrix of Modernism: Pound, Eliot and Twentieth-Century Thought* (Princeton: Princeton University Press, 1985).

Scott, R.F. and others, *Scott's Last Expedition*, 2 vols. (London: Smith, Elder, 1913).

Sewell, Elizabeth, *The Field of Nonsense* (London: Chatto and Windus, 1952).

Shakespeare, William, *The Tempest* in *Complete Works*, ed. by W.J. Craig (London: Oxford University Press, 1943).

Shires, Linda M. *British Poetry of the Second World War* (London: Macmillan, 1985).

Skelton, Robin (ed.), *Poetry of the Forties* (Harmondsworth: Penguin Books, 1968).

Spender, Stephen, *The Still Centre* (London: Faber and Faber, 1939).

Spufford, Francis, *I May Be Some Time: Ice and the English Imagination* (London, Faber and Faber, 1996).

Stanford, Derek, *Inside the Forties* (London: Sidgwick & Jackson, 1977).

Stephens, Christopher Buckingham, 'St Ives' Artists and Landscape (Unpub. Ph. D. dissertation, University of Sussex, 1996).

Stevens, Wallace, *The Palm at the End of the Mind: Selected Poems and a Play*, ed. by Holly Stevens (New York: Vintage Books, 1972).

Stevenson, Randall, *Modernist Fiction: An Introduction* (Hemel Hempstead: Harvester Wheatsheaf, 1992).

Synge, J.M. *Riders to the Sea in Plays, Poems and Prose* (London: Dent, 1975).

Tallis, Raymond, *Not Saussure: A Critique of Post-Saussurean Literary Theory* (London: Macmillan, 1998).

Tambimuttu, M.J. *Poetry in Wartime* (London: Faber and Faber, 1942).

Thomas, Dylan, *Collected Poems: 1934–1952* (London: J.M. Dent & Sons, 1952).

Treece, Henry, *Dylan Thomas: Dog Among the Fairies* (London: Lyndsay Drummond, 1949).

Trotter, David, *The Making of the Reader: Language and Subjectivity in Modern American, English and Irish Poetry* (London: Macmillan, 1984).

Valéry, Paul, *The Art of Poetry*, trans. by Denise Folliott (London: Routledge & Kegan Paul, 1958).

Waugh, Evelyn, *Unconditional Surrender* (Harmondsworth: Penguin Books, 1964).

Waugh, Patricia, *Metafiction: The Theory and Practice of Self-Conscious Fiction* (London: Methuen, 1984).

Weber, Max, *The Protestant Ethic and the Spirit of Capitalism*, trans. by Talcott Parsons (London: George Allen & Unwin, 1930).

Wellek, Réné, *Discriminations: Further Concepts of Criticism* (New Haven: Yale University Press, 1970).

Whorf, Benjamin Lee, *Language, Thought and Reality: Selected Writings of Benjamin Lee Whorf*, ed. by John B. Carroll (New York: John Wiley & Sons, 1962).

Whybrow, Marion, *St Ives 1883–1993: Portrait of an Art Colony* (Woodbridge: Antique Collectors' Club, 1994).

Williams, Raymond, *The Country and the City* (London: Chatto & Windus, 1973);

—— *Keywords: A Vocabulary of Culture and Society* (London: Fontana, 1976);

—— *Resources of Hope: Culture, Democracy, Socialism*, ed. by Robin Gable (London: Verso, 1989);

——*Culture and Society: Coleridge to Orwell* (London: Hogarth Press, 1993).

Wimsatt, W.K. and Monroe Beardsley, 'The Intentional Fallacy' in W.K. Wimsatt, *The Verbal Icon: Studies in the Meaning of Poetry* (Lexington: University of Kentucky Press, 1967).

Wittgenstein, Ludwig, *Philosophical Investigations*, trans. by G.E.M. Anscombe (Oxford: Basil Blackwell, 1963).

Young, Michael and Peter Willmott, *Family and Kinship in East London* (London: Routledge & Kegan Paul, 1957).

Index

www.ingramcontent.com/pod-product-compliance
Ingram Content Group UK Ltd.
Pitfield, Milton Keynes, MK11 3LW, UK
UKHW040638250425
457875UK00002B/110